The Jewish Experience

The Jewish Experience

BOOK I

Frieda Clark Hyman

United Synagogue Commission on Jewish Education

About the Illustrations

Cover: The prophet Samuel anointing David. From the unique frescoes of the third century C.E. synagogue at Dura Europos, a former city on the Euphrates. *Courtesy Yale University, Dura Europos Publications.*

Frontis: The mountains of Sinai. From a photo. *Courtesy Israel Government Tourist Office.*

Unit I: In the background is the Ziggurat at Ur as it still stands. The Semitic nomads in the foreground are from a wall painting in the tomb of Khnumhotep III at Beni-hasan, Egypt. Dating from c. 1900 BCE the accuracy with which utensils and weapons are rendered show the work of an eye-witness.

Unit II: In the foreground is a Semitic herdsman; and an overseer beating a slave. From the tomb of Puyemre at Thebes, 15th century BCE (and therefore from the time of the Hebrew sojourn in Egypt). In the background is the sphinx at Giza, which stood already before the Hebrew tribes settled in Egypt. Photo: *Black Star.*

Unit III: Semitic warriors from the Beni-hasan painting superimposed on an early 19th century photo of the Jordan. Photo: *Bettmann Archive.*

Unit IV: A ship of 'Tarshish' superimposed on a photo of the Gulf of Eilat, where ships like these sailed to India in the time of Solomon. The ship: from a relief in the palace of Ashurnasir-pal II, 9th century BCE, *courtesy British Museum.* Gulf of Eilat: *Courtesy Israel Government Tourist Office.*

Unit V: Hebrew prisoners being driven into exile by an Assyrian officer. From the relief in the palace of Tiglath-pileser, commemorating his victory over Gilead and Galilee (i.e. Israel) in the 8th century BCE. *Courtesy British Museum.*

Unit VI: The vision of Ezekiel as imagined by the artist of Dura-Europos. In all these paintings figures representing periods of Jewish sovereignty are generally depicted wearing Greco-Roman togas. Jews in exile are shown in Parthian dress. *Courtesy Yale University, Dura Europos Publications.*

Unit VII: An imaginary 19th century engraving of the battle between the armies of Judah Maccabee and Nicanor. In the background a photo of the hills of Judea. Engraving: *From the collection of Rabbi William Rosenthall.* Photo: *Leni Sonnenfeld.*

Design and map illustration by Robert Sugar

To my beloved Israel

acknowledgments

My thanks to all who encouraged me to serve our children: to my teacher and friend, Dr. Abraham Halkin, for reading the manuscript and for his helpful suggestions; to Dr. Azriel Eisenberg, for his friendship and interest; to Dr. Morton Siegel, for his warm understanding and support; to Rabbi Marvin S. Wiener for his helpful suggestions; to Mr. George Levine, for his splendid cooperation in supervising the production of this volume; and to Monica Shoffman for her painstaking labor in preparing the comprehensive index.

Most of all, I am grateful to my husband, not only for his help in this work, but for his matchless constancy and devotion. It is to him I dedicate this book.

Nevertheless, I, and I alone am responsible for the text.

F. C. H.

contents

Unit IV

Unit V

Unit VI

Unit VII

Unit I

The Lord said to Abram, "Go forth from your native land and from your father's home to the land that I will show you. I will make of you a great nation . . ."

GENESIS XII:1–2

chapter 1   How We Learn About Ourselves

ALL OF US LOVE TO HEAR STORIES OF when our parents were children. We love it so much, we ask them to tell us the same stories over and over again. For the same reason, we are eager to know about their parents, our grandfathers, and about the men and women who came before them. For by learning about them we are learning about ourselves.

We are both Jews and Americans. Americans for almost two hundred years; Jews for four thousand. In the public schools we learn about the founding fathers of our United States. But we have to attend Jewish schools to learn about the founding fathers of Israel. We have to go back four thousand years into history for this. Much longer than the, roughly, thirty years to the youth of our own parents, or the sixty years of the childhood of our grandparents.

Why is it important for us to know about our distant ancestors? Because they fashioned themselves and their children into certain kinds of human beings. They had special qualities, special goals, and a special way of life. And they created a special kind of nation.

We, our parents, and grandparents, are what we are today, because of what they were before us. If we get to know those forefathers, we will understand the reasons we behave as we do. We can also understand the unique way our people developed and grew throughout their four thousand years.

Fine, you say. But why do we need a new history of the Jews? Why not bring the one we already have up to date, instead of starting all over again?

The answer is simple. We know more today. Certain studies which we call "disciplines" have advanced rapidly within our century. These disciplines have imposing names. But they needn't awe you. For example, linguistics merely explains the beginnings and the forms of speech. Anthropology is the science of man, especially as regards his customs and beliefs.

What is the most helpful for us in the study of biblical history is the discipline known as archeology. Archeology is concerned with uncovering ancient cultures and civilizations by digging up the remains of these cultures from the earth. Much of what has puzzled students of the Bible has now become clear because of "digs" in the ancient Near East: ancient Mesopotamia, Canaan, and Egypt. Mesopotamia is now Irak; Canaan is now the Land of Israel; and Egypt is still Egypt, although the Arab

3

who lives there is not a descendant of the original Egyptians.

The men who dig within the layers of the soil are called archeologists. What they bring up out of the earth are called artifacts. These artifacts may be bits of pottery (potsherds), jewelry, household dishes, figures of gods and goddesses, temple columns and altars. Together with written records they shed very helpful light on the events of those days. These records are inscribed on tablets. They consist of stories, royal decrees, codes of law, tax receipts and accounts of battles.

Most frequently found are graves and tombs. This may not seem attractive to you, but the way the dead were buried and the artifacts found in these burial places tell the archeologist a great deal. They learn how the people lived then. They learn what they valued, what they believed. And they learn into what class of society the dead had been born.

Occasionally, a whole house like one uncovered some yards from the Western Wall of the Temple in Jerusalem is discovered. We can see how the inhabitants of that house lived, what their occupation was, and how they fashioned their tools. Perhaps the most exciting find of all was the Dead Sea Scrolls. These were scrolls stored away in jars within caves near the Salt Sea. Among them is a Scroll of the Prophet Isaiah. It is the oldest copy of this Book in our possession. It is a very valuable source for scholars. The Scrolls also tell us about men and women who lived separately during the days of the Second Temple.

The study of archeology is one of the most popular activities in Israel today. Whole programs on radio and television are devoted to it. Almost everyone is an amateur archeologist. Archeology is as much a part of the lives of Israeli youth as sports are of American youth.

For us, the most important source of our past has always been our Bible. Today its pages speak more clearly than ever because of the disciplines of the scholars. For example, we know from tablets in a city called Nuzi that part of the money a man paid to the father of his bride was set aside for the bride as her own dowry. Therefore, when Rachel and Leah, two of our Mothers, said: "Not only did he (their father) sell us, but he has used up the money he got for us . . . ," they were accusing their father of violating the family laws of their country. We could not have known this before 1925–1931. Not until then did archeologists dig in Nuzi and find these tablets.

At the end of this unit, you will read of other incidents in the lives of our ancestors. Because of the digs carried out in our century, these incidents are no longer puzzling to us.

However, we must always remember that, no matter how much these disciplines support the text of the Bible, they do not either add or subtract from the meaning of the text. For, though the Bible contains history, the Bible is more than history. It is the story of our ancestors who knew they were made in the image of God. These ancestors wanted to know the will of God, and to fulfill that will. In that way they knew they would become better human beings.

Therefore, it is our story as well. We, as they, are made in the image of God. And we, as they, are searching for that way of life which will make us as human as man can be.

There is no question that the men and women who walked across the pages of the Bible were real people. What is written of them did happen, although the way in which they were written may puzzle us. But then, the history of Israel puzzles most men. It is not an ordinary history.

Activities

Additional examples of how archeology helps us to understand the text of the Bible:

1. Read Chapter XVI of *Genesis.* You see that Sarah was unable to have children. Therefore, she gave her maid, Hagar, to Abraham for a wife. And Sarah said: "Perhaps I shall be built up . . ." through Hagar and the son she would bear.

Leah and Rachel also gave their maids to their husbands for the same purpose. All of these thousands of years no one truly understood why our ancestors did this. But now we do.

After six years of digging in Nuzi (near modern Kirkuk), four thousand tablets were recovered by the year 1931. These are the famous Nuzi Documents. They tell us about a people called Hurrians. These Hurrians were found throughout the Near East. At one time, the Egyptians called Canaan "Hurru Land," because so many Hurrians lived there.

Our Patriarchs lived among these Hurrians in Mesopotamia. They accepted certain of their customs. One of the Nuzi Documents reads as follows:

"If Gilimninu (a wife) bears children, Shennima (her husband) shall not take another wife. But if Gilimninu fails to bear children, Gilimninu shall get for Shennima a woman from the Lullu country (a slave girl) as a second wife. In that case, Gilimninu herself shall have authority over the child."

We see now that what Sarah, Leah, and Rachel did was what women of the upper classes did when they could not bear children. They gave their maids to their husbands as second wives. In those days, men could have more than one wife.

2. Later, Sarah asked her husband, Abraham, to send away both Hagar and the son she bore. It was a cruel request. And indeed, Abraham did not want to comply. But *Genesis* tells us that God assured him that his son, whose name was Ishmael, would become the head of a great nation.

It may be, however, that Sarah was actually giving Hagar and Ishmael their freedom when she sent them away. Why should we think this? Because, in a code of law, Lipit-Ishtar, it was written that when the son of a slave-wife is sent away, he gives up his inheritance in exchange for his freedom. This may be exactly what Sarah was doing.

3. Read Chapter XXXI of *Genesis,* especially Verse 19. You see that Rachel took her father's house gods.

Surely we must ask ourselves:

a. Why did Rachel take these idols?

b. Why was her father so upset about their loss?

Again, the Nuzi Documents explain this mystery. According to them, if a man possessed the house gods, he possessed proof of his inheritance.

Rachel knew her husband was entitled to a certain share of her father's estate. But she knew her father might try to cheat her husband. Therefore, she took the house gods to protect her husband's legal share.

Nelson Glueck was the president of Hebrew Union College in Cincinnati, Ohio. He was ordained as a rabbi there. He was also one of the foremost archeologists of our century. He was in Israel so much, one wonders how he could have attended to his duties in Cincinnati. Between 1951 and 1959 he identified over five hundred ancient sites of the Bible. Read about him, and about the books he wrote.

Yigal Yadin is another famous archeologist. He was the General of Israel's army in its War of Independence. We shall find his dig in Masada very helpful when we study the period of the Second Commonwealth. Do you think his archeological knowledge made him a better general?

Israel has built a special building for the Dead Sea Scrolls. It is called the Shrine of the Book. In case of an attack, the Scrolls can be lowered into the earth for protection. Find out how the Scrolls were discovered. It is better than a mystery story.

Francis R. B. Godolphin, a former Dean of Princeton, wrote an introduction to a history called *The Persian Wars.* This is the work of the great ancient historian, Herodotus. In his introduction, Dr. Godolphin makes the following point:

The character and distribution of potsherds is important for dating . . . but it may be that much which can be measured, and hence appears to be a scientific occupation today, is really less important than the written records which can convey human insights and aspirations together with an expression of the values and limitations of human life.

Discuss this in your class. Your teacher will explain whatever you find difficult.

Do you agree or disagree with Dr. Godolphin? State your reasons.

What is the written record of Jewish history?

I hope you will read some books on the Bible and Archeology. They make an excellent introduction to the study of Israel. Here are a few I know you will enjoy:

Worlds Lost and Found by Azriel Eisenberg and Dov Peretz Elkins. Of special interest for the period of Abraham: Chapters III, IV, V.
The First Book of Archeology by Nora Kubie. Material on Mesopotamia and Egypt.
Buried Treasure in Bible Lands by Lenore Cohen. Chapter VIII: Abraham, Father of a Faith.

Readings for teachers:

Land of Two Rivers by Leonard Cottrell. Ancient Mesopotamia.
Palestine Before the Hebrews by Emmanuel Anati. Whole book of value. Part Five of special value for history of Israel.

chapter 2   The Covenant, Our Family Tree

A COVENANT IS AN AGREEMENT BE-
tween two parties. Usually it is between
man and man, or nation and nation. For the
Jewish People the word, *Covenant,* means
the agreement between God and our forefathers, Abraham, Isaac, and Jacob.

Abraham was the first father of the Jewish People. We call him our first Patriarch.
It was with him, the Bible tells us, God
made a *Covenant.* Abraham, on his part,
was to live according to God's laws. By the
way he lived he would teach and encour-
age all men to obey these divine laws. God,
on His part, would make Abraham the
father of an important nation. Together with
this promise went the gift of the Land of
Canaan, to be renamed the Land of Israel.
Clearly God is more the Giver and Abraham more the receiver.

Let us pause here and elaborate on the
Covenant. Where does it first appear?
What was its influence on Israel's history?
How is it accepted by most Jews?

The *Covenant,* (Brit in Hebrew) is found
in the Bible:

Yahweh said to Abram,
"Go forth from your native land
And from your father's home
To a land that I will show you.

I will make of you a great nation,
Bless you, and make great your name,
That it may be a blessing.
And I will bless those who bless you;
And curse those who curse you;
And through you shall bless themselves
All the communities on earth."

(Genesis XII: 1–3)

These words are repeated with some
changes and additions from time to time.
Not only to Abraham, but to his son, Isaac,
his grandson, Jacob, and to men we shall
call agents or messengers of God.

This *Covenant* is one of the central
themes of Scripture; it is the foundation
upon which ancient Israel stood. It has pro-
pelled our people onto highways no other
people has ever walked. It is no exaggera-
tion to say that without this *Covenant* there
would not today be the State of Israel. Despite all this, can it be proved that this
Covenant actually was agreed upon by God
and Abraham? Even if its first pronouncement is found in *Genesis* XII, does it make
it necessarily true?

For many Jews it does. These men and
women, called traditionalists, believe that
the Bible is the living word of the living
God. According to them, God dictated the

8

Bible to Moses on Mt. Sinai. Therefore, its words cannot be questioned; they are true and good.

Modernists believe that truth and goodness are to be found in the Bible. Thus, the Bible for them, is God-inspired. But whereas the traditionalist says everything in life must be measured against the Bible to be judged true or false, the modernist says that the Bible must be tested against reason and experience to be accepted as true.

No one can decide how his neighbor shall view the Bible. For our purposes we shall deal with the Bible as modernists. Why? Because we don't have to convince the traditionalist. Modernists insist we use the disciplines of history as well as of science to make our point.

Let us, therefore, subject the verses above to these disciplines. Tradition has appointed Abraham specifically as the man who left in search of a new faith. That choice has not been contradicted by anything discovered so far. According to modern students, the author of *Genesis* XII, known as J, lived about the tenth century. He did not get his information from the files of a student, nor from cuneiform texts. By the tenth century these texts had been covered up for centuries, and were to remain buried for nearly three thousand years more.

From where then, could he have gotten it? Only from earlier Israelite traditions, which in turn, reached back all the way to patriarchal times. Embodied in every episode is a historical event and a description of real men and women. That is why this Chapter XII, which begins a new period in Abraham's life, deserves our respect. It is supported by what we call internal evidence from Biblical history and indirect testimony of such disciplines as archeology.

What do we mean by early Israelite tration? Simply that the descendants of Abraham recalled the life of this man, their ancestor. This memory was eventually shared by the whole family, clan, or tribe. It became, in short, a folk memory. Within the scope of this folk memory, J constructed this episode. He did it to explain why Abraham left his homeland. Indeed, in other episodes, we shall read that not only did God speak to Abraham, but Abraham replied: in speech as well as in deed.

How could this be? For the traditionalist, of course, there is no problem. There is no J. There is no need for folk memory. Does not the Bible itself explain that God revealed Himself in many ways: in visions, in dreams, in riddles, or even in an aspect of nature such as a burning bush? But for the modernist, it can only be that early Jewish history is portrayed by calling each important episode or crisis, a meeting between God and man. Therefore, as God spoke to Abraham, so Abraham answered Him, as described by in this case, J.

But no matter how the above verses are interpreted, all of us, traditionalist as well as modernist, can agree that this man, Abraham, felt the need to break with his past, to seek a new meaning in life. Indeed, that is why these verses come upon us so abruptly. Abraham was a pioneer. There had to be a first time, place, person, or group of persons. In the next Unit we shall elaborate upon these verses again, but more simply.

Right now, it is important for us to realize that whenever we say: "the Bible tells us" or "tradition tells us," the modernist can understand that no matter how the episode is described, its historical implications are valid. Remember always that it is one of the principles of the Bible itself, that it is written in the language of man. How else could man read it? But the language of man, is, by definition, a human skill. Therefore, it is subject to all the limitations of man.

To understand what this means, try to recall an extraordinarily beautiful sunset. Now try to picture it in words. Can you do complete justice to it? Does violet or purple or rose truly capture the color tones? And what of the quality of the air? And how much of your emotion is woven into your language?

Therefore, when the Bible tells us that God made a *Covenant* with Abraham, we should know that, at the very least, Abraham and his sons and all his descendants saw themselves as having a special relationship to their Creator. Furthermore, their God was the Creator of all men and of the whole universe. No gods or forces preceded Him. No magic could control Him. He had nothing in common with the gods in which other men believed.

This awareness of the character of God and of their partnership with Him, is inbedded in the *Covenant.* It is what later prophets will call "the knowledge of God." And this knowledge withstood, as you shall see, the attacks of many civilizations and creeds. Whether we be traditionalists or modernists, the *Covenant* made and makes life meaningful in ways only Jews can know. Rather than relinquish it, our fathers chose death. Had they not, we would not today be Jews.

From now on, therefore, if you read "the Bible tells us" or "tradition tells us," you may accept the telling either as a traditionalist or as a modernist. What is valid for both will be the force of the event upon the course of Jewish history, and therefore, upon us. Now, we can return to Abraham.

He had eight sons. The two most important were Ishmael and Isaac. Ishmael was his first born son. Hagar, his second wife, was Ishmael's mother. Ishmael became the Patriarch of the Ishmaelites. Arabs claim they are descended from him.

Isaac was Abraham's second son. Sarah was his mother. Isaac was chosen to fulfill the *Covenant.* He is, therefore, our second Patriarch.

Isaac had only one wife, Rebecca. She bore him twin sons, Esau and Jacob. Esau

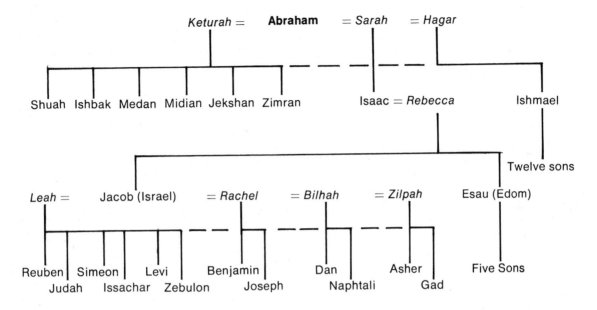

became the Patriarch of the people of Edom. Jacob, his younger son, was our third Patriarch. His name was later changed to Israel. He had four wives: Leah, Rachel, and their maids, Bilhah, and Zilpah. They bore him twelve sons. These twelve became the heads of the future tribes of Israel.

Sarah, Rebecca, Leah, and Rachel are our four Mothers, or four Matriarchs.

Above is a chart of the beginnings of our people:

Men who are descended from the tribe of Levi are called either Kohanim (which means priests), or they are called Levites. In ancient days, both Kohanim and Levites served in the Temple. Kohanim served at the altars. Levites had lesser duties. They played instruments, sang in the choir, and guarded the gates.

The rest of us are called Israelites. We are, in truth, the descendants of all tribes. Of Judah and Benjamin, for they were not, as you shall learn exiled by Assyria. Of Simeon, because Simeon merged with Judah early in her history. Of the others, known as the "lost ten tribes," because many of these northern tribes fled to the south, to Judah and Benjamin, for a variety of reasons. We shall speak of these "lost ten tribes" later in our history.

What is important for us to remember now, is that all Jews, we and our brothers all over the world, are the heirs and the guardians of the Covenant. As Isaac and Jacob inherited the *Covenant* from Abraham, so our fathers and grandfathers, right back to our Patriarchs themselves, received and renewed the *Covenant.* We are each a link in the chain that goes back to Abraham.

Activities

Questions

1. Do you know anyone whose name is Katz?
   Katz in Hebrew is spelled כ״ץ
   The כ stands for כהן Kohen
   The ץ stands for צדיק righteous
   כ״ץ means a righteous Priest.
   From what tribe are men descended, whose name is Katz?
2. What other names usually signify Priestly descent?
   Guess what names signify a Levite?

3. What privilege does a Kohen receive in your synagogue?
   What privilege does a Levite receive?
4. What does B'nai Brit mean?
   Do you know of any other organization or institution containing the word "Brit"?
   What ceremony is known simply as "Brit"?
   Actually it should be "Brit Milah." Look up Genesis XVII? Read from v. 1–14. Verses 10–14 explain precisely what a Brit Milah is.

Readings for Students

Buried Treasure in Bible Lands, by Cohen, Lenore, Ward, Ritchie Press, 1965. Chap. I–II–III–IV–V–VII–VIII.

Readings for Teachers

The Hebrew Scripture in the Making, by Margolis, Max, J.P.S., Philadelphia, 1922.

chapter 3   The World of Abraham

WHEN WE BEGIN THE STUDY OF OUR history, we discover many startling facts. One of these is that the home of the first known village settlement of the world was in southwest Asia, particularly in Mesopotamia. This part of the world is called the "Cradle of Civilization."

Immediately, you who have heard Bible stories, will say: "But that is where Abraham was born."

It was, indeed. Abraham, our First Patriarch, migrated first from Ur, a city on the river Euphrates in lower Mesopotamia, to Haran, in the west of Mesopotamia. From there, at the age of seventy-five, he continued on to Canaan. The first city of Canaan in which he built an altar, was Shechem.

We cannot be sure of the exact date of his migration. There are many estimates. Some believe his journey took place 1900 years B.C.E. (Before the Common Era). Others think it occurred about 1750 B.C.E. and even later. What we do know is that between 2000 and 1900 B.C.E., Ur reached the peak of her prosperity. She was then the foremost center of culture in the world. Men in Ur had already mastered mathematics. They were familiar with zoology, geography, mineralogy, and understood some medicine. Others were grammarians, and had even written a dictionary.

Besides the two great rivers of Mesopotamia, the Euphrates and Tigris, inland waterways irrigated the land. Many were farmers. And many were merchants.

Down from the north, in boats called keleks, goods were shipped to Ur on the Euphrates. Within this commercial world, merchants kept accounts the same way we do today. They issued monthly statements. And they divided up profits at the end of the year.

Ur was ruled by a complicated administration. She maintained a professional army and a police force. There was a large priesthood too. It served Sin, the moon god. Priests were able to control the lives of Ur's population, because they convinced the citizens that they alone could secure Sin's help for them.

It was in such a center Abraham grew up. Why then, did his father, Terah, leave? Some say because Elam, a kingdom to the north, conquered Ur in 1950 B.C.E. After that Ur no longer prospered.

According to the Bible, it was Terah's intention to go to Canaan. But he never did. Instead, he stopped at Haran, and remained there. Again, we must ask why?

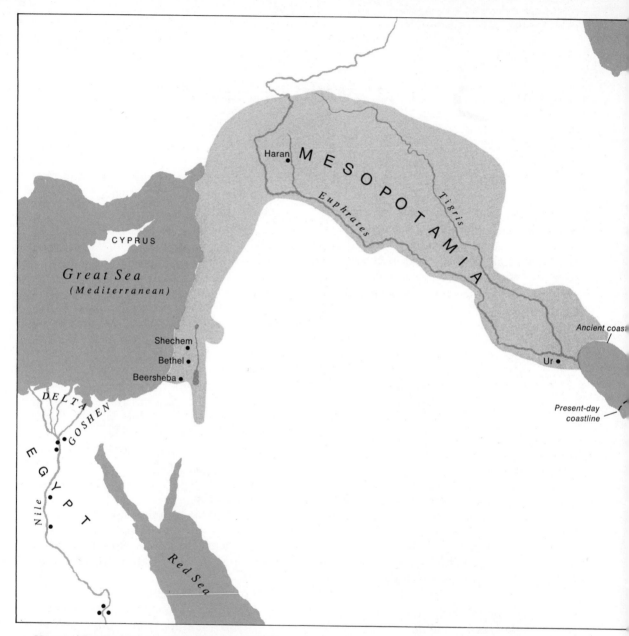

Map 1 Fertile Crescent (Around 1800 BCE)

Could it be because Haran, like the city of Ur, was also a center of the worship of Sin? Both cities, we know, had huge Temples for Sin, known as Ziggurats. Built like towers, these temples were called by different names. Three of these names were: the House of the Mountain; the House of the Link Between Heaven and Earth; and the House of the Foundation of Heaven and Earth.

We do know that the name Terah, as well as the names of other members of his family, were connected to Sin. Laban, for example, the great-grandson of Terah, means moon.

Hundreds of years later, Joshua, the future conqueror of Canaan, will speak of Terah thus: "Your fathers dwelt long ago beyond the River (Euphrates); Terah, the father of Abraham and the father of Nahor; and they served other gods."

Was Joshua referring to the worship of Sin? Our rabbis must have thought so. They said Terah made idols. And what better place to make idols than in Haran, the sister city of Ur? Was not Sin worshipped in Haran? And was not Sin the very idol Terah was supposed to have carved in Ur?

Nahor, one of Terah's two remaining sons, stayed with him. Abraham, the oldest son, did not. He carried out his father's original intention. He went down to the land of Canaan.

Why did Abraham leave father, brother, and relatives? Why did he take only wife, nephew, and followers, and go to a strange land? We have already discussed this in Chapter II. Now, let us look at it in the clear common-sense light of everyday events.

We are told Abraham was a semi-nomad. That means he owned sheep and cattle, and traveled on donkeys. But Abraham's brother also owned sheep and cattle. Surely, the land of Mesopotamia, with its great rivers and smaller waterways, was well irrigated. Surely, there was plenty of pasture for herds in Haran. We know how rich this land must have been: our ancestors believed the Garden of Eden was located in the valley of the Euphrates.

Perhaps you will say Abraham was one of the men driven south by barbarians who invaded the Near East in 1700 B.C.E.? Even if we could accept this late date for Abraham, why, then, didn't Nahor and Terah flee with him?

Before we try to answer, let us take a closer look, both at Abraham and at the lands in which he wandered.

The map above describes the Fertile Crescent. It is a half-moon circling along the line where the Arabian desert ends. Start at the Persian Gulf, not far from Ur on the Euphrates where Abraham was born, travel west across Mesopotamia (noticing Haran on the way); then south along the coast of the Mediterranean Sea, to Aram (Syria), Canaan, and winding eastward to Egypt.

During the time of Abraham, men moved freely around this Crescent. When there was no rain, crops didn't grow and people had no food. It was then they would migrate to Egypt. There the land did not depend on rain. There the great river Nile overflowed each year, and the soil on each side of the Nile was rich and black. With her abundant harvest, Egypt attracted starving men. An Egyptian frontier officer, for example, sent the following message to his superior, a "Scribe of the Treasury":

We have finished letting the Bedouins of Edom pass the fortress to keep them alive and to keep their cattle alive.

Obviously, there was famine in Edom.

The Bible tells us Abraham also traveled to Egypt because of famine. For the same reason, Abraham's grandson and great-grandsons would go down to Egypt.

The road to Egypt was, and is, through the Negev, the southern desert of Canaan. Abraham, Isaac, and Jacob moved up and down the Negev frequently. Isaac lived in the Negev for many years. Although parts of the Negev were always harsh and barren, other parts supported hundreds and perhaps thousands of people in the days of the Patriarchs.

We can see how our forefathers lived from the Bible and from archeology. They were tent dwellers, settling near, but not in, cities. But they were not crude or helpless. Despite their wanderings, they made alliances with kings; they trained and led small armies; and they possessed gold, silver, slaves, and herds.

Their gifts were royal; their hospitality, generous; and their independence, fierce. Nor were they limited to sheep and cattle raising. Both Abraham and Jacob bought fields in various parts of the hilly country. Isaac, the one Patriarch who never left Canaan, was a successful farmer. Wine, oil, grain, lentils, were part of their diet. Abraham's nephew, Lot, settled in a city. Some have even suggested our forefathers participated in the caravan trade.

Perhaps. Abraham, after all, had been born into an advanced civilization where commerce flourished. And men do not shed their past so easily. Our grandfathers, for example, continued their way of life when they came to America. Wherever they settled they built schools and synagogues. If they were craftsmen, they worked at their skills.

But we know why our grandfathers and great-grandfathers came to America. We know they were seeking a life which offered opportunities to every man, no matter what his race or religion. They moved from lands that kept them second-class or third-class citizens to a land of equality and freedom.

In Abraham's day, Mesopotamia was culturally superior to Canaan. We know this from the tablets of Mari, a city on the Middle Euphrates, and from the business documents of Nuzi. Abraham, it is clear, did not move from a lower level of life to a higher when he migrated to Canaan. Nor was he in search of riches. He did not come, as many nomads or semi-nomads did, to raid other people. He was not a member of the Hyksos nation that conquered parts of Canaan, and even ruled Egypt for two hundred years. On the contrary, he was, as you know, to become the founder of a brand new people: Israel.

The only answer that makes sense is that he was compelled by something within himself to leave Mesopotamia. He must have had a fresh new vision of the universe which could not be voiced in Haran. He could not accept the Mesopotamian ideas about the gods who ruled the world. So many of them were like men themselves: weak, fearful, and mean-spirited. Besides, many gods meant many conflicts. Conflicts bred indecision and hostility. You see this reflected in the great Mesopotamian story of *Gilgamesh*. How then could a man live at peace either with himself or his fellow man if his gods did not? And so, Abraham must have rejected the religious structure of his day, with its complicated families of gods.

He must have asked many questions. How could men worship idols, the work of their own hands? How could they believe in gods whose power was limited? How could they single out the separate forces of nature, like that which makes grain grow, or enables women to bear children, and worship those forces? How could they cringe before the sun, the moon, the ocean, the earth, or any part of the natural universe?

Our rabbis wrote stories or legends, to explain the words of the Bible. Legends are not history. But because they reflect the thinking of Israel, and because this thinking shaped the character of Israel, they are very significant for an understanding of Jewish history. These rabbinical stories, we call Midrash. Rabbi Hiyya, one of our Sages, wanted to show not only the folly of worshipping idols, but how reason or common sense is all man needs to reject idolatry. He therefore, wrote the following Midrash (Midrash Rabbah XXXVIII:13):

Terah was a maker of idols. He once left Abraham to sell his idols. A man came and wished to buy one. "How old are you?" Abraham asked him. "Fifty years," was the reply. "Woe to such a man," he exclaimed "You are fifty years old and would worship a day-old object," At this the man became ashamed, and departed. On another occasion, a woman came with a plateful of food and said: "Take this and offer it to the idols." So Abraham took a stick, broke the idols, and put the stick in the hand of the largest idol. When his father returned, he demanded: "What have you done to them?" "I cannot conceal it from you," Abraham answered. "A woman came with a plateful of fine flour and requested me to offer it to them. One claimed, "I must eat it first." Thereupon, the largest idol arose, took the stick, and broke them." "Why do you make sport of me?" Terah cried out. "Have they, then, any knowledge?" "Should not your ears listen to what your mouth is saying?" Abraham replied. ("You deny their knowledge, and yet you worship them!") Thereupon, Terah became so angry, he seized Abraham and delivered him to Nimrod, the king. Nimrod decided to find out whether Abraham really rejected the religion of his land. "Let us worship the fire," Nimrod proposed. "No," said Abraham, "let us rather worship water which extinguishes the fire." "Then let us worship water," Nimrod agreed. "No," said Abraham, "let us rather worship the clouds which bear the water." "Then let us worship the clouds," Nimrod agreed. "No," said Abraham, "let us rather worship the winds which disperse the clouds." "Then let us worship the wind." "No," retorted Abraham, "let us rather worship human beings who withstand the wind." "You are just playing with words." Nimrod said furiously, "we will worship nothing but fire. Behold, I will cast you into it, and let your God whom you adore come and save you from it." He seized Abraham and cast him into a fiery furnace, but God saved him from the flames of the furnace.

It is worth noting that while this Midrash proves indirectly the existence of God through reason, the Bible itself rarely attempts this or any proof. The Bible accepts God's existence as indisputable. Its very first verse reads:

In the beginning God created the heavens and the earth.

(Genesis I:1)

Were the Bible a Greek document, it would, no doubt, have begun thus:

In the beginning the heavens and the earth were created by God. But who is God? Let us define Him. . . .

Rabbi Isaac, another Sage wanted to teach that the universe was watched over by the Owner of the universe: By God Himself. Therefore, he wrote this Midrash:

A man was traveling from place to place when he saw a building in flames. Is it possible that the building lacks a person to look after it? he wondered. The owner of the building looked out, and said: "I am the owner of the building." In the same way, when Abraham saw the world being destroyed by the flames of evil deeds, he asked: "Is it conceivable the world is without a guide?" The Holy One, blessed be He, looked out, and said to him: "I am the Guide, the Sovereign of the Universe."

According to the authors of these Midrashim we see in what the spiritual quest of Abraham resulted. He discovered that God alone was the Creator of the universe. His mind had made him challenge what all men accepted. And his heart, which must have suffered before the evil and confusion that idolatry caused, made him recognize the One Father of all men.

Nevertheless, this does not explain why Abraham migrated to Canaan. Why couldn't he have remained in Haran. Surely, the Creator of the world was in Haran as well as in Canaan. Or was Canaan less idolatrous than Haran?

No, Canaan was, if anything, more affected by idolatry. In Canaan, human sacrifice, which had ceased in Mesopotamia, was still practised.

Stories of the Canaanite gods were, on the whole, more bloodthirsty and revolting. Canaanite religious customs were cruder and wilder.

In order to understand why Abraham left Haran, think back upon what you read. Remember that the governments of the Mesopotamian cities were very complex, that the power of the priests was very great. Furthermore, many of the Mesopotamian city-kingdoms were connected with each other. And while each had its own family of gods, these city-kingdoms were united in some ways. For example, they all sent offerings to En-lil, the lord of the storm, whose shrine was in Nippur.

It is clear, therefore, that an ancient and powerful tradition upheld Mesopotamia's way of life. Did it not take Abraham himself seventy-five years to reject this tradition? Certainly, such a way of life would resist any new or revolutionary belief. And what Abraham discovered was both new and revolutionary. It challenged everything the kings, nobles, priests, and even the masses of people held dear. But especially, it threatened the power of the king and priest.

Abraham had to find a land which was not governed by such strong civic and religious rulers: a land like Canaan.

Now let us return to Chapter Two, p. 8, and reread the verses of *Genesis.* Does this explanation make sense? The traditionalists among you might say NO! it was not Abraham's vision at all that made him leave his home. It was God's command. True, but had Abraham not discovered God already, he would not have recognized His voice. He could not. Moreover, to know God is to obey Him, to pursue Him, and to teach what He demands of us. This could not be done in Haran. It could in Canaan.

As for the modernists among you, no matter how you accept these verses, the conclusion remains inescapable. Abraham sought a new territory in which to live his new life. He had to find that land where the institutions of palace and temple were not so powerful, where he would have more freedom, both of thought and expression. Compared to the cities of Mesopotamia, Canaan was such a land.

Canaan's fertile region was made up of small kingdoms. Their rulers lived inside fortified walls. Outside the walls, peasants tilled the soil, paying tribute to the rulers for their protection. But, unlike Mesopotamia, the kings and priests within these small kingdoms had little connection with each other. City dwellers kept to their own territory. They fought their wars from the towers and walls of their kingdoms. Some of these small nations had to pay tribute to more powerful nations, even to nations outside of Canaan. The Bible, in Chapter XIV of *Genesis,* describes just this kind of situation.

In Canaan's semi-dry regions like the Negev and the Jordan, semi-nomads lived. Each of these different groups had a leader. Their names tell us they belonged to many races. They made war frequently on one another, formed small alliances, and tried to destroy other groups in order to take their land and their belongings.

Sinuhe, an Egyptian noble living in exile in northern Canaan, wrote of these groups and of the battles he fought against them:

"Every foreign country against which I went forth, when I had made my attack on it, was driven away from its pasturage and its well. I plundered its cattle, carried off its inhabitants, took away their food, and slew people in it by my strong arm, by my bow, by my movements, and by my successful plans."

Also, according to Sinuhe, Egyptians were constantly visiting Canaan. At the same time, people were swarming down from the north. Many people meant many and different ideas, different cultures, different religions. A land with so many differences would not be as angry or as afraid of new ideas as a land where everyone shared the same ideas.

In such a land, living near, but not in the cities, Abraham had little to fear from the civic or religious powers of the kingdoms. As for other semi-nomads, we know from the same XIVth Chapter of *Genesis* that Abraham was very capable of defending himself. Sinuhe would not have defeated Abraham.

The Bible lists the names of many nations that lived in Canaan at the time of Abraham. Besides these names, archeologists have dug up artifacts of many other people not identified by the Bible.

We have no artifacts that point to the presence of our forefathers in Canaan. The evidence of their existence comes from the Bible and from what we have learned about the civilizations of Mesopotamia.

Therefore, we should ask ourselves this question: What has happened to all of these other nations? Where are the Jebusites, the Amorites, the Hyksos, the Ammonites, the Moabites, the Elamites, the Horites, to name a few?

While we possess their artifacts, or some of them, they themselves have disappeared from the face of history. Why, then, has Israel survived? Is this an accident? Or is this part, as traditionalists say, of God's plan?

Furthermore, why have the great empires of Babylonia, Assyria, Egypt, Hitti, so little influence upon our lives today? Why is it that Israel has left her mark so deeply upon the world? Most historians will agree only Greece has had the same lasting influence upon the mind of mankind.

How can we account for such a fact? Can you find a clue in what you have just read? Think about it.

Activities

1. Write your own Midrash about the folly of idols. For an idea for your Midrash, look up what the Prophet Isaiah had to say about idols. You will find it in the Book of Isaiah, Chapter XLIV: Verses 14–19.
2. Do you think Abraham should have left his father, Terah? If you did not agree with what your parents believed, or with what your neighbors believed, what would you do?
3. Act out Rabbi Hiyya's Midrash.
4. In his book called Rivers of the Desert, Nelson Glueck tells us how he discovered hundreds of ancient settlements in the Negev. These settlements existed in the days of our Patriarchs.

   When Abraham traveled from Canaan to Egypt, he passed these small villages. Everywhere he found a welcome. Nelson Glueck calls this period in the Negev by the Latin name: Pax Abrahamitica. Can you guess what it means?

   Today, Jews are resettling the Negev.

   Do you think they are wise?

   What dangers are they facing?

   Would you choose to live in the Negev if you could?

Readings for Students

Voices from the Past, by Eisenberg, Azriel, Abelard-Schuman, 1959. P. 114.

Voices from the Past, by Mazar and Trone, Harvey House, 1967. Chap. I–II–III–V–VI.

Treasures Under the Sand, by Honour, Alan, McGraw-Hill, 1967.

The Three Brothers of Ur, by Fyson, J. G., Coward-McCann, 1964.

Readings for Teachers

The Dawn of Civilization, ed. E. A. Speiser, gen. ed. B. Netanyahu, Jewish History Publications, Ltd., Rutgers University Press, 1964.

From the Stone Age to Christianity, William F. Albright, Doubleday, Anchor Book.

Rivers in the Desert, Nelson Glueck, Jewish Publication Society.

Genesis, E. A. Speiser, Doubleday & Co., 1964.

The Midrash: Midrash Rabbah, trans. by Rabbi Dr. H. Freedman, Soncino.

The Heritage of Biblical Israel, Nahum M. Sarna, United Synagogue Commission on Jewish Education.

chapter 4 Why Monotheism Shocked Most of Abraham's World

MONOTHEISM IS THE BELIEF THAT ONE God created the universe and everyone and everything in it. Furthermore, God is unique, different from all forces and powers within nature. Nor did any force or power precede Him.

It may be that some men in ancient days conceived of monotheism, or of a kind of monotheism. What is undoubtedly true is that Abraham was the first man who not only conceived of one God, but taught this to his children and to all men who would listen to him.

When he migrated to Canaan, men and women, not of his family, accompanied him. If they were slaves obviously they had to follow their master. But if not, then they must have had another reason. What could it have been? They must have believed what Abraham taught. The Bible recognizes this function of Abraham to teach, when it says:

Shall I conceal from Abraham what I am about to do, since Abraham is to become a great and populous nation, and all the nations of the earth are to bless themselves by him? For I have singled him out, that he may instruct his children and his grandchildren to keep the way of the Lord by doing what is just and right, in order that the Lord may bring about for Abraham what He had promised him.

There is a very interesting Midrash* written by a Rabbi Judah in the name of Rabbi Johanan. It says that God lifted Abraham up above the vault of heaven and commanded him to look down from above.

Can you figure out what Rabbi Judah meant? Remember, that, according to the Bible, no one before Abraham, from Adam to Terah, had succeeded in fulfilling God's plan. It was to Abraham God then turned. Abraham was to do what others had not been able to do. But, in order for him to accomplish this, Abraham had to see the universe from God's position. Abraham was to be a prophet, not an astrologer. He was not to penetrate to God's will by reading stars, or by any other form of magic. He was to understand the purposes of God's commandments because these commandments were revealed to him.

God's plan, the Bible tells us, was, and remains simple. Men were to act justly, and to love mercy. Men were to live decently together as brothers. For this is a very im-

* Genesis XVIII:17–19.

portant lesson of monotheism. If God is the Father of all of us, then we must all be brothers.

This may not appear so amazing to you. But to the men of Abraham's day, this would have been considered shocking. How could men be brothers when they were of different nations and classes? And even within the same nation, could a slave be the brother of his master? Could a peasant be the brother to his king?

Even today, how many people really accept this doctrine? Didn't the Nazis claim to be a super race? Didn't they murder millions of innocent people to prove it? And what about us? What do we believe when we allow men, women, and children to go hungry and naked while we enjoy the gifts of the earth?

When Abraham looked about his world, he saw that, while men brought sacrifices to their gods, they did not serve their gods with the only gift that made sense: with good deeds. Why? Because men imitated their gods. And their gods were often furious, violent, unreliable: hardly concerned with good deeds.

In a pagan creation story, *Enuma Elish,* we read how gods battled with each other. We learn that when a god killed a goddess, heaven and earth were created out of the corpse of the goddess.

In another story, *The Epic of Gilgamesh,* it is written that the gods gathered around a sacrifice like flies. This is an ugly description. But clearly, if gods behaved like gluttons, why shouldn't men behave like gluttons as well?

Furthermore, if gods and goddesses are born, live, grow old, and die, they are then as dependent on natural forces as man. If even En-lil, the chief god of the Mesopotamians, did not always exist, then there had to be other powers before him. Therefore, man was dependent not only on the gods, but on the powers before the gods. That is why man sought by magic to control those powers. With such control, man thought he could change the natural order of life. Thus, magic became one of the most important sciences of pagan man. In both Mesopotamia and Egypt, magic would have been called a "discipline."

More often than not, the pagan kings considered themselves sons, or agents, of the gods. Their every deed was supposed to have meaning. The acts they performed, especially the religious acts, were supposed to influence the lives and destinies of their people.

First-born sons were also considered partly sacred. That is why they were taken by pagan priests as sacrifices to the gods. As Rabbi Isaac said, the world was on fire with evil and superstition.

Abraham and his sons taught the folly and danger of these beliefs by the way they lived. They drew people to them by their faith in El Elyon, the God of heaven and earth. They took possession of the lands as heralds do, in the name of their King. They were men who made mistakes too. But all their lives they sought to know God's will. They longed for justice and demanded it. Even of God Himself. In short, they spoke not only of monotheism, but of "Ethical Monotheism."

Chapter XVIII of Genesis tells of one of the central dialogues between God and man. It occurs when Abraham attempts to save the cities of Sodom and Gemorrah.

According to this episode the wickedness of these cities was so enormous, God decided to wipe them out. Abraham pleaded for them. Though he argued on the basis of justice, he was actually asking for mercy. He knew very well Sodom and Gomorrah deserved their punishments.

If modernists protest again, they do so with counter-arguments. All the author of this Chapter was trying to explain, they say, was how the once fertile plain of Sodom became the arid and desolate one it is today. Therefore, J invented this story of the destruction of these cities through a sulphurous fire. Besides, Abraham's nephew, Lot who lived in Sodom, had to escape and become the Patriarch of the nations of Moab and Ammon.

Even if this were valid, how could the author have invented any man epic enough to argue with God? Such a man must surely have lived and been preserved in the memory of the people. Abraham must have demonstrated by his deeds, the quality of courage, and above all, his passion for justice and mercy. Only from his mouth could J put so daring and challenging a demand:

Will You sweep away the innocent along with the guilty? Far be it from You to do such a thing, to bring death upon the innocent as well as the guilty, so that innocent and guilty fare alike. Far be it from YOU! Shall not the Judge of all the earth deal justly?

(Genesis XVIII:25)

No pagan man, and no pagan author would have dared use such language before his god. Pagan man brought gifts to the gods hoping the gods would not be his enemy. Most of the time he was satisfied not to be noticed by the gods at all. To challenge his gods would not only have shocked him. It would have terrified him.

How then, could Abraham have used such bold speech? How could J himself have dared ascribe such a demand unto a mortal? J knew how much guts it took. He, or as the traditionalists would say, Abraham, admitted it even as he pleaded for Sodom and Gomorrah.

. . . "Here am I presuming to speak to the Lord, I who am but dust and ashes . . .". . . "Let not the Lord be impatient if I go on . . ." Still he went on, "Please, let not the Lord be angry if I speak this last time: What if there are no more than ten?" . . .

(Genesis XVIII:27–32)

J could and did, only because such demands were true to the character of Abraham. As a matter of fact, Abraham's own experiences forced him to believe that the God for whom he had given up his past, his home, father and brother, had to be concerned for justice and mercy. He had staked his very life upon this faith. If this weren't true, then he really didn't care if God *did* blot him out.

But if, as he believed, God required justice and mercy of man, then how could He object when he, a man, also demanded this very justice and this very mercy?

According to this episode, Abraham was actually testing God. What he didn't know was that God was testing him. That is why, as we shall see more clearly in Chapter V, God made Abraham his first prophet by revealing to him what He might do. And, since a prophet is concerned for all mankind, Abraham becomes the first biblical man of history. When Abraham stepped out of Haran, he stepped out into history.

Slavery

Before we continue with our history, we should pause to consider the institution of slavery. For, how can we speak of monotheism, of all men being brothers, and own slaves. The very word "slave" is a horror to us.

Slavery in the ancient East is hardly a simple subject. But when we examine it in Israel as well, by the way, as in Arabia, we find a very different order of society. It bears no resemblance to the dreadful lot of the black man of the southern plantations of our own country, nor to the bestial conditions under which the Roman slaves of the latifundia (the lower class) and the Greek slaves of the potteries or mines lived.

Jewish and Arabic slaves were considered part of the family. Often they had more independence than sons or younger brothers. Indeed, before the birth of Ishmael and Isaac, it was Eliezer, a slave, who was Abraham's heir. Eliezer was called a "son of the house."

After Isaac's birth, Eliezer acted as a kind of older brother to Isaac. He made the marriage arrangements for him, bringing Rebecca back from Mesopotamia to be the wife of our second Patriarch.

This same familial relationship existed in Arabia. Not only ancient Arabic sources reveal this, but even a modern traveller, Freya Stark, tells us in her book *The Southern Gates of Arabia,* that "each boy is given a slave of his own age, and they grow up as good friends together."

Most significant is the fact that while the prophets of Israel condemned every sign of injustice against the poor, the orphan, the stranger, the widow, or the Levite, there is not one reference to the mistreatment of slaves. You will understand how telling this is when you study the nature of prophets.

When Psalm 116:6 says "I am your slave (or servant, for 'Eved' means both), the son of your handmaid (female servant or slave), he was saying: I am a very intimate member of your family. Moses' finest title was "Eved Adonai," Servant or Slave of God.

At the same time, you should know, there was a difference between Hebrew slaves and what were referred to as "Canaanite" slaves. The fact is no Hebrew slave could be enslaved for more than seven years. When he was sent away, he had to be equipped generously from his Master's goods.

On the other hand the Canaanite slave was protected in many ways. If hurt by his Master so that he lost a part of his body, even a tooth, he had to be freed. Nor could anyone return an escaped slave to his Master. Under the enlightened Hammurabic code, which had preceded Abraham's period, an escaped slave was either turned back to his Master or beheaded. The Bible on the other hand, specifically warns against oppressing a fugitive slave. Canaanite slaves were circumcised and shared the Seder meal. In a priestly house, they ate of the "holy food."

Post-Biblical literature speaks of how Canaanite slaves could be liberated. To fulfill a Commandment was one reason. We read that the Sage, Eliezer ben Hyrcanus freed his slave in order to make up a "Minyan." Female slaves were set free for purposes of marriage. This was for her protection and for society's as well.

As Jewish law evolved, the emphasis was on making the ownership of slaves a very expensive and uncomfortable affair. So much so, that it was said that he who owns a slave owns a Master.

After it is all said and done, however, we should know that any instrument which gives one man possession of another, is an abomination. "Unto Me the children of Israel are slaves," God says, according to one Midrash. They must not be slaves to any human being, it therefore, follows. Nor, we may add, should the children of any other nation.

Activities

Questions

1. Contrast Abraham's plea for the wicked of Sodom and Gomorrah with the silence of Noah before the announcement of the flood.
2. The Bible describes Abraham as "walking before God." How does the Bible describe Noah? Why?
3. Idolatry is the creation by man of a thing (idol), and his worship of that very thing.
4. Are we guilty of idolatry today? How?
5. Why is magic not only used by men who worship idols, but is itself idolatry?
6. Read how Abraham bargained with God for Sodom and Gomorrah. (Genesis XVIII:16-33).

7. Why was Abraham really pleading for mercy, though he demanded justice?

Readings for Students

Words in Genesis, by Asimov, Isaac, Houghton Mifflin Co., Boston, 1962.

Voices from the Past, by Mazar & Trone, Harvey House, 1967. Chap. V–VI–VII.

The Book of Legends, by Goldin, Hyman, The Jordan Publishing Co., 1937. Pp. 64–208.

Readings for Teachers

Buried Treasure in Bible Lands, Cohen, Lenore, The Ward Ritchie Press, 1965. Chap, VIII.

Commentary on Genesis, by Cassuto, Umberto, Part II, Magnes Press, 1961.

The Divine Drama, Travis, Marion Thomas Yoseloff Ltd., 1967.

Oriental and Biblical Studies, ed. by Finkelstein & Greenberg, Univ. of Pennsylvania, 1967.

Unit II

And it came to pass in those days, when Moses was grown up, that he went out unto his brethren, and looked on their burdens; and he saw an Egyptian smiting a Hebrew . . .

EXODUS II:11

chapter 5 Descent Into Egypt and Into Slavery

GO BACK TO CHAPTER 2, TO THE FAM- ily chart of our nation, and find Joseph. He is the first son of Rachel, one of Jacob's wives. It is Joseph Jacob favored above all his sons. Why? Because he loved Rachel more than he loved his other wives. When she died, he transferred that deep love to Joseph, her first son. He made the boy a special coat, like the ornamental coats worn by princes.

Naturally, his brothers resented this. And when Joseph lorded it over his brothers, their resentment swelled into hatred. They sold Joseph as a slave to merchants going down to Egypt.

When famine struck Canaan and the other countries of the Near East, Jacob sent his ten older sons to Egypt to buy food. Unknown to Jacob and his family, Joseph had become Vizier of Egypt: the most powerful man next to Pharaoh, the King. Because of Joseph's wise manage- ment, Egypt and the neighboring countries did not die of hunger. He saved substantial portions of grain during seven years of plenty, and with this surplus, fed popula- tions during the following meager years.

Read the story of the brothers and Jo- seph in the first Book of the Bible. It is one of the most exciting stories ever written. It is also the cause of our people's descent and settlement in Egypt.

There is a curious similarity between Abraham and his heirs. As Abraham had travelled down into Egypt and back to Ca- naan because of famine, so too did his son. As Abraham left Egypt with much cattle, gold and silver, so his children would leave. And as Abraham and Sarah were in danger in Egypt, so too were their de- scendants.

But Abraham's danger lasted a short time; Israel's two hundred and ten years. At first, Jacob and his sons came as guests of a grateful Pharaoh. On a scarab dated 1600 B.C.E. we read of a chieftain Ya'kob- her. Even the most cautious Egyptologist (student of Egypt) believes this referred to our Patriarch, Jacob.

For Jacob or this Ya'kob-her, Pharaoh could not do enough. He gave him and his sons the land of Goshen in the northeastern Delta, where their cattle would have ex- cellent pasture, and where they and their families would live in comfort. But after many years a new Pharaoh arose who, as the Bible says: "did not know Joseph." We realize he did not *want* to know him, did not want to remember that Joseph had pre- vented a killing famine. Instead he began to oppress them, and finally made slaves of them.

It is important for us to study the culture of Egypt. Our people, after all, spent over two centuries there. Except for Canaan, Egypt and Mesopotamia's civilizations influence Israel's early years the most. Indeed, you cannot truly understand the Bible, which is the record of those formative years, unless you realize the Bible is constantly combating the evils of both Egypt and Mesopotamia.

Therefore, let us go back to Egypt's early history: first, to her technical and scientific accomplishments of 2000 B.C.E. We find that Egypt had some knowledge of metals: producing bronze from tin and copper. She devised the 365 day calendar centuries before it was in use elsewhere in the world. Her mathematicians and architects laid out huge structures with very little error. Her scientists had some knowledge of anatomy and surgery and recognized that the heart carried essential fluids to all parts of the body. In fact, Egyptians came close to discovering the circulation of the blood. But they did not investigate further because they feared the gods. For everyone knew it was gods and demons who caused disease. And who would tamper with what the gods desired?

These are exciting and impressive skills. But no one skill is as significant to the development of Egypt as her geography. As Herodotus, a Greek historian said, Egypt is "a gift of the Nile."

If you examine the map on p. 14 you will see why. Egypt is a semitropical country with no rain to speak of. Yet she bears two or three crops a year. How is this possible? Because of the Nile: her great river. Every year the Nile rises above her banks. Her muddy waters coming from Equatorial Africa and the highlands of Abyssinia, carry with them refertilizing soil.

At first man did not know how to use this water wisely. It would rush over its banks without restraint, spreading thinly beyond the river marshes and jungles, then drain off quickly into the sands. It probably took thousands of years of prehistory before man cleared the jungle and swamps that existed along the river's edges. It probably took centuries more for man to create methods of holding the waters against the greedy desert sand.

Gradually Egyptian man learned to channel the yearly overflow into canals. In this way he irrigated and enriched the earth. Upon this mud, Egypt exists to this day.

The map shows you the Nile winding her way through the middle of Egypt to the Mediterranean Sea. Like a huge black serpent it moves from south to north. On either of her sides, the blackness suddenly turns red, and deserts unroll eastward and westward. One can stand with one foot on the living earth, and one foot on the lifeless desert sand. If you look inward toward the river valley you see vegetation, bustle, life; outward, you see sandstone hills, silence, desolation.

The Nile not only fed Egypt, but shaped her character, her beliefs, and her form of government. Because all productivity was along the river's banks, all settlement was there as well. As a result, Egyptians developed a kind of city-civilization. They had an alphabet made up of signs we call hieroglyphics; they wrote on papyrus, a reed which grew in the Nile, and from which our word "paper" is derived. Even their quills were fashioned out of thin reeds of the Nile.

Because of this concentration of population, Pharaoh, whose name meant the Great House, could control his Egyptian subjects with ease. He did not have to depend on too many governors, as do rulers whose land is scattered over distances. He was an absolute monarch. All of Egypt belonged to him. Even the priesthood, the next most powerful force, was appointed by Pharaoh.

Furthermore, the country was separated from other lands by long stretches of deserts and hills. For hundreds of years, therefore, Egyptians felt confident and secure. So much so, they considered their king, unlike the kings of Mesopotamia, to be not an agent of the gods, but a god himself. He was Horus, god of the distant spaces of the sky; a falcon.

It was easy for the Egyptian to accept the divinity of his Pharaoh. Under a warm and constant sun, he saw all his world in one steady light. He did not distinguish as most people did, between life and death, between human and animal, between human and divine. Bear in mind this god-state of Pharaoh. It will explain the epic encounter between Pharaoh and the man who was to defy him.

In Chapter 3, you read of a people called Hyksos who swept down from north and northeast Asia into the Near East. These Asiatics were a military horde, using horses and chariots, and so fierce, they actually defeated Egypt in 1800 B.C.E. The Hyksos kings ruled her 160 years. This conquest shocked and humiliated Egypt. From that time on, Egypt's sense of security was severely shaken. Nevertheless, Egypt did learn how to use war chariots and other weapons from the Hyksos.

Some historians believe that the Pharaoh who made Joseph his Vizier was a Hyksos. If this is so, it would follow that as soon as the Egyptians drove out these Hyksos rulers (known by some as Shepherd Kings), they would turn against anyone, or any group close to their detested conquerors.

For these historians, it is obvious why our people were enslaved by the Pharaoh who "did not know Joseph." He must have been an Egyptian Pharaoh. But if we read the Bible carefully, we can see that this is not necessarily true.

In the *Book of Genesis* 43:32, we read that the Egyptians would not eat with Joseph's brothers, "since that would be abhorrent to the Egyptians." In 46:34 we read, "for all shepherds are abhorrent to Egyptians." Could it be that men who were themselves former shepherds would hate other shepherds? Or men who were themselves Asiatics, would abhor other Asiatics? What do you think?

There is no doubt the Egyptians continued to hate Asiatics even after they drove the Hyksos from their land. During the post-Hyksos period, Egypt conducted a constant campaign against many tribes in Canaan, seeking to revenge their humiliation. The prisoners she brought back from those battles, she enslaved. It follows that any Asiatic within Egypt would be considered an enemy. Did we not put Japanese-Americans in detention camps during World War II?

Nevertheless the story is hardly that simple. Let us trace the history of our people in Egypt and see why. At first, as you already know, Jacob and his sons lived comfortably in Egypt in the rich Delta lands of the north. They were made Shepherds of the royal herds. Still they probably missed the simple and rural life of semi-nomads. Remember, though they lived near cities in Canaan they had never settled within those cities. And then, of course, there was that slight, very slight sense of domination that they had not experienced before. For though our Patriarchs were the heads of their tribes, they did not rule as tyrants. Quite the contrary, they consulted the Elders. At times, we get the feeling they were ignored. Rachel, Jacob's own wife, did not tell him that she had taken her father's *teraphim*. At other times they were defied. Jacob's own sons defied him.

But Pharaoh, an absolute monarch, was a different matter. True, Joseph's Pharaoh was kind to them. *Genesis* tells us, when Jacob died, they had to get permission from Pharaoh to take their father back to Canaan for burial in the family tomb of Machpelah. And they left their children, their wives, and their herds behind. Why? Were these hostages? Was this the beginning of a kind of bondage? Was the change from freedom to total slavery gradual? Instead of guessing, let us see what history reveals to us.

According to some historians Israel left Egypt and slavery during the reign of the Pharaoh, Mer ne ptah. This departure we call the Exodus. *Exodus* is also the name of the Second Book of the Bible. According to others, the Exodus occurred in the reign of Ramses II, his father. There are still others who put it 200 years earlier. If we accept the date 1220 B.C.E., then Mer ne ptah must be the Pharaoh of the Exodus, because Ramses II's reign ended in 1225 B.C.E. Seti I, the father of Ramses II, would be the Pharaoh who forced Israel into bondage.

These Pharaohs were part of what we call the Nineteenth Dynasty. On the surface, this period seemed an era of peak glory and power. Egypt was one of the two strongest Empires of its day. The other Empire was Hatti, country of the Hittites. After many battles against Hatti, Ramses II finally made a treaty of peace with her. Later he married a Hittite princess.

Yet the fact remains that only five years after Ramses' death, our forefathers marched out of this mighty Empire. Historians point to conditions outside of Egypt to explain this Exodus. They mention the Rise of the Sea People, for example, who threatened Egypt. Or the Libyans, who joined with the Sea Peoples and attacked Egypt from the west. Or rebellions in Canaan against Egyptian rule.

Perhaps. Yet Egypt defeated the Libyans, and put down the rebellions. Of course war and rebellions can cause national upheavals. Also the plagues described in the Bible, point to natural catastrophes. It may even be that after the death of Ramses II, the tireless builder, that there were no extensive building projects. The slaves, therefore, might not have been closely supervised.

But before we decide how the Exodus came about let us study the years that preceded it.

One fact is clear: our ancestors were dragged downward from the position of Royal Shepherds to the shameful state of slavery. How was this accomplished? How was a free people transformed into slaves?

According to the *Book of Exodus,* first Pharaoh accused them of a crime against the state: "Behold the people of . . . Israel are . . . mightier than we . . . and . . . when war comes they will join up with our enemies and fight against us. . . ."

Then he arrested them and did everything he could to dehumanize them: to make them forget they were made in the image of their God. Each step that follows was cleverly planned.

Grind them down with constant toil. Make their living and working conditions unbearable. Force them to make bricks and refuse to give them straw: the raw material they need. Choose overseers from among them so that slave will turn against slave. Should they still have some spirit left, crush it by murdering their sons. Order the infants killed at birth. And when that doesn't work, compel the mothers themselves to throw their babies into the Nile. The very source of Egypt's life must become the grave of Jewish children.

What can any sensible person make of this? Why refuse the straw? Why murder babies? Without straw, production of bricks must decline. Without children, there can be no future slaves. There is no profit in such a program for Pharaoh himself. Why should he have adopted it?

In the face of such irrational and cruel behavior, what could our ancestors do? Nothing much, except dream of liberation. These dreams were made of the one thing no Pharaoh could take from them: their folk memories. Handed down from father to sons, these recalled the steadfast Abraham. Some claimed that God Himself had revealed this very bondage to Abraham in an episode known as *The Covenant of the Pieces.*

Traditionalists accept this revelation without doubt. Modernists, however, cannot. J, they say, described this event for comfort's sake. In what way could a prophecy of slavery comfort our ancestors? By disclosing, at the same time, that they would be freed. Liberation as well as bondage would then be part of the same divine plan. Included in this plan was the land: a land of milk and honey; a land that awaited their return.

No matter what the details of this Covenant of the Pieces, it can hardly be doubted that these memories kept alive hope of eventual return. It prepared them, in some measure, for the Exodus.

Who their liberator would be, they could hardly know, except that he too must be a Hebrew. Who else would care? And so, they must have wondered if he was among them chopping straw for bricks, hauling stones from the quarries, climbing the ramp of the pyramids, burning beneath the violent sun of Sinai's desert as they dug for turquoise and copper.

They could hardly suspect he was in none of these places. Less, could they imagine it was from Pharaoh's own family, from the Great House that he would come. Or that he would bear one of the most distinctive Egyptian names: Moses.

One scientist connects the disappearance of the island of Atlantis with the Exodus. According to him, the destruction of this island in the eastern Mediterranean unleashed wide-spread catastrophes. He believes it brought Minoan civilization on Crete to an end. He also believes the various plagues described in the Bible, such as insects, darkness, lightning, etc. were direct results of this violent upheaval.

Indeed, he quotes the prophet Amos as proof. For *Amos* IX:7 seems to connect these two events:

Have I not brought up Israel out of the land of Egypt
And the Philistines from Caphtor (Crete).

Activities

Questions
- What European country of our century enslaved Israel and other nations?
- Did this country repeat Pharaoh's program? If so, how?
- Were its goals the same as Pharaoh's? How, the same? How, different?

Readings for Students
Legends of Joseph and His Brothers, Skulsky, Shulsinger Bros. N.Y.
The Book of Legends, by Goldin, Hyman E., The Jordan Publishing Co., 1937. Vol. I.

Readings for Teachers
The Culture of Ancient Egypt, Wilson, John, Phoenix Books, University of Chicago Press.
Moses and the Vocation of the Jewish People, Neher, Andre, Harper Torchbooks, N.Y.

The Torah: New Translation, J.P.S.
Egypt of the Pharaohs, Gardiner, A Galaxy Book, Oxford University Press, N.Y.

Understanding Exodus, Moshe Greenberg, Melton Research Center Series. (Vol. II, Part 1.)

chapter 6 Moses: Rebel of Egypt

MOSE MEANS SON. WHETHER ROYALTY or commoner, Egyptians bore such names as Thut mose, Amenmose, Ptah-mose, and Ra-mose: sons of the gods, Thut, Amen, Ptah, and Ra.

But Moses was son to none of these. He was born to Jochebed and Amram of the tribe of Levi, Jacob's third son. He was saved by Pharaoh's daughter from the graveyard of the Nile, and adopted by her as her son. Legend says he became one of Egypt's greatest generals and heir to Pharaoh. The Bible names him the greatest prophet of history.

What do Egyptian records tell us? Nothing; absolutely nothing. Is it possible? Can it be that the man we call the noblest of men never drew one word of comment from Egypt? Or is it all legend?

Not if you know the way of Egypt. Precisely this total silence concerning Moses can be the most conclusive proof not only of his existence, but of his importance. For it was the practise of Pharaohs to erase the name of anyone they considered an enemy.

A man's name was considered a vital part of his being. By blotting out his name from his tomb, Egyptians believed you destroyed his continued existence in the next world. If you erased it from records you ended his earthly success which was important to his survival.

When Akh-en-Aton, (a Pharaoh of whom you shall read later) tried to destroy the worship of the god, Amon, he systematically hacked Amon's name out of every document he could. Even a god, therefore, existed as long as his name was part of a single record.

What could Moses have done to warrant such a fate? Moses, *Exodus* reports, rebelled against Egypt. Reared in the midst of power and wealth, he threatened both the power of the Great House, and the wealth of the aristocracy.

He killed a man, most likely a taskmaster who was beating a Hebrew slave. Surely you must wonder how a man could be so dangerous because he killed an Egyptian? After all life was cheap in Egypt. Not only the life of the slaves was unbearable, but the life of the masses of workers was almost as wretched. In a papyrus of Turin we read: "for the last 18 days we (workers) have been putrefying with hunger. . . ." In a famous bas-relief, we see an Egyptian peasant lying full length on the ground being beaten by agents of Pharaoh's treasury. In another papyrus we read of a mason that "his fingers are his bread." And a Scribe who wants his students to work diligently reminds them that "the plebeians (workers) stink." He had nothing against the workers. He was merely warning them they would become workers if they were lazy. In fact the misery of workers led at times to revolts against the government.

It was not always thus in Egypt. Around twenty one hundred B.C.E. almost one thousand years before this period of Israel's slavery, Egypt had come to grips with the need for social justice. In *The Eloquent Peasant,* a story of that time, the most important goal we are told was social justice. For in that period, ancient Egypt believed that all men have equal rights or opportunities, or should have.

It is a pity this vision which Egypt once had of the worth of each man, faded. By the nineteenth dynasty, the lot of the lower classes was desperate. Why then, you may ask, was the death of an unidentified taskmaster by a Royal Prince, so crucial? Because the taskmaster was the *representative of oppression.* By killing him, Moses has lifted his hand against Pharaoh himself. He challenged the very system and structure of slavery.

Egypt's magnificent temples, huge storehouses, royal tombs, royal cities, were wonders of the ancient world. We know Egyptian architects and mathematicians were advanced. But what machines did they invent that could lift massive stones, crushing weights? What tools did they devise that could plant a very forest of stone colonnades?

The answer is simple: slaves. Slaves were the cheapest tools. There were tens of thousands in Egypt. Not only our people, the Hebrews, were enslaved, but many other national groups as well: Sardinians, Libyans, Negroes, Lycians. . . . If one slave slipped and was crushed by the stones he was shoving up a ramp, no matter. There was another to replace him immediately. In many pictures, in fact, slaves were drawn as part of a mass. They were not seen as individuals. "They had no hearts," the Egyptians said of the slave. They meant he had no personality. Therefore, the slave, for all practical purposes, was an inanimate object, a thing, incapable of emotion.

The two cities of Pithom and Ramses of which the Bible speaks were built by our ancestors. These were probably Pi-Tum and Pi-Ra'Messe, Great of Victories, Ramses II's royal home of the north.

Can you imagine what it meant to strike at the very foundation of such a system? Without slaves who would have built the pyramids, temples, royal cities? Anyone who threatened such a way of life, commoner or prince, would have to be put to death, and his name blotted out.

Moses must have been a young man at the end of the reign of Seti I. In the famous temple at Karnak, there is a picture of Seti I and his son, Ramses II, as Crown Prince. Beneath the figure and name of Ramses, another figure and name has been erased. One Egyptologist believed that Ramses gained the throne through cunning and then erased the name and form of an older brother.

But might it not have been Seti himself who erased that name? This may sound far-fetched, but the possibility cannot help but tease us. For might not Seti have chosen his daughter's adopted son as his heir? She, the adopting mother, must have been very special to her father. How else would he have allowed her to keep Moses, a baby of the Nile, in the first place? Of course, we can only speculate.

Slaves do not learn from their masters. Pushing stones up a pyramid's ramp, slaves do not take time out to discuss Egyptian philosophy with the Royal Architect.

But even if they had been invited into the palace itself, what would they have learnt? That the Egyptian, from their king down, saw gods everywhere? In the peace treaty Ramses II made with Hatti, he called as witnesses:

a thousand gods of the male gods and of the female gods of them of Hatti, together with a thousand gods of the male gods and of the female gods of them of the land of Egypt.

In a land where whole groups of people know poverty, hunger, toil, Ramses II sought only the glorification of himself. He was not content with his 90 foot statue at Tanis, or with the one thousand ton statue in his tomb, or with his cliff temple at Abu Simbel, or with his mighty Hypostyle hall in Karnak. No, he used the monuments of his ancestors as well: either adding his name to theirs, or destroying them in order to use their stone for his own building projects.

Moses, on the other hand, did see this. He may very well have been witness to many treaties. He must have walked beneath many columns, scanned many temples, pyramids, obelisks.

Yet all these trappings of power, vanished before his sight when he met with cruelty. He killed the taskmaster who beat a slave.

When he fled to Midian, his first deed, the Bible tells us, was to defend women who were being driven away from a well by men. Moses, it is obvious, could not be still, or silent, when the strong oppressed the weak.

For forty years he became, like the Patriarchs, a shepherd. For forty years he tried to forget the sights and sounds of slavery in the desert of Midian. He even, the Bible records, went "beyond the desert." To no avail.

The summons came to him, as it was to come to all prophets of Israel. Before a Burning Bush that would not be burnt, before a Voice that would not be stilled, he was commanded to return and liberate his brothers. To traditionalists, the Burning Bush was a revelation of God to one man. To modernists, it was the conscience of Moses. Its result was the same. Moses began the task for which he had been preparing all his life. He went back to Egypt.

Activities

Questions

- What qualifications would a man need in order to undertake the task of liberation?
- What qualification, according to the Midrash, did God consider most important?

When Moses our teacher . . . was tending the flocks in the wilderness, a kid escaped from him. He ran after it until it reached a shady place . . . From a pool of water there, the kid stopped to drink . . . Moses said: "I did not know that you ran away because of thirst; you must be weary!" So he placed the kid on his shoulder and walked away. Thereupon God said: "Because you have mercy in leading the flock of a mortal, you will surely tend my flock, Israel."

- Do you agree that compassion is the most important qualification for a liberator? Why?
- You read in Chapter 5 that the Bible constantly combats the evils of Mesopotamia and Egypt. Here are some laws which demonstrate this. All are from the Book of Deuteronomy.

A king shall not keep many horses . . . he shall not have many wives . . . nor shall he amass silver and gold to excess.

When he is seated on his royal throne, he shall have a copy of this Teaching written for him by the levitical priests. Let it remain with him and let him read in it all his life, so that he may learn to revere the Lord his God, to observe faithfully every word of this Teaching as well as these laws. Thus he will not act haughtily toward his fellows or deviate from the Instruction to the right or to the left, to the end that he and his descendants may reign long in the midst of Israel.

(XVII:16–20)

You shall not turn over to his master a slave who seeks refuge with you from his master. He shall live with you in any place he may choose among the settlements in your midst, wherever he pleases; you must not illtreat him.

(XXIII:16)

You shall not abuse a needy and destitute laborer, whether a fellow countryman or a non-citizen in your communities. You must pay him his wages on the same day, before the sun sets, for he is needy and urgently depends on it; else he will cry to the Lord against you and you will incur guilt.

(XXIV:14)

You shall not destroy the rights of the stranger or the fatherless; you shall not take a widow's garment in pawn. Remember that you were a slave in Egypt and that the Lord your God redeemed you from there; there-

fore do I warn you to observe this commandment.

(XXIV:17)

• Bring in five more examples of the Bible's
opposition to the evils of Egypt.

Readings for Students

Worlds Lost and Found, Eisenberg and Elkin.
(Chapter III)
Words from the Exodus, Asimov, Isaac, Hough-
ton Mifflin Co., Boston, 1963.
Moses, by Flight, John, Beacon Press, 1942.

Midrash Rabbah-Exodus, Soncino Press, Lon-
don. P. 49. Read Midrashim on Moses.
Understanding the Midrash, by Miller, Amos
W., Jonathan David, N.Y., 1965. (Interpreta-
tions on Exodus.)
This Man Moses, by Weisfeld, Israel, Bloch
Publishing Co., 1966.

Readings for Teachers

Antiquities of the Jews, Josephus.
(Read Book II, Chapters IX, X, and as much
as you find interesting. Josephus gives us
the legendary personality of Moses.)

chapter 7 The Meaning of Freedom for Israel

HOW DOES ONE LIBERATE SLAVES? WE in the United States had to fight a Civil War to abolish slavery as well as to keep our country together. Before the war men and women known as Abolitionists organized an Underground Railroad to transport slaves from the south up to the north and to freedom. At the most, they saved a handful. But woe to those Abolitionists if they were caught in the south. And woe to the slaves caught escaping.

Yet the slave owners of the south were not absolute rulers like Pharaoh. Nor was the south a mighty Empire. Could any one man, or even two, oppose Pharaoh and his warriors? Is it likely Pharaoh would agree to give up such cheap labor?

It is only natural then that Moses should fear such an assignment. He tried to refuse. We read in *Exodus* how he argued, first, that he was not suitable: "Who am I that I should go to Pharaoh and free the Israelites from Egypt?" he asked. Then he protested that neither the slaves nor Pharaoh would believe God had sent him. At this God, *Exodus* continues, revealed his name to him, not for magical purposes, but to identify Him to the doubters. In addition He gave Moses three signs by which he would convince slaves and Pharaoh.

Nevertheless, Moses continued to object, claiming he could not speak properly. Still patient with him, God assigned Aaron, the brother of Moses, to be his spokesman. But when Moses still refused, God commands him to Egypt.

Moses obeyed. What else could he do? But, as he had feared, it was a bitter and frustrating experience with Israel, and more so, with Pharaoh. Nine times he pleaded with Pharaoh to release Israel. Nine times Pharaoh refused. Each refusal God punished with a plague. The last one, the killing of the first born of both man and beast, brings Pharaoh to his knees. He begs Moses to take the people and leave. He also begs him to pray for him. The Egyptians load the slaves with gifts, and the Exodus begins.

This will, no doubt, prove too much for modernists. Surely, they maintain, we cannot accept the plagues, as history. Perhaps they cannot. But they can agree that there must have been a series of natural upheavals which the author interpreted as the intervention of God, or as the Bible itself puts it as "the finger of God." Any of the nine plagues, they must concede, could have occurred. Certainly if the scientist in Chapter 5 is correct, the plagues

43

cease to be a mystery altogether. As for the tenth, the threat to Pharaoh's very life, this was the only one, they would have to admit, that could drive so stubborn a man to let Israel go. Indeed, the Rabbis point out, Pharaoh had to be that obstinate to be in any way a worthy opponent of the Creator of all men. For that matter, Moses too had to undergo change to deal with the ruler of this mighty empire.

In the encounters between Moses and Pharaoh we see this change take place. The very Moses who cried out "Who am I that I should go to Pharaoh . . ." develops into a towering and heroic personality. Pharaoh may be a god to his people, indeed, according to one Egyptologist, the chief of Egypt's gods; before Moses, he is an obstinate mortal who must be made to acknowledge the God of Abraham, Isaac, and Jacob, as the Ruler of the world.

And he does. At the end of this harsh education the tables are turned: Pharaoh pleads; Moses commands.

Nothing we have learnt about Moses, neither his royal upbringing, nor his horror before cruelty and injustice, prepared us for this man of men. It is fair to say Moses himself never suspected the quality of his own courage and resourcefulness.

On the shores of a body of water, the Bible tells us, this Exodus Moses leads almost comes to a halt. This water is called by some the Sea of Reeds; by others Lake Sirbonis. At its edge, Pharaoh and his army overtake the Israelites. For it had not taken long for Pharaoh to regret losing his slaves.

Suddenly Israel, we read on, is trapped between Pharaoh's chariots and water. "Were there no graves in Egypt?", the people weep, "That you brought us to die in the wilderness." To their amazement the water parts:

And the children of Israel went into the midst of the sea upon the dry ground: and the waters were a wall unto them on their right hand and on their left. (*Exodus* XIV:22)

Israel is delivered. The pursuing Egyptians drown. Israel rejoices: they sing and dance.

This episode, known as the Splitting of the Red Sea, is cited as another of the miracles of the Exodus. Modernists point out that such an event is not uncommon in folk tales. The Pamphylian Sea was supposed to have drawn back and given passage before Alexander the Great when he marched against the Persian king, Darius. A Roman historian, Livy, records that when Scipio the Elder was laying siege to the city of New Carthage, the god Neptune aided him by causing the waters of a canal to recede so that he could cross it.

On the other hand, in 1495 and again in 1645, a strong wind drove back the waters of the Rhone into the Lake of Geneva for a distance of about a quarter of a league (three miles = a league).

It looked like a wall of water! (See above) . . . and the inhabitants could go down on dry ground between the bridges and pass from one band to the other.

So too in 1738, when the Russians were fighting the Turks, they were able to enter the Crimea at the Isthmus of Perekop because a strong wind suddenly blew upon the waters of the Putrid Sea, causing them to recede. It is recorded also by an eyewitness that the waters of Lake Menzaleh at the entrance to the Suez Canal were driven back seven miles by the east wind!

Let us pause here for an instant. What you have just read was not written for the sake of proving or disproving any one episode. Indeed, rationalists dismiss this whole discussion. For them the explanation is very simple. The Sea of Reeds was at low tide. Anyone could cross it. By the time the Egyptians arrived the tide had shifted and the Egyptians perished.

No matter what the conclusion one fact remains. The Sea of Reeds did loom between Israel and safety. And Israel did escape.

For traditionalists this passage which is recorded in the famous Song of Moses, is one of the crucial moments of Jewish history. The Song of Moses from the *Book of Exodus,* is reprinted in the Prayer Book. It is recited every morning of every day of the year. Its imprint upon the personality of our people is so deep, one Midrash tells us that the maid servant who beheld the splitting of the waters, saw more of God's plan than did the prophet, Ezekiel.

Both traditionalists and modernists rise when the Song is chanted from the Bible. Both stand when reciting it at prayer.

Why is it so memorable and awesome an occasion? Because it was the decisive blow that brought tyranny to its knees. And because it is both end and beginning: it ends the chapter with Israel's former master; it begins the new life which is to lead to complete freedom. For Moses it will mean continued responsibilities, pain, and yes, satisfaction too. He will need every ounce of strength and wisdom. For out of this horde of slaves, he has to create a nation.

Slavery does not ennoble man. Nor does a desert soften him. Although not as barren as its name suggests, the desert is not hospitable. Water is scarce. Food is hardly abundant. Heat shortens tempers. The danger of warlike tribes like Amalekites who attacked women, children and old men first, terrified them. Little wonder these former slaves tormented Moses during their forty years journey across the desert of Sinai.

If it is amazing that Moses bore with them, it is more amazing that he loved them. True, he became impatient, and even furious at times. But when the fate of the nation hung in the balance, he stood firm. When God, according to Scripture, despaired of the weakness and cowardice of the people and offered to make Moses the founder of a new people, Moses refused. He preferred death with his people rather than the glory of such a future.

When Joshua, the man who will lead Israel into Canaan, begged Moses to punish two men who were prophesying, Moses asked: "Are you jealous for my sake? Would that all the Lord's people were prophets. . . ." How would a Pharaoh have reacted to anyone who invaded his privileges or power?

And yet, we must not make the mistake of underestimating Israel. The fact is that these slaves were asked to go out into an unknown desert. As far as they knew only hot sand, deadly snakes, and burning winds awaited them. Yet they went. At the right moment they found the necessary courage to obey the command of history. Perhaps that is the greatest miracle of the Exodus? Greater than the signs, plagues, or parting of the water?

In this desert, forty-nine days after they left Egypt, days in which they were provided with manna, quails, and most of all, with water, they arrived at the foot of Mt. Sinai. Before the Burning Bush, Moses and Israel had been commanded to serve God upon this Mountain.

The Bible tells us they had been led towards it in the daytime by a pillar of cloud; in the night by a pillar of fire. This divine fire, first beheld in the Burning Bush by one man, now lodges with the people itself. At Sinai the meaning of the Exodus is made clear.

To be set free is not enough. The Amalekites who atacked the weakest were free. How free men live, makes freedom a blessing or a curse.

At Sinai, these former slaves take the most decisive step for themselves and for us: they accept the *Covenant*. With one voice they said: "All that the Lord has spoken, we will do!"

Not just Moses or the Elders, but all of them, we read in *Exodus,* entered into the responsibilities and blessings of the *Covenant.* Each heard exactly what his neighbor heard. From now on each would have to yield only that measure of personal freedom which would keep society orderly and peaceful. Other than that, each now knew he served no one but God. Thus he became completely free from human domination. This, then, is the second heroic act of our ancestors. For all their shortcomings, it is an undeniable fact that they knew how to respond at the crucial moments.

Now the fire of the Bush, and the guiding fire that led them through darkness, is revealed at its source. Mt. Sinai, the Bible tells us, was altogether on smoke, because the Lord descended upon it in fire.

This awesome description of this central event of Jewish experience we call theophany, or Sinai: Revelation of God to man. The greatest of minds have grappled with Sinai. Traditionalists, without question, accept its historicity (historical truth). Yet even among them there are differences. Some claim all of the Ten Commandments, also called the Decalogue, were spoken by God. Others, only the first two: "I am the Lord your God," and "You shall have no other god before Me." Then the people could not endure the divine voice, and Moses was forced to communicate the other commandments to them.

The great rationalist and philosopher, Maimonides (Rambam) (1135–1204) developed the idea that Moses was the interpreter of the divine voice even further. A man who carried Maimonides' concept to its ultimate conclusion was one of the outstanding Hasidic saints, Rabbi Mendel Torum of Rymanov (d. 1814). He said that not even the first two commandments were revealed to Israel. All they heard was the aleph of the first word of the first commandment: Anochi.

What could Rabbi Mendel have meant? After all to hear an aleph is to hear very little. The aleph is only the preparation for all heard language. In itself it has no specific meaning. Therefore, each ear could hear what it was capable of hearing or what it chose to hear.

But if the Decalogue was to become the foundation of religious authority, it had to be translated into a human language. According to Rabbi Mendel, this is exactly what Moses did. Thus every statement became a human interpretation of a divine commandment.

A similar idea was expressed by the philosopher, Franz Rosenzweig (d. 1929). For him the immediate content of revelation was revelation itself. He pointed out that when we read: "And the Lord came down upon Mt. Sinai . . ." (*Exodus* XIX: 20), God gave Himself, surrendered Himself, revealed Himself to Israel. In coming down, therefore, theophany was completed. But, he continued, when we read: "And He spoke . . ." (*Exodus* XX:1), it meant interpretation began.

The modernists of the Reform Movement saw revelation thus:

God reveals Himself not only in the majesty, beauty, and orderliness of nature, but also in the vision and moral striving of the human spirit. Revelation is a continuous process confined to no one group and to no one people. Yet the people of Israel, through its prophets and Sages, achieved unique insight in the realm of religious truth. The Torah, both written and oral, enshrines Israel's ever-growing consciousness of God and of the moral law . . . The Torah remains the dynamic (forceful) source of the life of Israel . . .

The viewpoint of Mordecai Kaplan, founder of the Reconstructionist Movement, is as follows:

The modern-minded Jew cannot consider the miraculous events . . . in the Torah . . . as other than legendary. By far the most significant of these miraculous events was God's self-revelation . . . on Mt. Sinai . . .

And according to Rabbi B. Z. Bokser, one of our present day theologians, the Biblical story is to be read:

. . . as a poetic elaboration of the doctrine that God was the inspiration for the truths which Israel pledged itself to uphold at Sinai . . .

But regardless of how one interprets Sinai, one radiant truth shines forth: for the first time in history a whole people, men, women, and children, agreed to live by law: to live justly and mercifully.

It is significant that everything connected with this episode in *Exodus* is unconcealed. Revelation and acceptance are public acts. All see the smoking mountain with their own eyes; all hear the commandments with their own ears.

Because all witnessed this revelation, all recognized that the laws they heard, moral as well as cultic, were the absolute will of God. They were not the code of wise men nor kings, nor even the wisdom of a god like the Egyptian Thoth who revealed laws along with other matters of arts and science.

Remember the Midrash about Abraham. He was to be a prophet not an astrologer. He was not to read the stars; not to use any form of magic. He was to know God's will because it would be revealed to him.

Revelation, then, is the experience of prophecy. The morality demanded of Israel at Sinai derives not from the wisdom of man. It does from prophecy. Furthermore, this morality can no longer remain a personal concern. The Covenant accepted by the nation, becomes the responsibility of the nation.

Little wonder so many Midrashim were written about Sinai. They describe how terrified the people were, how the heavenly hosts crowned each Israelite, how an absolute silence gripped the universe. These are exciting and instructive stories. Read them.

But there is one Midrash that seems to turn this Sinaitic experience upon its head. It says:

When the whole nation . . . approached Sinai, God lifted up this mountain and held it over the heads of the people like a basket, saying to them: "If you accept the Torah, it is well, otherwise you will find your grave under this mountain."

Where we must ask, is freedom of choice? Where the exultant response: "All that the Lord has said, we will do?" What could the author of this Midrash have meant? He surely knew he seemed to be contradicting the very spirit of the Bible.

Perhaps the answer lies in this message Moses brought Israel before they responded so enthusiastically:

If you will obey Me faithfully and keep My covenant, you shall be My treasured possession among all the peoples. Indeed, all the earth is Mine, but you shall be to Me a kingdom of priests and a holy nation.

(Exodus XIX:5–6)

Isn't the Midrash telling us that the Covenant is the reason for Israel's appearance upon the pages of history? Without it we cease to be a living people. To refuse Torah, therefore, is for Israel to refuse life itself: to invite death to crash down upon us. Certainly this concept is found throughout our whole history. If you look, you will find it in our Siddur, in the Maariv Service, said every day of our lives.

The idea of selection found in the phrase: ". . . you shall be to Me a kingdom of priests and a holy nation" is summed up in the words "The Chosen People." Many, traditionalists and modernists alike, accept it as a fact of history. Others reject it. These claim that this concept is common to almost every people. For example Egyptians called themselves simply "the people" in contrast to foreigners. Greeks spoke of all others as "barbarians." An Athenian orator named Demosthenes defined them thus:

"Barbarians are slaves; we, Greeks, are free men."

Moreover this concept can be mischievous. For if people believe they are special, they will think they are superior to the rest of mankind. If they are superior, then it should follow that they must rule. It is not difficult to see the dangers of such thinking.

The answer to all of this has been given over and over again. Choseness never meant superiority. It meant above all responsibility. Indeed, as you shall see when you read of the Classical Prophets in Unit V, that because God chose Israel to carry out His Commandments, He would punish Israel more severely for failing to do so. As the Midrash above implies: Israel will bring her own death upon herself if she is unfaithful to the *Covenant.* In addition it must be added that according to tradition not only God chose, but Israel did as well. Israel chose God. Israel chose Torah.

At Sinai we accepted our *Covenant.* At Sinai the Exodus came to an official end. At Sinai we became a nation. The Ten Commandments spoken there, are engraved not only upon tablets of stone, but upon our hearts. They are basic to our lives and to the lives of all decent men and women. Here they are:

1. I am the Lord your God who brought you out of the land of Egypt and out of the house of bondage.

2. You shall have no other gods beside Me.

3. You shall not swear falsely by the name of the Lord your God.

4. Remember the Sabbath Day and keep it holy.

5. Honor your father and mother.

6. You shall not murder.

7. You shall not commit adultery.

8. You shall not steal.

9. You shall not bear false witness against your neighbor.

10. You shall not covet your neighbor's house, or anything that is your neighbor's.

(Exodus XX:2–14)

These Ten Commandments, or the Decalogue, were not new in every detail. They have some things in common with the Babylonian Code of Hammurabi (1945–1902 B.C.E.), while now and then they remind us of the Egyptian *Book of the Dead*. But in their aim, character, and usage, they are Jewish. For example in the *Book of the Dead,* the soul of a dead man, pleads before the god Osiris: "I have done no murder." The Decalogue, on the other hand, makes moral conduct a duty. "You shall not murder!" "You shall not steal!" etc.

As for the Code of Hammurabi, there are more differences than similarities. According to this Babylonian law, there are thirty-four crimes for which the death penalty is inflicted. Among them we find every kind of theft, including receiving and buying from servants. In Israel the death penalty for property crimes is abolished.

Indeed the eighth commandment: "You shall not steal," is interpreted by some Rabbis to mean "You shall not kidnap." Why? Because while the Rabbis respected property, they never considered it as sacred as life. Disgusting as it is to steal, it was not to be grouped with murder, adultery, or idolatry. Therefore, they believed the only reason "You shall not steal," was included in the Decalogue, was because it referred to the dreadful theft of a human being.

The first statement: "I am the Lord your God . . ." looms over the rest of the Decalogue. The belief in one God who insists on freedom is basic to all of Jewish law. Of the other nine, it is the fourth commandment "Remember the Sabbath Day and keep it holy," which is so revolutionary. Masters, slaves, even animals were to rest every seventh day.

That a noble should be able to rest, could be understood. But a peasant, a slave, an animal! And to rest because it was his right! What could be more absurd. More clearly than any other law, the fourth taught that every living creature was under the same divine law.

It is an interesting fact that we sealed our *Covenant* in a desert; and received these Commandments there. Wouldn't you have expected all this to have taken place in the land of Israel? After all, that land was promised to our Patriarchs and to us.

There is good reason for this. The *Covenant* is independent of the land of Israel. Fulfillment of the *Covenant* will lead to possession of the land. But even if driven from the land, the *Covenant* holds.

That is why our people never despaired of their partnership with God even in exile.

They knew, as we should know, that the *Covenant* endures forever, regardless of where we are.

As a matter of fact, it is written, that only two of the men and women who were twenty years or older when they left Egypt entered Canaan. Yet the *Covenant* belonged to all the men of the Exodus.

Moses himself, we are told, was permitted to see the land from the top of Mt. Nebo. He died in the land of Moab, and God Himself, the Bible tells us, buried him in its valley. No one knows his burial place to this day.

The Importance of Slavery

Most people boast of their ancestry. Pharaoh claimed he was the son of a god. Aeneas, a Trojan hero, that he was descended from Venus; Romulus and Remus founders of Rome, were the sons of Mars; and Hercules, was the son of Jupiter.

We Jews are not ashamed of our family tree. It is no light thing to count Abraham, Isaac, and Jacob, among our ancestors. As for Moses, there can be no nobler lineage. A great poet once said even Sinai seemed puny next to Moses.

Nevertheless we do not conceal the fact that our people were once slaves. On the contrary, we speak of it constantly. Why? What is so grand about being another man's tool; of not having freedom of choice; of not being accountable for one's life? What can be more debasing?

Why then is this chapter of our history recalled so frequently in our literature? Why does one of our festivals revolve around it?

Would you end so many commandments with the words: "for you were slaves in Egypt . . . ?"

What do you make of this sentence of the Bible: "You shall not hate an Egyptian, for you were a stranger in his land. Children born to them may be admitted into the congregation of the Lord in the third generation."

What do you make of this Midrash:

When Israel stood by the Red Sea (Sea of Reeds) before them the rolling waters, and behind them the hosts of Egypt, then, too, the angels appeared to sing their daily song of praise to the Lord, but God called to them, "Forbear! My children are in distress, and you would sing."

How do we symbolize our sympathy at the Seder for the drowning Egyptians?

In what way did the history of slavery in Egypt affect the slaves of our country?

Readings for Students

Moses, K. B. Shippen, Harper and Brothers, N.Y.

The Ten Commandments, ed. by Robinson, Armin, Simon & Schuster, 1944. Chap. I.

Readings for Teachers

The Legends of the Jews, Louis Ginzberg, J.P.S. (Vol. III, p. 32, p. 92, From the Exodus to the Death of Moses).

The Wisdom of the Talmud, by Bokser, B.Z. Philosophical Library, 1951. Chap. IV.

The Sabbath, by Heschel, Abraham J., Farrar, Straus and Young, 1951.

chapter 8

The Ten Commandments, the Torah, and the Covenant

THE MOST PRECIOUS POSSESSION OF our people is our Torah. Whenever a Synagogue is in danger we rush in to rescue the Torah. Wherever we go, we take our Torah with us.

When you hear the word "Torah" you think of the Scrolls in the Ark of your Synagogue. These Scrolls contain what is called the first five books of Moses: Genesis בראשית; Exodus שמות; Leviticus ויקרא; Numbers במדבר; and Deuteronomy דברים. Around the Ten Commandments of Sinai these Books developed.

If we accept the meaning of Torah as these five Books, then Torah becomes part of a more inclusive Book: Tanach תנ"ך. The best translation of Tanach would be Scriptures.

Actually Tanach is an abbreviation that stands for three groups of Books. The ת stands for Torah תורה, the five Books listed above. This is considered the holiest portion of the Tanach.

The נ stands for N'veem נביאים, Prophets. This is next in sanctity. The ך stands for Ketuvim כתובים, Writings. Put each letter together and you have תנ"ך Scriptures, or The Bible, or sometimes called Holy Scriptures. Bible, by the way, is a Greek word which means "paper." Even-

tually it meant "book." Today it means *The Book*, the Tanach.

Often when we say Torah, we mean, not just the first five Books, but the whole Tanach. Or at times we mean Teaching: the instruction that shows us how to be faithful Jews. Or Law.

We have two types of Torot: a Written Torah and an Oral Torah. The Written is simply the Tanach. The Oral is the interpretation of the Tanach. Once this Oral Torah was not written down lest it be considered as holy as the Tanach. But eventually it became apparent that it would be forgotten if it were not recorded. Therefore, certain of our Sages wrote it down for the generations to come. The Books, i.e. Tractates, which contain the Oral Torah are called the TALMUD.

Talmud, in turn is made up of two parts: *Mishna* which details and expands the scope of the commandments of the Tanach; and *Gemara,* which enlarges upon *Mishna*.

Some people use Torah and *Covenant* interchangeably. Actually Torah is the direct consequence of the Covenant of Sinai. Torah records that *Covenant*. Torah also helps us to keep our share of the *Covenant* by supplying us with the guide lines we need.

At Mt. Sinai the *Covenant* we accepted was in fact the same *Covenant* Abraham, Isaac and Jacob accepted. According to the *Covenant* Israel was to fulfill two duties. First, to reveal the will of God to the whole world. And second, to be a holy nation.

In Abraham's case the first duty is made clear when his name is changed from Abram to Abraham. Abraham means a Father of a multitude of nations. Abraham was to be the example of a God-fearing man to all mankind. The second is stated when we read that Abraham was singled out "that he may instruct his children and grandchildren to keep the way of the Lord by doing what is just and right. . . ."

At Sinai we saw the same division. Remember the message Moses delivered to Israel. To be "a kingdom of priests and a holy nation." Kingdom of priests refers to our universal duties; a holy nation, to our national ones.

The Ten Commandments we received at Sinai are the laws we are supposed to spread throughout the world. With these we become a "kingdom of priests." The other commandments found throughout Torah are supposed to train us so that we become indeed, a holy nation.

Holiness in Hebrew consists in "separation from" and in "dedication to." For Israel this means separation from all that is opposed to the will of God, and dedication to His service.

To meet the demands of holiness we have but to follow the directions of Torah. And that in our tradition, refers to both the Written and the Oral Torot.

Activities

Questions

1. What nation of this century rejected every one of the Ten Commandments and almost destroyed Europe?
2. Do you think there is the possibility of world-wide destruction today? Why?

Readings for Students

Our Religion, by Kolatch, Alfred J., Jonathan David Co., N.Y., 1951.

Readings for Teachers

Judaism: A Historical Presentation, Isidore Epstein, A Pelican Book: Penguin Books.

chapter 9 Moses, Magic, and Monotheism

IN CHAPTER 4 YOU LEARNED WHY monotheism, first taught by our Patriarchs, was a revolutionary doctrine. For Moses this oneness and unity of God is central. Every event is an opportunity for him to emphasize it, to teach it. It is one of the reasons why we call him Moshe Rabbenu: Moses our teacher.

Also in Chapter 4, you learned that magic was a discipline of ancient Mesopotamia. Ancient man believed it controlled the gods and nature; compelled them to do the magician's will. Magic was as much a discipline in Egypt and throughout the whole Near East.

"There is no witchcraft in Jacob," the Bible states. Diviners, soothsayers are forbidden. No one may consult ghosts or spirits or the dead. No one may cast spells. And rightly so. For that would mean trying to impose one's will upon God. Yes, man can plead with Him, argue with Him, as Abraham did for Sodom and Gomorrah, praise Him, worship Him. But to resort to tricks of magic is a very denial of monotheism. It implies that there are mysteries or powers that are stronger than God.

Yet in the Tanach we come upon incidents that seem to employ magic. Before the Burning Bush, for example, God Himself teaches Moses what appears to be tricks of magic. These, as you know, are to convince Israel and Pharaoh that Moses speaks the word of God. Can it be that God who forbids magic is commanding Moses to use magic. Let us analyze what these signs mean. The lesson these teach us is the same lesson all such future incidents teach.

Now if these signs are truly magic, Moses should, as magicians did, use words of incantation: secret words; wonderworking names; weird chants. But none of these are spoken.

Then there should be special tools: chemicals, vessals, animal parts like wings of bats or stings of scorpions. No, all Moses uses is what he normally has about him: his shepherd's staff; his own hand; and water.

Then surely there must be a difficult or secret act Moses performs. Yet all we read is that he casts his staff down, puts his hand in his bosom, pours water. These are acts each one of us does often. True, what happens to the staff of Moses or to his hand or to the water, never happened to us. The staff becomes a serpent, Moses' hand becomes leprous, the water turns into blood. But none of it is due to Moses. In fact, Moses is terrified by the serpent, and jumps backward. No magician, worth his name, would flee from the work of his own hand. What is clear, is that each transformation is accomplished by the will of God.

If anything these signs mock magic. They teach Egypt and her magicians that magic is useless. The magicians of Egypt learn this after the third plague. These plagues, which are only further demonstrations of God's power, are called by the magicians "the finger of God."

With the sixth plague the poor magicians are so helpless they cannot even face Moses. They, who are supposed to control gods and nature, suffer as much as the rest of Egypt from the plague.

So this lesson which follows from monotheism is spread throughout Egypt: magic is an empty discipline. He who practices it, denies God. Only God can reverse the order of nature. Only He is above nature. Only God can keep a burning thorn bush from not being consumed by the fire. Thus every wondrous act of the Tanach comes to pass because God wills it; not man.

Pagan man consulted diviners or oracles when he wanted to know the will of the gods. There were famous oracles throughout the ancient world, like the one at Delphi in ancient Greece.

When our ancestors wanted to know the will of God they consulted prophets and priest. Monotheism will have nothing of oracles. Recall again the midrash in Chapter 4. God lifted Abraham above the vault of heaven. Abraham was to be a prophet not an astrologer. He was to understand the will of God because God would reveal His will to him: not by reading the stars or by any other false science.

Abraham, as we shall see, was the first prophet. But Abraham was given no *specific* task. He was never sent to any one man or king. By the example of his own life he was to raise up a nation loyal to God. He was to take possession of the land not by conquest, but simply in the name of God. It is Moses who is sent to fulfill a definite mission: to liberate slaves. He becomes a messenger of God, the first of the prophet-messengers. But prophet-messengers must never be confused with oracles.

First of all, prophet messengers spoke up before waiting for anyone to consult them. Most of the time they challenged the ruling power, as did Moses.

Secondly, prophet-messengers are never paid. More, they scorned payment. Oracles always expected rewards. Third, prophet-messengers did not speak in riddles like oracles, but in plain language that all could understand immediately. And most important of all, prophet-messengers never spoke as did oracles, in absolute terms. Prophet-messengers always held out hope. They always used the word "if." They taught man could avoid punishment, *if* he repented of evil. For ancient man, there was no avoiding the oracle's pronouncement.

Looking back into history, we realize how

ahead of his age Moses was. Who else but he could have liberated a rabble of slaves and forged a resolute nation of them? Who else could have brought them to Sinai and stood between them and God? And who else could have set Torah in their midst, and drummed its words into their hearts?

Moshe Rabbenu taught them that though they were God's unique people, God was the Father of all men. God was not only above nature, but above prejudice as well.

But because they were His unique people, they had to keep the *Covenant*. Whether they liked it or not (remember the Midrash), they were partners of God. Their deeds affected history.

The duty to reveal God's will to mankind comes down from the Patriarchs through Moses, through other messenger-prophets to Israel itself. Inevitably each Jew becomes a bearer of the word of God. Because Israel became a covenanted people, she had to become a prophetic people.

This relationship of God to man is a direct outgrowth of monotheism's rejection of magic and of monotheism's revolutionary doctrine. Everything Moses does, he does openly, before the very eyes of the people. Only when he ascended Sinai, did he remain concealed. And that led to disaster.

The crossing of the Sea of Reeds with its dancing and singing celebrated a religious festival that was historical; not a stage in the life of a god. And Moses, a prophet-messenger, not a magician, had accomplished this redemption.

What made Moses so unique is that he did not pretend that what he wanted was the will of God. He never tried to be more than man. He refused to let God make a nation out of his seed alone. He shared his power with as many as he could. He accepted sound advice. He forgave those who slandered him.

No matter how severe he appears, especially when he combats idolatry, he never ceases to love Israel. In the *Book of Numbers* 13:3, we read: "Now Moses was a very humble man, more so than any other man."

The very last sentences of the Bible read:

Never again did there arise in Israel a prophet like Moses, whom the Lord singled out, face to face, for the various signs and portents that the Lord sent him to display in the land of Egypt, against Pharaoh and all his courtiers and his whole country, and for all the great might and awesome power that Moses displayed before all Israel.

Deuteronomy XXXIV:10–12

Humility and awesome power! A curious combination, is it not? Yet both were true!

Activities

Questions

1. Shavuot, which commemorates Sinai, is called Atzeret in the Talmud. Atzeret means to close up.

What event does Shavuot bring to a close?
Why does Sinai make Israel truly free?
Which of the Commandments of the Decalogue emphasizes this? Explain.

2. Look up the Code of Hammurabi. Compare the laws governing slavery, theft, and murder with those in the Torah.

3. Do you think the grave of Moses should have remained unknown? Explain your point of view.

4. In what way did the history of slavery in Egypt affect the slaves of our country?

5. How did the Founding Fathers of our country use the story of the Exodus to express their revolt against George III?

Readings for Teachers

The Legends of the Jews, Louis Ginzberg, J.P.S.
(Vol. III, p. 92, 93.)

Passover: Its History and Traditions, T. H. Gaster, Henry Schuman, N.Y. 1949.

Religious Authority and Mysticism, G. Scholem, *Commentary,* November, 1964.

The Jacobs Affair: Anglo Jewry in Crisis, I. Maybaum, *Judaism,* Fall, 1964.

Atonism and Monotheism

The Egyptologist, James Breasted, claimed that the concept of monotheism came from Egypt. He said Moses learnt it from the Pharaoh, Akh-en-Aton who ruled 1369–53 B.C.E. The man who disproved this theory was Breasted's own pupil: John A. Wilson.

Wilson proves conclusively that the Hebrews took absolutely nothing worthwhile from Egypt. Furthermore Atonism, that faith that Akh-en-Aton initiated, was not monotheistic.

There were two gods central to Atonism not one. Akh-en-Aton and his family worshipped the Aton, pictured as the round disk of the Sun, and everybody else worshipped Akh-en-Aton as a god. It was an exclusive faith of the god-king and his family. In the famous hymn of Akh-en-Aton to the Aton, the Pharaoh stated that this was his personal god: "Thou art in my heart, and there is no other that knows thee except thy son (Akh-en-Aton) whom thou hast initiated into thy plans, and into thy power." The scenes in the tombs of Akh-en-Aton's period show Pharaoh serving the sun-disk, while all his courtiers bow in adoration to him.

Unlike God, Aton was concerned only with creating and maintaining life: in other words, with the physical aspects of life. Man might be grateful for life, but in no text about Aton can we find that he had to show his gratitude by an upright life in his social relationships or in his innermost heart. Nowhere do we find that the Aton insisted upon law.

The other proofs that Breasted offers, his pupil, Wilson, disproves. There is no connection between Atonism and Monotheism. Moses continues in the footsteps of the Patriarchs. Akh-en-Aton continued in the tradition of his ancestors as far as his own divinity was concerned.

Monotheism, the belief in the oneness of God and in the Unity of His creation is the discovery and contribution of Israel to mankind.

Activities

Questions

- What men of our century tried to take on the power of God?
- What did they accomplish?
- Can you think of other men who want to be more than "man"?

- Even if Akh-en-Aton had not considered himself a god, why was Atonism a form of idolatry?
- Why is any belief idolatrous when the worshipper claims that God is only his, and no other's?
- What good is faith without deeds?
- Contrast Akh-en-Aton's private relationship to Aton with Sinai?

Readings for Students

More World Over Stories, ed. Schloss and Epstein.
(p. 50, A Golden Earring in Morocco by M. Dluznovsky.)
The Drama of Ancient Israel, by Flight, John, Beacon Press, 1949. Chap. I.

Readings for Teachers

History of Egypt, Breasted, Scribner, N.Y.
Understanding Exodus, Greenberg, Moshe, Behrman House, J.T.S., 1969, N.Y.
The Culture of Ancient Egypt, by Wilson, John, Phoenix Books, University of Chicago Press.

Unit III

Your wives, your little ones, and your cattle, shall
abide in the land which Moses gave you beyond the Jordan;
but ye shall pass over before your brethren
armed, all the mighty men of valor . . .

JOSHUA 1–14

chapter 10   Before the Conquest

LET US TAKE A CLOSE LOOK AT ISRAEL after the death of Moses. The adults, except for two men, could not be older than fifty-nine years. Anyone twenty or over at the Exodus, had perished in the desert. Most were much younger. They had been born during the forty years of wandering.

All the younger men had fought successfully in at least two wars on the eastern side of the Jordan River: against Sihon, King of Heshbon; and against a giant—King Og, of Bashan. Also twelve thousand Israelite warriors had defeated Midian. The one battle Israel lost was at the hand of a Canaanite king of Arad. Because of this defeat, Israel was prevented from entering Canaan by the most direct route: from the south. We can see, therefore, that the Israelite soldier was a tried and tested veteran.

Transjordan is the land on the eastern side of the Jordan River. In Transjordan, Edom, Moab, and Ammon, also dwelt. But Israel did not challenge them. Their lands were assigned to them as Canaan had been to Israel. Heshbon and Bashan, however, were divided up among two and a half tribes: Reuben, Gad, and half of Manasseh. These tribes needed the grassy plains of Heshbon and Bashan for their cattle. The soldiers of these two and a half tribes settled their families in Heshbon and Bashan and then joined the rest of Israel. Together they would conquer the western side of the Jordan.

Look then, at these tough warriors as they are poised before the Jordan. Their reputation terrified the countryside. In vain the king of Moab had hired a professional diviner, Balaam, to curse Israel. Balaam had been forced to bless Israel instead.

But it was not with Balaam's blessing or curses these warriors were concerned. Rather the words of Moses still rang in their ears. How often their leader had reminded them of their duties and responsibilities as partners of God. As long as they remained true, worshipping only Yahweh, they could be sure of Yahweh's blessing. But if they served false gods, they would be driven from the very land they were about to possess. It was up to them now. And to their new leader, Joshua ben Nun.

But could any man take the place of Moses? And what did they know of Joshua? That he was a competent General? Yes: had he not defeated the ferocious Amalekites? That he loved Moses? Yes; had he not wanted to punish those Elders who had prophesied? His very title, "Msharet

Moshe," Attendant of Moses, testified to his devotion. And that he was undaunted? Unquestionably. He and Caleb ben Yephunneh were the only ones of the Exodus courageous enough to be allowed into Canaan.

Joshua and Caleb were two of twelve spies Moses had sent from the great oasis of Kadesh Barnea to spy out Canaan. They had returned bearing huge clusters of grapes, as well as figs and pomegranates. All had agreed it was a "land of milk and honey." But ten had added these discouraging words: "The people are fierce . . . the cities are fortified . . . the land eats up its inhabitants . . . they are so tall . . . we appear like grasshoppers. . . ." Only Joshua and Caleb had contradicted them. "We shall go up at once and possess it; for we are well able to overcome it!" they urged.

Joshua and Caleb had not been able to convince Israel. "Let us make a Captain and . . . return to Egypt." Israel had wept. Do you understand why these adults had to die in the desert? How could they have stood up to Sihon, or the giant, Og? What would they have done when Arad defeated them? And how could they conquer Canaan, or build an independent nation there?

From now on we shall get our information about this period of the conquest and settlement of Canaan from two books of the Tanach: *Joshua* and *Judges,* and from the *El Amarna Letters.* These letters are messages from the petty rulers of Canaan and Syria to their master, the Pharaoh of Egypt.

The episodes of these two Books of the Tanach are exciting and vivid. They were written with a powerful pen that spared no one: neither Israelite nor Canaanite, neither man nor woman.

Certainly the author of the *Book of Joshua* must also have wondered about the reaction of Israel to any man who succeeded Moses? For we are told that the Jordan gave Israel dry passage as the Sea of Reeds once had. Every man woman and child had to understand that as God had been with Moses and Israel, so He would be with Joshua and Israel. Indeed, we read that it was not Moses who chose Joshua, but God.

The holding back of the Jordan's waters was also intended to spread the terror of Israel upon all Canaan. The land was to learn immediately that God ruled here as He did in Egypt.

On the western side of the Jordan at last, they encamp at Gilgal, east of the city of Jericho. It is the tenth of Nisan. In four days they will celebrate the first Passover on their own land. Joshua prepares them. They eat Matzot and whatever grows before them. For the manna ceases forever. Only from what the land yields, are they now to live.

It is clear from the *Book of Joshua* that Gilgal is the first shrine of Israel in Canaan. Here Joshua circumcised all males born in the wilderness. Surely after that first Passover before the Exodus, this one in Gilgal must have been the most meaningful of our history. Gilgal which means a circle, is given the additional meaning, "to roll away." What is rolled away is the shame of not being circumcised. Hence we read in the *Book of Joshua:* "This day have I (God) rolled away the reproach of Egypt from off you." Sinai decreed nationhood. Canaan, is to build nationhood.

What did they know of this land they were about to possess? Moses had seen it from a mountain peak. Joshua and Caleb had covered its length. The rest of them knew very little. Only what had been told them. But they yearned to occupy it.

For most of the forty years they had camped at Kadesh Barnea: the biggest and greenest oasis of the desert. They had probably sowed some seed and reaped small harvests there. In all other ways they were desert nomads. Their eyes were accustomed to horizons of mists; their ears to the silence of sand. They lived in tents as their Patriarchs had. Yet they knew from their fathers that men could use bricks or stone for homes. Manna, though always available, eventually became tasteless upon their tongues. Hundreds of years later, prophets would look back longingly upon this austere existence. Men weary and polluted by city life, would return to the desert for peace and cleansing. But for these who had endured it for years, it held little attraction.

They were thirsty for the milk and hungry for the honey. They did not know, nor would it have mattered to them, that Canaan was the least fertile of the Fertile Crescent. They were unaware that Canaan's rivers were so much smaller than Egypt's or Mesopotamia's, or that no boats of commerce plied their waters. Nor had they heard that her riverbeds were too deep to be used for irrigation.

As for areas of cultivation, these were limited by the many hills and ridges. Besides rain fell in one season, and even this was meagre the farther south one went.

What mattered was that the time had come for the fulfillment of the promise made to Abraham, Isaac, and Jacob. And they were ready. Indeed, impatient.

Activities

Questions

- These are the twelve sons of Jacob: Reuben, Simeon, Levi, Judah, Dan, Naphtali, Gad, Asher, Issachar, Zebulun, Joseph, Benjamin.
- These are the twelve tribes of Israel: Reuben, Simeon, Judah, Dan, Naphtali, Gad, Asher, Issachar, Zebulun, Ephraim, Manasseh, Benjamin.

- Which sons of Jacob have no tribe in their name?
- Why?
- Would you have awarded two tribes to Joseph?

- Do you think it fair that Levi should be given no tribal allotment of land?

- Read Chapters 33 and 34 of Deuteronomy. You will see there is no blessing for Simeon. Chapter XII may explain the omission. Read on.

Readings for Students

Buried Treasure in Bible Lands, by Cohen, Lenore, The Ward Ritchie Press, 1965. Chap. X–XI–XII.

Silent Cities, Sacred Stones, by Landag, Jerry, McCall Books, 1971. Chap. III.
The Land of Canaan, Asimov, Isaac, Houghton Mifflin Co., 1971. Chap. III.

Readings for Teachers

Numbers
Deuteronomy
Joshua
The Macmillan Bible Atlas, Aharoni and Avi-Yonah, The Macmillan Co., N.Y.
(Map on p. 15)

chapter 11   Canaan and Her Conquest

THOUGH OUR ANCESTORS WERE IMPATIENT, we need not be. Let us pause and examine Canaan in detail. On her northern border, Phoenicia sits. "Phoenicia" is the Greek translation for reddish-purple (phoenix). Canaan also meant purple. Eventually Canaan took on the secondary meaning of "merchant."

What connection is there between the land and purple? The connection is the murex shell. It was found along the coastal waters of Canaan and Phoenecia. From this shell fish a purple dye, the famous "Tyrian purple" was manufactured. Since this dye was used for expensive cloth, the cities along the coast became centers of the textile trade. In the ancient city of Ugarit, to which we shall refer again, tablets mention the cities Ashdod, Ashkelon, and Acco in Canaan as these textile centers. In Phoenecia, it was Tyre, of course.

Both countries together with Syria were inhabited mainly by Canaanites. Their cultures were in most ways, identical. When we speak of Canaan, we mean only that land on the western side of the Jordan, which will become Eretz Israel. The eastern side of what will become Eretz Israel, we shall refer to as Transjordan. Throughout hundreds of years, Eretz Israel was also known as Palestine.

Today this old-new nation of our people is Israel again. But Transjordan, which was once part of Eretz Israel, is now Jordan.

You know something of the political structure of Canaan. She was made up of separate city-states, ruled by a king. The classes closest to him, were the priests and the nobility. The other two classes were peasantry and slaves.

From 1550 B.C.E., Egypt controlled these city-states. The kings sent tribute to the Pharaoh. In return the Pharaohs maintained order, and protected the land.

The petty kings were what we call vassals of the Pharaohs. So too, were the nobles. But both the king and his nobles lived on the sweat and toil of peasants and slaves. The taxes the kings sent Pharaoh, they wrung out of the lower classes.

This was very similar to the feudal system of the Middle Ages. The social order created by grinding down peasant and slave, existed as long as no one questioned it. But the moment a voice was raised challenging the justice of this injustice, king, noble, and eventually the Pharaoh himself, was threatened.

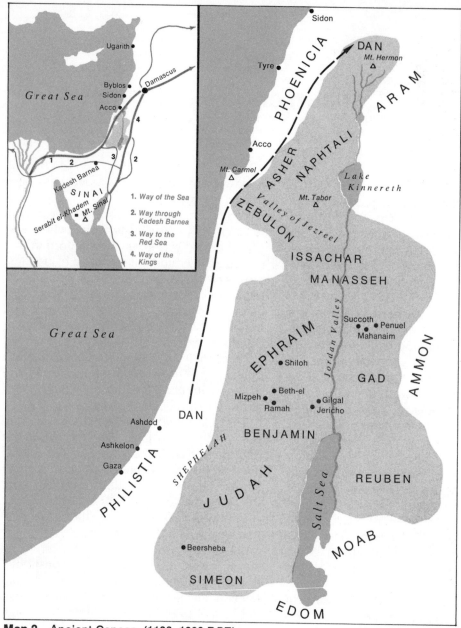

Map 2 Ancient Canaan (1100–1000 BCE)

The kings were safe within their castles for centuries. They ruled with an iron hand. Their power was supported by paid soldiers (mercenaries) and by their warrior nobles. The land about their walls were tilled by peasants and serfs. Most of the produce and the increase of the cattle was snatched by the kings.

But a change was in the making. From north, south, and east, nomads pervaded Canaan. At the same time, the population of Canaan was increasing. New settlements developed. Before long there was friction between these new city settlers and the nomads. Both were competing for the same land and water.

Among these nomads a group called the Habiru appeared. According to the El Amarna letters, they were largely responsible for the disruption of Canaan's society. They helped set peasant and slave against nobility and king. They also incited the populations against Egypt. You can see how eagerly, oppressed people would rally around anyone who promised them relief from their misery.

For many years scholars believed the Habiru were Hebrews. Now many assert the Habiru were not a national group at all, but a social class.

During the reign of Pharaoh Akh-en-Aton there was a serious disruption of political and social life in Canaan. In an El Amarna letter we read:

Dagantakala to the king. Asks for rescue from the Habiru and the Shutu. . . . let my lord protect his land from the hand of the Habiru. If not, let the king, my lord, send chariots to fetch us, lest our servants smite us.

So bad had conditions become, one prince deserts his own class and goes over to the other side. But the pharaohs after Akh-en-Aton, succeeded in restoring order. One hundred years later, the Pharaohs of the 19th Dynasty whom we know, are still busy suppressing their colonies in Canaan.

But they cannot, as you have learnt, suppress dreams. Peasants and slaves yearn, yes, dream, of freedom. By the time Israel appears upon the doorstep of Canaan, the kings cannot rest easily behind their walls. They knew their subjects would rise up at the first opportunity.

Egypt's power is also dwindling. Campaign though they do, the Pharaohs will not be able to protect their vassal kings much longer. To cap it all, these separate city-states were never interested in the fate of their neighbors. An archeologist comments: The individual kings were so jealous of each other "That union for a common purpose, even for the public safety, was out of the question."

We shall see that this is not entirely true. Some Canaanite kings will unite, but by then, it will be too late. Joshua shall defeat thirty-one of them.

The fact is that the conquest of Canaan

is really the clash of two cultures. On one side is a structure consisting of vassal and tyrannical kings living on the sweat of other men. On the other, a tribal democratic system of nomads. It is obvious slaves and peasants will not rush to defend rulers who oppress them.

Until 1929 it was believed the Canaanites were backward people. But with the "dig" at Ras Shamra, that ancient Canaanite city Ugarit on the coast of northern Syria, we discovered how wrong we had been. There we found hundreds of tablets. Among the sagas found, there was one about the resurrection of the god, Baal, and another about Dan'el and his son.

A book of the Tanach is called *Daniel.* It has no connection with the Canaanite Dan'el. Both Daniels, however, were wise and just men. The prophet, Ezekiel, who lived 400 years before the man who wrote the *Book of Daniel,* refers to this Canaanite Dan'el twice. Other than their wisdom and sense of justice, there is no resemblance between them. In addition we also learned from these tablets of Ugarit, that their language was, at times, very similar to the verses of our own Psalms.

In another Syrian city, Byblos, we brought to light a syllabic script containing 100 phonetic signs. This was an obvious improvement over the thousand which was used before.

More revolutionary than this, however, were two other scripts. One, a cuneiform alphabet, with 32 signs, was found in Ugarit; the other of southern Canaan was called the Sinaitic script. This last one contained 22 letters as in our own Hebrew alphabet, and was, indeed, similar to it.

We can hardly appreciate what a contribution simple scripts were to the advancement of man. Up until 2000 B.C.E. the two international scripts were Mesopotamian cuneiform and Egyptian hieroglyph. Cuneiform is a wedge-shaped character pressed on metal or clay tablets. Hieroglyph is picture writing which conveyed ideas. That is why it is often referred to as "ideographic writing." These scripts contained more than 600 signs. They were used by the governing aristocracy and priestly class.

These new alphabets, however, made writing available to everyone. The ten examples of Sinaitic Script unearthed so far, were written by ordinary men. They were inscribed on pottery vessels and other popular utensils of daily and religious use. In Sinai, in the mining region of Serabit al-Khadem, similar inscriptions are believed to have been written by Canaanite captives or slaves. Some even suggest that perhaps Moses himself was inventor of this Sinaitic Script, or the author of these inscriptions.

The Sinaitic Script became the father of modern language: Hebrew, Phoenician, Greek, Etruscan, Roman, and all the other languages derived from them.

Alalakh, another Canaanite city of Syria revealed proof of rare artistic ability. A curious stylized ram's head and stately statues of lions were found there.

Other than a talent for ivory carving, Canaan showed little creative spark. Most of the known art objects found in Canaan, such as cult figures, statues and steles, came from Syria, Egypt, and the central Mediterranean areas. In the south of Canaan it appears the desert nomads influenced whatever artistic creations were discovered!

The religious life of the Canaanites was primitive and brutal. They beheld gods and demons in every aspect of nature. At their shrines they became drunk and debased. Men and women cut their flesh, sacrificed their children. Serpent worship with its cruel gods was common. Indeed, they imagined many of their gods and goddesses as bloody, vengeful, and deceitful. How then, one wonders, could they see themselves?

But being debased, does not necessarily make people militarily weak. For all her ugly rites, Canaan should not have been conquered. As a matter of fact, some of her cities, were never taken. Her fortifications and watch towers were too strong. Her canals and aqueducts which guarded the precious water supply, were solidly engineered. Her numbers were greater, her weapons better. Especially her deadly war chariots terrified the Hebrews.

But before we discuss the actual conquest let us examine this map. We can see how Canaan's geography affected her history and development. Canaan is situated within a desert area, stretching from the African Sahara to the Persian Desert. She lies between the Mediterranean Sea and the Syrian-Arabian Desert. Were Canaan not made up of so many mountains and plateaus, the desert would have swallowed her up completely.

If you were a hungry nomad of the Syrian-Arabian Desert, you would gaze westward longingly: at the settled agricultural villages. If the border nations of Transjordan were weak, you would not be afraid to swoop down upon these settlements on both sides of the Jordan and plunder harvests and cattle.

If you were a would-be conqueror from Crete or the Aegean Islands, you would invade Canaan from her western and permanent border: the Mediterranean Sea. Philistines, a nation of Sea People, did exactly that. They settled on Canaan's southern and central coastland. It is from them the name "Palestine" is derived.

Although in 1200 B.C.E. many coastal cities of Canaan were important centers of international trade, Canaan will never develop into a major Sea Power like Phoenecia. But were you a land merchant, Canaan would always have suited you. She contained excellent international highways for caravans. Two of them: "The Way of the Sea" and "The Way of the Kings," joined Egypt to Damascus in Syria. Then they ascended farther north into Mesopotamia, to Babylon. These roads threw off many side routes like "The Way of the Red Sea" which descended to the Gulf of Eilat. Another route crossed the Sinai Desert up to Kadesh Barnea, passed over Edom, and continued northward through Transjordan to Babylon.

They, of course, also served armies. The greatest soldier-Pharaoh, Thutmose III, marched across the "The Way of the Sea" to shatter a league of Canaanite kings. But it was "The Way of the Kings" that served the Pharaohs each day. Up and down its length their messengers rode, bearing commands to their vassal kings.

Because Canaan is a bridge between three continents, many armies marched across her. During World War I, the British General, Allenby, used the Tanach as a guide while fighting in Palestine. Many armies brought many ideas and cultures. Canaan received these new ways of life placidly, and sometimes, gratefully. For pagan man there was room for all gods and cults. Indeed, they adopted each others gods happily.

Not so for Israel. True our ancestors were affected by their surroundings. But in the long run, their influence upon the nations they confronted was the greater. It seems very unlikely, that from these crude nomads, saints and prophets shall come forth: men who would change the thinking of western man. Nor that the Tanach, the autobiography of Israel, with its stories, poetry, laws, and visions, would continue to be read throughout the ages. Our own Founding Fathers as you know drew the necessary courage and faith from the Tanach, to leave the tyranny of their pharaoh, George III and cross over their own Sea of Reeds.

Canaan is an amazing land. Hardly bigger than the state of Vermont, she contains a variety of climates and terrains: from the snow-capped Mt. Hermon in the north, 9000 feet high, to the burning sands of Sodom, 1300 feet below the earth's surface: the lowest point of our globe.

The Jordan is perhaps the most famous River of history. Her name appears in Spirituals and poetry time and again. The names of the settlements along her banks reflect her ancient sanctity: Jericho, Succoth, Penuel, Mahanaim, Gilgal. In Jericho a Captain of the Lord's Hosts commands Joshua: "Take off your shoes . . . for the place upon which you stand is holy." These exact words were spoken to Moses before the Burning Bush. Our Patriarch, Jacob, saw God's Hosts at Succoth and Mahanaim. And at Penuel he wrestled with an Angel, and received the new name "Israel."

Jordan means descent. And the river does descend from the north, enters the harp-shaped Lake of Kinneret, and continues southward until she empties into the Salt Sea. This Sea is in the arid plain, The Arabah. The intense heat evaporates her waters. As they dry, the waters leave behind rich deposits of valuable chemicals.

Our Sages called it the Sea of Sodom, and permitted both bathing in her, and the drawing of her water on Shabbat for health reasons. Now we understand why: she contained many medicinal chemicals like bromide and magnesium. Also her asphalt was excellent for the treatment of certain skin diseases.

The Pharaohs used asphalt for embalming as well as for caulking their ships. Today we need it for building, insulation, and roads. The Salt Sea is a very valuable source of raw materials for modern Israel.

Unlike the Nile or the Euphrates, the Jordan does not unite the country. In the *Book of Joshua,* we read of how the two and a half tribes of Transjordan set up stones as a sign they were brothers to the tribes on the western side of the Jordan. Why? Because they feared the river would divide them.

Jericho, according to the Tanach, is the first city Israel conquers in Canaan. She was one of the oldest cities in the world, if not the oldest. Though very warm, she was watered by powerful springs, and so grew an abundance of date palm and balsam trees. She probably developed the cultivation of wheat and barley. But more significant was the trade she carried on, because of her access to the riches of the Salt Sea. She exported the precious asphalt and salt, as well as balsam, dates, and wine. She imported obsidian and other stones from Mesopotamia, turquoise from Sinai, cowries from the Red Sea. Her stone walls 12 feet high and 6 and one half feet thick, would not impress us today. But to eyes shaped by deserts, they were awesome.

Certainly as Israel will become more familiar with this land, her character and products will continue to astonish. The Negev, Israel's desert of the south, while rich in copper and iron, was also farmed. Our Patriarch, Isaac, reaped huge barley harvests there. It should come as no surprise that barley is one of the successful Negev crops today.

In her central area, the mountains of Judah and Ephraim climb. At the foot of Mt. Judah on the west, is an area of flat land: the Shephelah. This is excellent soil for farming. On one of the highest hills overlooking the Shephelah, is Jerusalem. It will take another two hundred years before Jerusalem is captured.

Other very lush areas were the Sharon, north of the Shephelah, and the two valleys: Jezreel and Jordan. Canaan was always a land of wheat, barley, grapes, date, pomegranate, and olive. From grapes and dates wine was made. From olive, oil was pressed. But more than these, it was a land of cattle and fruits. Can you imagine how such wealth dazzled the eyes of nomads?

Mt. Judah and Mt. Ephraim are but two of many mountains. We find more in the Negev and Transjordan. The Galilee which is the northern section of Canaan, consists of two ranges of mountains: an Upper and a Lower. Most beautiful of the Lower Galilee is Mt. Tabor. Her round dark head hovers majestically and mysteriously above the valleys at her feet.

In the Upper Galilee, the mountains are composed of distinct and separate chains, enclosing narrow valleys. The communities in these valleys were isolated from each other. Consequently, it was known as "Galilee of the Nations": a stronghold of separate kingdoms.

There was always a marked difference between the populations of the mountains and the plains. Since the international highways cut through the valleys, their inhabitants came into contact with new goods and new ideas. They possessed among other things, better weapons. That is why Israel could, at first, only occupy and hold the hilly country. Not until years later would Israel conquer the richer lowlands.

After Jericho, Israel conquered Ai. Terrified by these fearsome warriors, the city of Gibeon made a treaty of peace with Israel. Gibeon's delegation appeared before Joshua in rags and with worn water skins and mouldy bread. They pretended they came from a distance.

When the truth was out, Israel kept the peace treaty. The Gibeonites were not attacked. They became servants of the Sanctuary and eventually Jews. 600 years later they are still listed in the Tanach as a separate group.

After these events, the conquest of the balance of the land was decided by two campaigns: south and north. In the south the King of Jerusalem convinced four other kings to unite with him and resist Israel. In the north, the king of Hazor gathered many allies. Both of these alliances Joshua smashed.

Some historians believe that while the *Book of Joshua* gives us a true account of the *results* of the conquest, the actual battles did not occur exactly as they are recorded. They insist that the conquest was a gradual affair. According to them, it took place many more years than the *Book of Joshua* indicates.

The tribe of Asher, they said, was already living in northwestern Canaan. And of course, if the Habirus were Hebrews, they would also have been there before the conquest. This would mean that neither Asher nor the Habiru were ever enslaved.

Still others believe that the tribes of Judah and Simeon together with men called Kenites pushed into Canaan from the south. Furthermore, they say, these tribes brought the concept of monotheism to the rest of Israel.

The Tanach, these historians assert, presents an "idealized" account of the conquest. Why? Because the *Book of Joshua* wanted to present the conquest as the joint venture of all Israel.

If so, we must ask ourselves: why are we told of unconquered cities? Wasn't the "ideal" conquest supposed to include those cities? As for slavery is it so noble a state that we should lay claim to it for all Israel if it were not true?

Actually the conquest is narrated in parts. At the beginning of the *Book of Judges,* we find that the Conquest was a long process in which each tribe conquered its own territory.

In the *Book of Joshua,* we read that Joshua led a league of tribes. By his brilliant tactics he conquered a substantial part of Canaan.

These descriptions neither contradict nor exclude each other. Joshua's campaign was simply the most important event in a larger struggle. Each tribe must have taken a more active role in holding and settling its area.

Activities

A LIGHT CAST BY MIDRASH

Before the fall of Jericho, Joshua commanded the people not to touch any of the spoils. All of it was to belong to the Sanctuary. A man named Achan, disobeyed. As a result, all Israel suffered.

Among the things Achan took, was "a goodly Shinar mantle." According to a Midrash Jericho imported this mantle from Babylon, for Shinar is the Hebrew name for Babylon. We know that the plain of Shi-

nar was famous for its manufacture of gorgeous robes. It bears out our theory that Jericho's early development was due more to commerce than agriculture.

DEAD SEA

The Salt Sea is often referred to as the Dead Sea. Aristotle knew it as the Sea of Death. A Roman described it thus:

"The waters are very salty and evil-smelling, so that neither fish nor any living thing can live beneath the surface; and even though great rivers flow into it with their cool and sweet waters, yet the evil smell overpowers them and swallows everything."

In 1941 a scientist discovered tiny organisms existing in the Sea composed of microbes and sea-weed. He concluded that there is life in this "Dead Sea," both in its soil and waters.

Never does the Tanach call it Dead. The Tanach calls it The Salt Sea, The Sea of the Arabah, and The Eastern Sea. Later Hebraic sources refer to it as The Asphalt Sea as well as The Sea of Sodom. In fact no ancient Hebrew Literature which was based upon close contact and observation ever used the word "dead."

Pretend you are either a nomad, merchant, or warrior. Draw a map which would contain those features most significant for you. Explain it to your class.

Readings for Students

Worlds Lost and Found, Eisenberg and Elkins, (Chapters II, VII, and XII.)

Legends of Joshua, Slutsky, Shulsinger Bros., N.Y.

Buried Treasure in Bible Lands, by Cohen, Lenore, Ward Ritchie Press, 1965. Chap. XI–XII.

Voices from the Past, by Mazar & Trone, Harvey House, 1967. Chap. IV–VIII.

Voices from the Past, by Eisenberg, Azriel, Abelard-Schuman. Pp. 72–106.

At The Walls of Jericho, by Taslitt, Israel, Boch Publishing Co., 1961.

Readings for Teachers

Ancient Towns in Israel, Samuel Abramsky, Youth and Hechalutz Dept., W.Z.O., Jerusalem 1963.

The Worlds of the Bible, Jirku, The World Publishing Co., Cleveland 1967.

The Macmillan Bible Atlas, Aharoni and Avi-Yonah, The Macmillan Co., N.Y. (Maps pp. 11–23)

A History of the Jews, Sachar, Abram.

The Life of the People in Biblical Times, by Radin, Max, J.P.S., 1943.

chapter 12   Tribes and Their Leaders

IT MUST HAVE BEEN APPARENT TO Joshua that Israel would not conquer all of Canaan before his death. He had planned to take all of the land west of the Jordan to the Mediterranean Sea, and north to the Euphrates. (Whenever the Tanach speaks of the River, it means the Euphrates). Also south to the Wilderness of Zin, where the Brook of Egypt, the Wadi el-Arish of the Negev empties into the Mediterranean. But he never did. Which is why Canaanites continued to live near or around Hebrew cities.

As you know, Reuben, Gad, and a half of Manasseh had been given their portions in Transjordan by Moses. On the western side of the Jordan, Joshua had already awarded Judah, Ephraim, and the other half of Manasseh their inheritances. There were thus seven tribes still without land. To these Joshua now divided the remaining conquered territory.

But first he set up a central Sanctuary at Shiloh. It contained the Ark with its tablets of the Ten Commandments. This was intended to unify the people.

And it did. For the sense of group loyalty will not desert Israel during this period. At no time would one tribe join an enemy to fight against another tribe as Greeks fought Greeks during the Persian Wars. Nor will any tribe ever claim the land of his brothers.

For a good reason. The division of the western side of the Jordan was done by lots, before the Sanctuary of Shiloh in the presence of the High Priest and the Elders. Land was not granted at the whim of a man as was done in America. How many kings of Europe sliced up this continent for the sake of their favorites?

When the tribes are settled, and the tribe of Benjamin behaves wickedly, the others punish her. But they saw to it that Benjamin continued to exist and that her inheritance remained intact in their midst.

Each Israelite's portion had to be acknowledged as a gift from God. And what God had bestowed, was not theirs to take, or destroy.

Some tribes, however, did lose their identity. Simeon in the south merged with Judah. Asher in the north took to the sea and was eventually lost among those expert Seafarers next to them: the Phoenicians.

Not all tribes could possess the land assigned to them. Dan found itself at the mercy of its powerful neighbors, the Philistines, and had to leave its inheritance and migrate to the north. Thus, the phrase which described the length of the land of Israel became "From Dan to Beersheba."

Not only Dan, but all the Hebrew tribes were hemmed in by hostile nations. Warfare was constant. No mercy was shown by either side. Communities were destroyed "with the edge of the sword." It was a savage and tense period.

The *Book of Judges* describes in detail this historical era. When the Hebrews were attacked and spoiled by their enemies, the author of *Judges* wrote: "And the children of Israel did that which was evil in the sight of the Lord, and the Lord delivered them into the hands of an enemy."

"Evil in the sight of God" meant that they imitated the religious practices of their pagan neighbors. Some deserted Yahweh for the local gods: the male Baal and the female Astarte. These gods were supposed to assure bountiful crops and abundant cattle.

Others tried to serve both Yahweh and Baal. Yahweh, they said, was the God who watched over all the tribes. . . . Baal was the god who watched over each separate territory, the giver of harvests. Still others tried to combine Yahweh and Baal by transferring to Yahweh all the titles, powers and forms of worship of the local gods. This is known as "syncretism."

When the oppression of the other nations became too harsh, the Hebrews, according to Judges, repented, and God always sent them a leader. This leader was called a Judge. Many think of these Judges as local chieftains, skillful in war. But not the Tanach; to the author of Judges these men were agents of God. Not one acted for himself. None set up a dynasty, which would make his son a king after him. They were not concerned with their own imperilled tribe alone. Nor did they employ great armies to defeat the enemy. As though they knew that with God on their side, there was no need for much human aid. Ehud slays Eglon, king of Moab, unaided.

One of the most stirring poems is found in the *Book of Judges:* The Song of Deborah. She is a Prophetess and a Judge who rallies many of the tribes to defeat the Canaanite king and Sisera, his General. Hear how she mocks the tribe of Reuben. They cannot decide; they hide among the sheep; they do not answer the call of their brothers.

Among the divisions of Reuben
There was great resolves of heart.
Why did you sit among the sheepfolds,
To hear the pipings of the flocks?
At the divisions of Reuben
There were great searchings of heart.

(Judges V:15–16)

Contrast the "pipings" to the blast of the Shofar? Listen now, to the description of the battle itself: how the rains and the brook bog down the war chariots of the Canaanites:

They fought from heaven,
The stars in their courses fought against
Sisera.
The brook Kishon swept them away,
That ancient brook, the brook Kishon/
O my soul, tread them down with strength.
Then did the horsehoofs stamp
By reason of the prancings, the prancings of
the mighty ones.

(Judges V:20–22)

And now the awful description of how
Sisera was slain:

Blessed above women shall Jael be . . .
Water he asked, milk she gave him:
In a lordly bowl she brought him curd . . .
With the hammer she smote Sisera, she smote
through his head,
Yes, she pierced and struck through his
temples.
At her feet he sunk, he fell, he lay;
At her feet he sunk, he fell;
Where he sunk, there he fell dead.

(Judges V:24–27)

How dreadful the line: "In a lordly bowl she
brought him curd!", when we know what
she really intends. And the slow terrible
descent of death.

The anxiety of Sisera's mother is tragic.
But so too is the looting and enslavement
that a victorious Sisera practised. Listen to
how all is woven into these lines:

Through the window she looked forth and
peered,

The mother of Sisera, through the lattice:
"Why is his chariot so long in coming—
Why tarry the wheels of his chariots?"
The wisest of her princesses answer her
Yes, she returns answer to herself:
"Are they not finding, are they not dividing
the spoil?
A damsel, two damsels to every man;
To Sisera a spoil of dyed garments,
A spoil of dyed garments of embroidery for
the neck of every spoiler?"

(Judges V:28–30)

Deborah's cry of triumph pierces the very
marrow of our bones:

So perish all Your enemies, O Lord;
But they that love Him be as the sun when
he goes forth in his might.

(Judges V:31)

The Book of Judges gives us such vivid
accounts right along. The personalities of
the men and women leap out at us from its
pages. In the case of the strong-backed but
weak-minded Samson, we read of how the
Philistines blinded him and then brought
him into their Temple of Dagon to make
sport of him. What they don't realize, was
that his hair, which was supposed to be the
source of his strength, had grown back.
When he grasps the columns upon which
the Temple rests, he bends them, thus
bringing the Temple with its mocking thousands crashing to their death.

But what kind of story is this? Can hair
make one strong? Doesn't this smack of

magic? Listen to what Samson cries out before he destroys the Philistines:

O Lord God, remember me, I pray You and strengthen me, I pray You, only this once, O God, that I may be this once avenged of the Philistines for my two eyes.

(Judges XVI:28)

And finally, his fervent prayer: "O let me die with the Philistines." Samson behaved badly. He took a Philistine wife. With a fine sense of justice, this wife is the one who weakens him and leaves him a prey for his enemies. But when he repents, it is to God he turns. And it is God who gives him back his former strength. Thus, Samson becomes once more an agent of God.

According to the *Book of Judges,* there were 12 Judges. Judges were supposed to rule over all the tribes. Actually they led the tribes nearest to them. However, only five are described in detail: Ehud, Deborah, who judged under a palm tree, Gideon, Jephthah and Samson.

These men and woman resisted one enemy after another. At the end of this era, the worship of Yahweh is firmly established in the north with Shiloh as its central Sanctuary. There Hebrews went at festival times with their wives and children. The religious lives of the people centered mainly around their local shrines, called High Places. These usually contained a stone altar for sacrifices, and sometimes a hall where families ate the Sacrificial feast.

If there were also pillars and sacred poles, they were not pagan symbols. Nor did they affect the purity of the cult of Yahweh.

By throwing off pagan rulers, the Judges kept the Hebraic character of the tribes intact, until a king united them. Perhaps that is the theme of the *Book of Judges:* the need for one unifying ruler. The last line of the Book seems to imply this: "In those days there was no king in Israel; every man did that which was right in his own eyes."

Activities

THE STRUCTURE OF THE TRIBES

It is time we defined a tribe. According to the Tanach a tribe is a group of people related to each other because they have one ancestor in common.

Let us analyze the following name in the *Book of Joshua:* Achan the son of Carmi, the son of Zabdi, the son of Zerah, of the tribe of Judah.

Carmi was Achan's father. Therefore we say Achan belonged to the house of Carmi.

His grandfather was Zabdi. Therefore Achan belonged to the household of Zabdi. We see, then, that households were made up of separate houses.

Achan's great-grandfather was Zerah. Therefore Achan belonged to the family of Zerah. Families, then, contained households. All these families were descended from Judah, Jacob's son. They made up the tribe of Judah.

How do we remember our grandfathers and great-grandfathers today?

Can you name the Joseph tribes? The Rachel tribes? The Leah tribes?

Some of the men of the tribe of Levi were called Aaronides. Why?

The Kenites who lived in the south of Canaan, near Judah, were culturally superior to the Israelites. They were a musical people. And they knew how to use metals. They were supposed to be related to Jethro, the father in law of Moses.

• Would they be related to the rest of Israel? How?

• Jethro had other names. How would you go about discovering them?

Readings for Students

Voices from the Past, by Mazar & Trone, Harvey House, 1967. Chap. VIII–X.
Buried Treasure in Bible Lands, by Cohen, Lenore, 1965. Chap. XI–XII.
The Drama of Ancient Israel, by Flight, John, Beacon Press, Boston, 1949. Chap. II–III–IV–V–VI–VII.

Readings for Teachers

Judges
The Hebrew Scriptures: An Introduction to their Literature, Samuel Sandmel, Knopf, N.Y. 1963.

chapter 13 Achievements of Joshua and Judges

LET US VIEW THIS TURBULENT PERIOD through the eyes of the authors of *Joshua* and *Judges.* For them, the conquest and settlement of Canaan was the fulfillment of God's plan. We are given many indications of this. The dry passage through the Jordan River is the first sign. To commemorate this event, Joshua sets up twelve stones and connects the incident with the Sea of Reeds of the Exodus. Thus it was another step forward into freedom.

The capture of Jericho is another sign. The veteran fighters are not permitted to storm her walls. Instead the Tanach tells us that merely the blowing of Shofarot and the shouting of people bring Jericho's walls down. As though that were not enough, the people are forbidden to profit by this victory. Why? To emphasize that not they, but God has defeated this mighty city.

After the capture of Ai, Joshua leads the people near Shechem, situated between two mountains: Mt. Ebal, the mountain of cursing, and Mt. Gerizim, the mountain of blessing. After reminding Israel of her duties, Joshua carves upon stone a copy of the Law before all: men, women, children, and strangers.

Surely this is a strange intermission. That a General should take time out to build an altar; to proclaim blessings upon purity, justice, order, truthfulness; and curses upon impurity, disloyalty, injustice, and deceit, was never recorded before in the history of mankind. Notice too that "strangers" constitute a distinct class: men and women who have voluntarily joined themselves unto Israel. This was not a sizeable group. It will take a thousand years before strangers will flock to Israel in droves.

But for strangers to be included at all was a kind of revolution. For while pagan man tolerated all gods, he feared the stranger. Rarely did he allow the stranger to participate in his cultic acts. This fear of strangers, which modern man shares, is called "Xenophobia." Israel, on the other hand, tolerated no gods, but welcomed the stranger. More, Israel took him into his community as an equal member. He worshipped Yahweh with him.

The capture of Canaanite cities is described without concealment: the cities and their inhabitants are destroyed. The author of the *Book of Joshua* reminds us: "There was not a city that made peace with the children of Israel except . . . the inhabitants of Gibeon." What do you suppose he was telling us? That if others had "made peace," there would have been no wars?

Cruel as these battles were, they were in no wise as bestial as the warfare of the nations of antiquity. The following boastings of an Assyrian king, Assur-Nasir-Pal, is an example of how men fought:

> . . . and the rebellious nobles who had revolted against me and whose skin I stripped off, I made into a trophy: some on the midd!e of the pile I left to decay; some on the top
> of the pile on stakes I impaled; some by the side of the pile I placed in order on stakes; many within view of my land I flayed; their skins on the walls I arranged . . .
> many soldiers I captured alive; of some I chopped off the hands and feet; of others the noses and ears . . .

If you think this kind of warfare has ceased, read the accounts of Nazi atrocities. You will see that in our centuries the spirit of Assur-Nasir-Pal lives on.

But rarely in the history of Israel will you find cruelty for cruelty sake. The Prophets, you will learn, cherished peace as the ultimate good for mankind. To this day, war is a horror to our people. When you come to the Chapters on Modern Israel, you will be given an insight into the minds and hearts of today's Israeli soldiers. There are no more passionate lovers of peace than these veterans of three wars.

From the Tanach's point of view, the destruction of Canaan is the result, not of Israel's superiority, but of the Canaanite's evil. This land the Tanach teaches us, could not endure them any longer.

Nor is Israel spared. When she rebels against God, she is punished severely. For her Golden Calf, as well as for her idolatry with the god, Baal Peor, she pays dearly. And she is warned that any future misdeeds will bring the same death and expulsion to her, as it did to the Canaanites. However, it must be added, the land remains Israel's: always ready to welcome her back.

Before his death, Joshua again gathers Israel to Shechem and reminds them of their past, and cautions them about their future. Their conquest, he emphasizes, was the decision of God. Then he gives them, as Moses had at Sinai, the opportunity of choosing whom they would serve. As a people they reply: "Far be it from us that we should forsake the Lord . . ."

Joshua replies: "If you . . . serve strange gods, then He will turn and do you evil . . . You are witnesses against yourself that you have chosen the Lord to serve Him."

According to the *Book of Judges,* Joshua's warning is borne out. Israel did imitate Canaan, and paid for her disloyalty. It should be worth while to ask ourselves now, how much of Canaan's ways did Israel accept?

If Canaan's influence had been strong, we should expect to find it in Israel's political life. Canaan, as you know, was made up of separate city-states, unallied to each other except for emergencies. Yet, as you also know, Israel did not lose her tribal structure during this period. Though not all tribes answered the cry for help from their brothers, many did. And as we saw, the two and one-half of Transjordan worried lest they be separated from their kin on the western side of the Jordan.

Nor did any Judge, except for an upstart schemer, named Abimelech, allow himself to be crowned king. When kings appear in Israel they will be appointed by God at the hands of prophet and priest.

Israel did not even imitate the Canaanite methods of war, as Egypt imitated the Hyksos. When Joshua captures war chariots, he burns them. Why? Because there was no Canaanite to teach him or his warriors how to use them? But we read that the Canaanites did live nearby. Perhaps then, there was no real contact between the two nations?

What then of Canaan's religious influence. Does not the author of the *Book of Judges* accuse Israel of "doing evil in the sight of God"? We should certainly expect to see pagan practises in Israel's festivals?

Since most of Israel were farmers, her calendar was an agricultural one. It was based on both the sun and the moon in order that the festivals would fall in their proper seasons. But no life of a god is tied up with Israel's calendar, as Baal's is with the Canaanite calendar.

Remember the story found in Ugarit: the one about the resurrection of Baal. Baal had to return from death (winter) and revive the world. Therefore Canaan's festivals were intended to bring him back to life. Otherwise he would not be able to prepare the earth to receive the life-giving seed.

In Israel's festivals, Yahweh and Yahweh alone, blesses the earth and makes it fertile.

Then perhaps Israel took over the Canaanite sanctuaries? But we know that no Hebrew Sanctuary precedes the Patriarchs. It was they who blessed certain sites. Yet they never built temples or sanctuaries there. They set up pillars as Jacob did at Bethel, or altars, as Isaac did at Beersheba. When Israel builds her Sanctuaries, and eventually, her Temple, it is because God commands it. Never will a Prophet rebuke Israel with having worshipped Yahweh in a pagan temple.

There is little doubt that Israel's language and alphabet were affected by Canaan. The Psalms, as we learnt, use similar phrases as do poems found in Ugarit.

Literary forms do spread from country to country. But form is not the essential. It is not how one writes, but *what* one writes that counts. The content of the *Psalms* reflect the relationship of man to Yahweh. These are lyrical poems. Therefore the concern of the poet is more with how he feels toward his Maker, than with national or group responses. But there is no trace of pagan influence in this poetry.

What Israel did do at times, was to make idols and call them by Canaanite god-names: Baal, Astarte. But the idols had no histories: they were not born, they did not grow, they did not die. Neither prophet nor poet ever saw them as anything but wood and stone. Israel, we see, never accepted the myths of the Canaanites.

At the end of the *Book of Joshua,* the great General cautions Israel: "Put away the strange gods which are in the midst of you, and incline your hearts unto the Lord, the God of Israel."

And Israel answers: "The Lord our God will we serve and His voice will we obey."

The fact remains, that at the end of the *Book of Judges,* Israel worships Yahweh.

Activities

Questions

1. If you were Joshua, would you have given Israel a choice again? What might have been the consequences had Israel refused to serve Yahweh?
2. Shechem is not listed among the 31 city-states captured by Joshua. Yet we know it is near Shechem Joshua goes to renew the Covenant, not once, but twice: after the capture of Ai and before his own death. Among other things, he builds an altar there.
3. How can we account for the choice of Shechem as a sanctuary? Is it likely Joshua would have dared to assemble the people there if he were surrounded by enemies?
4. The following Unit will show that Shechem becomes the center of the northern tribes. In fact both Solomon and his son Rehoboam go there after being anointed king in Jerusalem. What explanation for this can there be?

Readings for Students

Joshua
   (Chapters VII, XXIII, XXIV, XXV)
The New World Over Story Book
   (p. 250)
Joshua and the Sun, Stein.
The Walls of Jericho, Campbell.

Readings for Teachers

Joshua
   (same as above).
The Religion of Israel, Yehezkel Kaufmann, U. of Chicago Press, 1960.

Unit IV

And King Solomon made a navy of ships in Ezion-geber, which is beside Elath, on the shore of the Red Sea . . .

KINGS I IX:26

chapter 14 Samuel and Saul

FOR TWO HUNDRED YEARS THE TRIBES lived under the constant threat of plundering nomads and raiding nations. Time and again Israel's Judges drove off enemies. Jepthah defeated Ammon, Gideon routed Midian as well as Amalek, and Tribes of the East. Deborah, together with a warrior, Barak, was victorious over the Canaanite king and his General, Sisera. Ehud killed Eglon, king of Moab.

As for Samson, despite all his deeds of courage and resistance, the Philistines succeeded in making life too harsh for Samson's own tribe, Dan. The Danites finally abandoned their inheritance in the south and migrated to the north.

These enemy nations, as you will see, will continue to threaten Israel for many years. But the greatest danger of all was Philistia, the Sea People. They had learnt the Hittite secret of making iron. They used this new and deadlier metal to forge swords and spears. Their chariots with iron scythes extending from each side, terrified Israel.

They settled in five city-states along the southern coast: Gaza, Ashkelon, Ashdod, Gath, and Ekron. Unlike the Canaanites, they were a united force. They were not Semites, like the Hebrews. They came from Crete and the Greek Islands, where their splendid Mycenaean civilization had been shattered by invaders. You may remember that for a while they threatened Egypt. However, they were checked there, especially by Ramses III.

Gaza, one of the five Philistine cities, became so wealthy and magnificent, she was known as "the outpost of Africa, the door of Asia." Caravans from Edom, southern Arabia, and Mesopotamia poured their wealth into her.

The Philistines built stunning temples to Dagon and to their other gods. When they wiped out the last of the native inhabitants along the southern coast, they turned their attention to Israel.

Slowly, but surely, they subdued most of Israel. Their power, at its peak, extended as far north and east as the valley of Jezreel which separates the mountain of Ephraim from the northern mountains of Galilee.

They maintained garrisons throughout the conquered territory to put down any attempt at rebellion. Indeed, they would not permit Hebrew blacksmiths to practise their craft "lest the Hebrews make swords or spears." In order for an Israelite to sharpen his farming tools such as ploughs, axes, and pitchforks, he had to pay a Philistine smith to do it, and pay dearly.

The hand of the Philistines bore down more heavily as the days and months passed. The people groaned. Who would deliver them now? True, they had a Judge. But he was different from the Judges of the past, for he was not a warrior. His name was Samuel.

Samuel had been raised and trained in the Sanctuary of Shiloh by the High Priest and Judge, Eli. In this very Sanctuary, Samuel's mother had prayed that she might give birth to a son. The name, Samuel, is supposed to mean "asked of the Lord." Listen to the words, Hannah, the mother used:

O Lord . . . if You will indeed look on the affliction of Your handmaid, and remember me . . . and will give unto Your handmaid a man child, then I will give him unto the Lord all the days of his life, and no razor shall come upon his head.

(Samuel I I:11)

If you have read the stories of the Judges, you should remember that Samson too, was born to a childless mother. He too was forbidden to use a razor. Such men were known as Nazirites. They were dedicated to God. But there is a great difference between Samuel and Samson.

Samson was only a Judge. He loved his people and he fought for them with his enormous strength. But his will power was as weak as his muscles were strong. That is why he took Philistine wives. When his second wife, Delilah, betrayed him to the Philistines, there was a kind of grim justice in that betrayal. For if an ordinary Israelite was forbidden to marry a foreign wife, how much more so a Samson, a Nazirite?

Samuel too was a Judge; in fact, the last Judge of Israel. But he was more. He was a prophet and a priest. He could no more pamper himself or break the Commandments, than he could bow to a Baal. Yet he was as human as other men. When his love for another clashed with the will of God, he grieved so deeply, he was rebuked by God Himself.

After the destruction of Shiloh by the Philistines, Samuel became the head of Israel. Eli, the old priest of Shiloh was dead, and Eli's two sons, who had been corrupt priests and worthless men, were also dead. They were among the 34,000 men of Ephraim and Manasseh slain by the Philistines at Aphek. At Aphek, too, the Ark of the Lord was captured and lodged in the Philistine temple of Dagon.

This final humiliation was unendurable. However, it taught Israel one lesson: no enemy as strong as Philistia could be resisted by a few of the tribes. They had to unite, all twelve of them, and behind a warrior.

But Samuel was not a soldier. Once it did appear as though he had defeated the Philistines. It happened after he had called a national assembly at Mizpeh to remind the people of the *Covenant.* He did not anticipate that the Philistines would attack.

The Philistines, however, were suspicious. Might not Mizpeh turn out to be another Aphek? Thus they came at the Israelites with their iron swords and scythed chariots. As in the case of Deborah, Gideon, and others, Yahweh fought for Samuel and Israel at Mizpeh. Thundering and earthquake drove off the enemy. But only for a while. For though the *Book of Samuel I* describes the Philistine as subdued during Samuel's lifetime, Philistia became the Master soon after.

With Shiloh no more, Samuel returned to his birthplace, Ramah, a city in Ephraim. Ramah now became the main Sanctuary of the land. The others during Samuel's days were Gilgal, Beth-el, and Mizpeh.

There will be other Sanctuaries after Samuel: at Nob, at Gibeah, at Gibeon, at Hebron, at Beersheba. Shechem was, as you know, an important Sanctuary during the days of Joshua. Others think there were also Sanctuaries on Mt. Carmel and Mt. Tabor.

In order to supplant a corrupt priesthood, (remember Eli's sons), Samuel raised up men who would spread the word of God. These were called the "sons of the prophet." In a school at Naioth, they were taught music and oratory. They would visit the Sanctuaries in groups, chant hymns, and urge the people to serve Yahweh. Often they worked themselves up into ecstasies.

Samuel was called father by these "sons." Prophets after Samuel would continue to support these schools.

Samuel did not travel with the "sons of the prophet." He went alone between Ramah, Gilgal, Bethel, and Mizpeh. He performed sacrifices, judged, taught, and counselled Israel. He saw the misery of the people. How could he not? But he must have advised patience.

Does this sound cowardly? Shouldn't free men refuse to subject themselves to foreign rulers? Surely the sight of Philistine garrisons was hard to bear. Not to mention the drafting of Israelites into Philistine armies, or the constant tribute Philistines exacted.

Why then was Samuel willing to bear this yoke? Because the Philistines did not interfere with the religious life of Israel. You will meet with this attitude many times in the future. Prophets and Sages hated war. It was always a last resort for them. Yet they would have been the first to take up the sword if the *Covenant* were in danger.

As Samuel grew old, his sons, like Eli's before him, behaved dishonorably. Dissatisfaction spread. Where was there another general like Joshua or Gideon? But not just a general. These came and went. They wanted someone who would defend all Israel always. Someone whose son after him would assume the same responsibility. Someone to whom every Israelite would be able to swear allegiance. In short, a king.

And so the Elders demanded that Samuel appoint one so that they could be like the other nations. Samuel refused. He saw this request as a rejection of Yahweh. For how could a human being be king when God was King? Monarchy suited pagans: men who did not acknowledge Yahweh as the Ruler of the universe. In asking for a king, Israel was disloyal to the Covenant.

Nevertheless, Samuel, the Bible tells us, is commanded by God to comply:

. . . they have not rejected you, but . . . Me, that I should be king over them.

(Samuel I VIII:7)

For God, according to Scripture, the *Covenant* is still in force. Despite themselves, they cannot be like other nations. Even with a king, Israel must continue to fulfill the Commandments. Moreover, the king shall understand that he is permitted to rule by God. He can maintain his position only as long as he is faithful to Torah. Remember this, for it shall hold true for the first and last kings of Israel.

But what of Samuel the Prophet? Shall he become a subject of the throne. Yes. But he shall also be the king's master. This is what we call a paradox: two facts which contradict each other, yet are each true.

No genuine prophet will ever remain silent if a king breaks the *Covenant*. And with but few exceptions, every king will accept the prophetic rebuke. Nor will there be any clear divisions of power in Israel. No one will say: this the king can do; and this the prophet can do.

Everything the king does, is the prophet's business. Everything in life can be, and should be done according to what is honorable and just. Everything, as Torah teaches, must be sanctified. For there are only two categories for the Jew: what is holy, and what is not *yet* holy.

With a heavy heart, Samuel obeys the voice of God. However, first he describes the perils of monarchy. This is one of the most stirring antimonarchial speeches in the history of mankind. It is found in the *Book of I Samuel,* Chapter VIII:10–18. These are just a few sentences:

. . . he will take your sons, and appoint them unto him, for his chariots, and to be his horsemen; and they shall run before him . . . and they . . . shall plow his ground . . . reap his harvest . . . make his instruments of war . . . and he will take your daughters to be perfumers . . . cooks . . . bakers . . . and he will take your fields . . . vineyards . . . oliveyards . . . and give them to his servants . . . and you shall cry out in that day because of your king . . .

The people, however, persist:

No, but there shall be a king over us that we also may be like all the nations, and that our king may judge us, and go out before us, and fight our battles.

(Samuel I VIII:20)

Samuel finally chooses a king. Notice that it is a prophet, an agent of God, who selects. But as you will see, the people will have to approve the selection. With this decision, the period of the Monarchies begins.

Most of our information will come from the following Books of the Tanach: Samuel I, Samuel II, Kings I, and Kings II. The Greek translation of the Tanach, we call Septuagint, classifies them simply as Kings I-IV. Also from the Tanach are Chronicles I and Chronicles II. The other sources for this period are the histories of neighboring countries. By comparing what went on in them with what happened in Israel we acquire many fresh insights into the history of our people. Archeology, especially, has uncovered much new and illuminating material.

Kings I-IV contain both approval and disapproval of the very idea of monarchy. When you read these Books, and you surely should, you will notice these two different points of view. It is as though the writers can never lose sight of this basic truth: Israel's king is Yahweh. The man who sits on the throne should not have been there in the first place.

But since God permitted it by word of the prophet, we have to accept it. In addition, we must be aware that these same Books reflect the feelings of the authors. Men who came from the tribe of Benjamin might not be fond of the king who was born in Judah. The author from Judah might be hostile to the king of Benjamin.

Samuel chose Saul ben Kish, a young man from Benjamin. This tribe was severely punished by the others for an evil deed. As a result, Benjamin had become the smallest of the twelve tribes. Nevertheless, Benjamin now takes away the leadership of Israel from Ephraim. Remember that Joshua was of Ephraim. Shiloh had been in Ephraim. And Samuel too, was born in Ephraim.

Saul was a handsome youth, taller than all other men, "from his shoulder and upward." He was accepted by his fellow Israelites, but only half-heartedly. In fact there were some complained aloud: "How shall this man save us?" And *Samuel I* adds: ". . . and they despised him, and brought him no present."

But Saul did not answer them. Perhaps he was himself truly overwhelmed? When Samuel offered him the crown, these were his words of protest:

Am I not a Benjamite, of the smallest of the tribes of Israel? and my family the least of all the families of the tribe of Benjamin: wherefore then do you (Samuel) speak to me in this manner? (about becoming King.)

(Samuel I IX:21)

Yet Saul was hardly as insignificant as he claimed. *Samuel I* tells us that though the Philistines took away every Israelite's weapons, Saul and his father did not give up theirs. Obviously the house of Kish was not made up of timid men.

Samuel anointed Saul with holy oil. When Aaron and his sons were named priests, they too were anointed. This special oil was supposed to cleanse. Also it set the anointed apart. His person was sacred. He had a special relationship to God. In Hebrew we call him "Mesheach Adonai." You can recognize the English word "Messiah" in "Mesheach." Messiah merely means anointed. The king, therefore, was the anointed of the Lord.

At the same time Samuel drew up a Constitution for both Israel and her king. This Constitution he set before God and man for the guidance of future kings of Israel. Thus Samuel made one of the greatest contributions to the political thought of man: the truly democratic theory of the relation between the governor and the governed. Each had his duties and his rights.

Unlike pagan kings, Israel's could never have absolute power. Why? Because of Torah. Torah was above both nation and king. The king had not written it. It was given to him as to every other Israelite. His job was to administer it.

It did not take long for Saul to prove himself. The king of Ammon was besieging the city of Jabesh-Gilead in Transjordan. The men of that city were willing to surrender, but the Ammonite King demanded more. He wanted the right eye of each man as a mark of subjection. In despair Jabesh-Gilead turned to Saul.

The "king of Israel" was plowing his field when the messenger arrived. For Saul had merely returned to his home in Gibeah after his election. He had no palace built for his family. He wore no crown. But when he read the letter of his brothers in Transjordan, he became every inch a king. He slew his oxen and cut them up into twelve pieces. To each of the tribes he sent a piece with this warning:

Who ever does not come forth after Saul and after Samuel, so shall it be done to his oxen.

(Samuel I XI:7)

Who would dare refuse? They came from every corner. Saul led them across the Jordan and smashed the army of Ammon. This rescue of Jabesh-Gilead will never be forgotten by the men of this city.

Those who had grumbled at Saul's appointment, now feared for their lives. This Benjamite was no weakling. He might not live in a palace, but he was a king! Indeed, there were those among Saul's men who were ready to punish them. But Saul would have no revenge:

No man shall be put to death this day, for today the Lord has delivered Israel.

(Samuel I XI:13)

Now that Saul was accepted by all, Samuel called Israel to Gilgal to publicly confirm Saul's position. For it is the people who must approve. At the same time, Samuel recalled the history of Israel since the Exodus, as Moses and Joshua had done before him. Like them too, Samuel was jealous for his own honor. He demanded that Israel witness against him before God whether he had ever oppressed or robbed anyone. Then he promised the people that he would never desert them.

Nor did he. Samuel kept a tight rein upon Saul. Perhaps too tight. For it did not take long before trouble erupted between Samuel and Saul. This conflict shall come to the surface between all future kings and prophets. All prophets spoke in the name of God. They demanded absolute obedience. For a king such demands became oppressive. Often they interfered with affairs of state.

An example of such a clash springs from the war with Amalek. Samuel ordered Saul to exterminate the Amalekites. For Samuel, that tribe was like the Nazis of our century. What Samuel meant was that all were to be put to death, and no spoils were to be taken. This was called "herem."

We find "herem" outside the Tanach. Mesha, king of Moab, boasted he had massacred the entire Israelite population of Nebo, herem to his god, Ashtar-Kemosh.

This was considered a holy war, but not as Muslims or Christians fought: for the sake of spreading their faith. Israel only fought for survival. And the Amalekites more than any other nation, threatened her existence. Philistia, Israel's chief enemy, oppressed her. But Philistia did not seek to destroy Israel as Amalekites did then, or as the Nazis did in our time.

In a war of "herem" the soldiers were called the troops of God or the armies of Yahweh. Victories were commemorated in the *Book of the Wars of Yahweh,* a volume which has disappeared. Before battle, sacrifices were offered. Most important, Yahweh was consulted by means of the Ephod the priest wore, or by the sacred lots. Yahweh, therefore, it was emphasized, decided when to go to war. He marched in front of the army.

The visible sign of the presence of Yahweh was the Ark. When the Ark was lifted, the people shouted: "Arise, Yahweh, and let Your enemies be scattered. . . ." When it was brought back to its place, they said: "Return Yahweh, to the countless thousands of Israel. . . ."

The Ark, you recall, had led them through the desert, across the Jordan, and encircled the walls of Jericho. The capture of the Ark at Aphek was the worst catastrophe to Israel. More than any other factor, it caused the death of Eli. Even the Philistines had been terrified by its presence. These are their words:

Woe unto us! Who shall deliver us out of the hand of these mighty gods? These are the gods that smote the Egyptians . . . (but) Be strong and quit yourselves like men O you Philistines . . . don't be servants unto the Hebrews as they have been unto you . . . quit yourselves like men and fight.

(Samuel I IV:7–9)

It is obvious that the author of *Samuel I* does not conceal his admiration for the Philistines, the enemy of Israel.

Whoever engaged in a holy war had to be convinced he would be victorious. That is why Gideon dismissed 22,000 men who were frightened. A different reason is given in the *Book of Deuteronomy* for sending fearful soldiers away. But the basic reason remains: fear is a sign of little faith.

During battle Yahweh fought. *Judges* makes this very clear. Against Sisera He sent rain, thunder, and earthquakes. At Mizpah He did the same against the Philistines. For Gideon He confused Midian. For Joshua we read, He held up sun and moon.

Thus the spoils belonged to Yahweh alone. Achan, who took among other things that "goodly mantle of Shinar," brought punishment upon all Israel. As herem was directed against every Canaanite object of worship, so too it was to be applied against any Israelite city that denied Yahweh.

This is a harsh and dangerous concept. But we must ask ourselves how much agony our world would have been spared if Hitler and his original tribe of Nazis had been exterminated immediately. Besides our own six million, there were fourteen more million men, women and children who might still be alive. And what of the suffering the Nazi caused? And what of the vicious heritage the Nazi left behind: that life is cheap; that man can be used as a thing; that one can do anything he wants as long as there is no one stronger than he?

Some believe Samuel was wrong in ordering herem for Amalek. One of our foremost theologians believes Samuel did not hear God correctly. What do you think?

Saul differed with Samuel. He spared Agag, king of Amalek. He also allowed the people to take the choicest of the cattle to sacrifice unto God.

Samuel's response to Saul is famous:

Has the Lord as great delight in burnt-offerings and sacrifices,
As in heeding the voice of the Lord?
Behold to obey is better than sacrifice,
And to listen than the fat of rams.
For rebellion is as the sin of witchcraft,
And stubbornness is as idolatry and teraphim.

Then Samuel added:

Because you have rejected the word of the Lord, He has also rejected you from being king.

(Samuel I XV:22–23)

Despite this grim prophecy, Saul continued to protect Israel against her enemies: Moab and Ammon in Transjordan; Edom in the southeast; Zobah, a nation in the north; and of course, Philistia. He picked his army carefully, seeking not quantity, but quality. He remained in Gibeath-Shaul, now a fortress-home, living without pomp or glitter.

He ruled with the advice of a Council of State which met informally. It was not below his dignity to sit in state under a tamarisk tree, as Deborah used to judge under a palm tree. He was a generous king and a most courageous man. Surely his reign should have been established firmly. His eldest son, Jonathan, should have succeeded him.

None of this took place. Saul, with all his courage and generosity, was unstable. He was overly suspicious. He thought men plotted against him. He suffered from sudden fits of terror, unreasoning rage, and on occasion, from uncontrollable violence. The *Book of Samuel I* describes it thus:

Now the spirit of the Lord departed from Saul, and an evil spirit from the Lord terrified him.

(XVI:14)

For the author of *Samuel I* both good and evil were equally in the power of God, and therefore the spirit that afflicted Saul had to come from Him. But if we bear in mind the break between Saul and Samuel, we can understand how this must have affected the king.

Because Saul was subject to such black moods, his counselors enlisted a young shepherd to soothe him with the music of his harp. The name of this country musician was David.

David was of the tribe of Judah, the youngest of eight sons of Jesse of Bethlehem. He is described as a good-looking boy with red hair and beautiful eyes. Not only can he compose songs, he proves himself the greatest warrior of Israel.

The career of David begins spectacularly. He defeats the taunting Philistine giant, Goliath. As a result he is made Saul's armor-bearer, accompanying the king into battle. Eventually he marries Saul's daughter, Michal, thus becoming a son in law of the royal household. Perhaps the closest bond of all to the house of Kish, is the friendship that grew between David and Jonathan, the heir to the throne. We might expect Jonathan to resent or to fear David's popularity in Israel. But nothing could rupture the relationship of these two youths. Our Rabbis called it the noblest type of love.

Saul, however, is different. When he hears the women sing: "Saul has slain his thousands; David, his ten thousands," his fear and jealousy are aroused. He is convinced David intends to usurp his throne.

This suspicion gives Saul no rest. So driven is the king, he tries to kill David. With the aid of Michal and Jonathan, David escapes with his life.

He flees into the stern Judean hills, gathering a band of loyal men about him. Saul pursues him. Twice David has Saul at his mercy. Each time his followers urge him to kill the king. Each time David refuses. Saul was Mesheach Adonai: the Lord's Anointed. No hand may touch him.

One of the most moving passages of *Samuel I* occurs after David proves to Saul that he is no threat to him. Listen to Saul's reply:

Is this your voice, my son, David. And Saul wept, and he said. "You are more righteous than I, for you have rewarded me with goodness, though I have done evil to you . . . therefore the Lord reward you good for what you have done unto me this day . . ."

(XXIV:18–20)

Though the author was an admirer of David, he could not prevent the nobility of Saul from shining through. We see that when Saul was not sick, he was a tragic and honorable human being.

The death of Saul is the death of a hero. Convinced he and his sons will be slain in battle, he nevertheless goes valiantly to meet the Philistines. Jonathan and two other sons are killed on Mt. Gilboa. Saul, mortally wounded, begs his armor-bearer to slay him, rather than let him fall into the hands of the Philistines. His armor-bearer refuses, and Saul falls upon his own sword. The Philistines cut off the heads of the king and the princes as trophies, send their armors to their temple, and fasten their mutilated bodies to the walls of nearby Beth-Shan.

When the men of Jabesh-Gilead hear of this indignity, they march all night, take down the headless bodies, bury them under a tamarisk tree in Jabesh, and fast seven days in mourning. Thus they repaid Saul for his kindness to them. Later David will remove these bones to the burial tomb of the house of Kish in Benjamin.

Activities

THE ARK OF THE LORD AND MAGIC

As you know, the Philistines captured the Ark at Aphek. They placed it in their temple of Dagon in Ashdod. What you don't know, is that they returned the Ark to Israel. Why?

Because they believed that Yahweh had sent a plague upon Ashdod as a punishment. Therefore, the men of Ashdod transferred the Ark to their sister city of Gath. The same plague erupted there. Gath sent it on to Ekron. And the plague accompanied it there.

By this time the Philistines were beside themselves with terror. What could they do? Their diviners advised them to return the Ark with "boils of gold and mice of gold."

Mice were a symbol of the plague-god. Thus the Philistines intended to expel the plague by transferring the demon of the plague to these images. By sending the Ark back with these images, they hoped to spread the plague in Israel.

The author of *I Samuel* knew nothing of such magic. How could he? He believed in God. To him these golden figures could only be gifts to Yahweh. And so he put these words into the mouth of the Philistine diviners:

Why do you (Philistines) harden your heart as the Egyptians and Pharaoh hardened their hearts? When He had done His work among them, did they not let the people go . . . Take the Ark of the Lord, and put jewels of gold which you return to Him for a guilt offering . . .

(Samuel I V:6–8)

Questions

• The exact words of *Samuel I* are: "God's hand was upon the Philistines all the days of Samuel." But the same book denies this. How can this be? One commentator explains that "all the days of Samuel" meant while Samuel was the sole authority. As soon as his sons shared authority, the Philistines returned to plague Israel. Can you offer another explanation?

• Since Saul did not seek the kingship, do you think history dealt fairly with him?
• Why was Samuel so anxious to have his name cleared? Consider his antimonarchial speech and his family? What other factors might have influenced him?
• See if you can find where Moses too cried out that he had never taken another man's property? It is in *Numbers* XVI.
• Did Joshua ever become rich? How did he treat the men of his own tribe when they demanded more land?
• An Ephod was a special garment worn by the priest. Find out how it was made, and how it was used.
• On Mt. Gilboa Saul and his sons went into battle like men. Who else expected defeat, yet fought? What does this tell us of the author of *Samuel I*?

Readings for Students

Samuel I.
Our Peop'e in Olden Days, by Israel, Ben Kindey Buch Publishers, 1956.

Readings for Teachers

Ancient Israel, Roland de Vaux, McGraw Hill Book Co., Inc., New York.
Samuel I.

chapter 15 David

THERE IS NO NAME IN JEWISH HISTORY that evokes more delight and hope than that of David the son of Jesse of Bethlehem, Judah. See if you agree after you have finished this Unit. Of course, you will be in a better position to judge if you read both *Samuels.*

Whoever wrote *Samuel II* was, without question the first great historian of the world. He gave us a realistic picture not only of national events, but of the intimate life of David's court. No doubt this author loved David. But neither his love nor his loyalty ever defer to his honesty. The truth is told, however unflattering to David.

Let us begin with the messenger who brought the news of Saul's death to David. Certainly this man expected some reward for what he considered happy news. After all, hadn't Saul pursued David, sought to kill him? To insure his reward, the messenger lied. He claimed he had killed Saul. He even brought Saul's crown and arm bands to David as trophy and proof.

David, however, hardly agreed.

How were you not afraid to destroy the Mesheach Adonai? . . . Your blood be upon your own head, for your mouth has testified against you saying, "I have slain the Mesheach Adonai."

(Samuel II I:14–16)

The messenger's reward was death.

David mourned for Saul and Jonathan in one of the most poignant dirges ever composed. Here is part of it:

Your beauty O Israel, upon your high places is slain!
How are the mighty fallen! . . .
You mountains of Gilboa
Let there be no dew nor rain upon you . . .
Saul and Jonathan, the lovely and the pleasant
In their lives, even in their death they were not divided;
They were swifter than eagles,
They were stronger than lions . . .
I am distressed for you, my brother
Jonathan; . . .
Wonderful was your love for me . . .
How are the mighty fallen,
And the weapons of war perished.

(Samuel II I:20–27)

With the defeat of the army of Saul on Mt. Gilboa in the Jezreel Valley, there seemed no hope for Israel. The only remaining son of Saul was Ishbaal, a weakling who fled to northern Transjordan. His throne was supported and maintained by Abner, General and uncle of the dead Saul.

The southern territory of Israel was defenseless before its enemies. David, who had fled there from Saul, roamed the mountains of Judah, hiding in their many caves. When Saul's pursuit had increased, David had taken refuge with Achish, the Philistine king of Gath. To keep David away from his capital of Gath, and yet to retain him as vassal, Achish gave David the city of Ziklag. From Ziklag, David pretended to raid Israelites in the Negev. Actually he attacked the enemies of Israel.

When the Philistines were ready to march upon Saul at Gilboa, Achish wanted David to accompany him. David might have had to take up arms against his own people! Fortunately, the four other Philistine kings refused to accept David as an ally.

During these "vassal years" David endeared himself to his own tribe of Judah. He sent gifts from whatever spoils he captured, to the elders of the strongholds of Judah. In addition he married Abigail, a rich, soft-spoken and wise widow of the tribe of Caleb, thus drawing the Calebites closer to him. David was ever grateful to Abigail. She had prevented him from shedding the blood of Nabal, her former husband, a stingy and arrogant landowner. She had supplied David with the provisions Nabal had refused him. At the same time she had persuaded David not to attack Nabal.

Also during these years David developed a crack military machine. 600 expert soldiers constituted the bulk of his army. A bodyguard of 30 Gibborim made up a select corp of knights. The highest rank consisted of just three warriors. One of them, Adino, was supposed to have slain 800 men at one time.

Once three Gibborim risked their lives to get David a cup of water from a well in Philistine hands. David refused to drink it. Pouring it out as a libation to God, he said:

Far be it from me, O Lord, that I should do this. Shall I drink the blood of the men that went in danger of their lives . . .

(Samuel II XXIII:17)

It may be that David learnt much about warfare from the Philistines. After he became king of a united Israel, his famous mercenaries were of Philistine origin: the Cherethites and Pelethites. One of his chief commanders was Ittai of Gath. When David was in mortal danger because of his own son, Absalom, he tried to persuade Ittai to leave him.

Why should you also go with us? Return for you are a foreigner and also an exile from your own place . . . Return and take your brother with you . . .

(Samuel II XV:19:20)

To which Ittai replied:

As the Lord lives, and as my lord, the king lives, surely in what place my lord, the king shall be whether for death or for life, there also will I be.

(Samuel II XV:21)

With the death of Saul, David moved his forces to Hebron, capital of Judah. It may be the Philistines helped him establish himself there. Surely it suited them to have two rulers in Israel: Ishbaal and David. Can you figure out why?

But the Philistines could not foresee the future. They could not know there would be a rift between Ishbaal and his General, Abner. Nor that Abner would transfer his allegiance to David. Indeed, so weak did Ishbaal become, two of his own captains crept into his house while he rested, assassinated him, and brought his head to David.

Their reward was also not what they expected. This is what David said:

. . . when one told me that Saul was dead . . . I slew him . . . instead of giving a reward for his tidings. How much more when wicked men have slain a righteous person in his own house upon his bed, shall I not require his blood of your hand and take you away from the earth?

(Samuel II IV:10–11)

Nor did Abner benefit from his desertion of Ishbaal. David had probably promised Abner command of his army. If this is so, it was a threat to Joab, the present commander. And Joab and his brothers were mighty and loyal warriors. They were also David's nephews. We should not be surprised, therefore, that Joab killed Abner in the gate of Hebron.

Was Joab justified? It is true, that before this, Abner had killed one of Joab's two brothers. But he had done so in self defense. And Joab knew it had been self defense. It can be assumed that Joab was revenging his brother's death, as was his duty. But then, why did he wait for just this moment to act?

In order to judge, remember that Abner was of Benjamin, an uncle of Saul, a member of the royal family of Kish. He could very well have become a rallying personality for the Benjamites and the northern tribes. And these tribes were ever quick to oppose David and his throne if they thought they were slighted or wronged.

With Ishbaal and Abner dead, the North of Israel was leaderless. It was inevitable that the Elders should come to Hebron, and appeal to David.

Behold we are your bone and your flesh . . . when Saul was king . . . it was you led Israel . . . and the Lord said unto you: "You shall feed my people, Israel, and you shall be prince over Israel."

(Samuel II V:1–2)

David made a covenant with them and was anointed king. For seven and a half years David had ruled over Judah in Hebron. For thirty-three more years he was to rule over a united kingdom. The leadership of Israel, which had descended from Ephraim (Joshua and Samuel) to Benjamin, (Saul) now descends further south, from Benjamin to Judah. It remains a living force until today.

Now the Philistine hope for the disunity of Israel was dashed. They lost no time in attacking David. After a series of retreats and skirmishes, David dealt Philistia a decisive blow by capturing the city of Gath. An enduring peace was concluded. From that time on Philistia never dared set foot on Israel's soil.

Unity was always a dream of Israel's leaders. It will find its most poetic expression in the vision of the great prophet: Ezekiel (Chapter XXII.) For David, it had to be achieved immediately. He knew he had to create a national religious center as Joshua had at Shiloh, as Samuel had at Ramah. Being a warrior, David would seek a place that was easily defended.

He decided on the Jebusite stronghold, situated on the top of Judean hills. Except for her northern flank, she seemed inaccessible and invincible. Also her springs and conduits supplied her with sufficient water at that time. In addition, she was close enough to Benjamin to be included within Benjamin's southern border. The most important reason, however, was that in Jebusite hands this stronghold would always interfere seriously between north and south. Her position hindered unification.

So invincible did she appear, the Jebusites boasted even their blind and lame could defend her. But they did not reckon with a Joab. This amazing warrior found a tunnel leading into her fortress. With his most daring soldiers, Joab crawled up its length and took the city.

David named the whole citadel, together with the additional land he developed, the city of David. Her enduring name is Jerusalem: the city of Peace. For us, she is the city of God.

Her sacred character was stamped upon her by David. He linked Jerusalem to the religious tradition of Sinai, Shiloh, and Ramah, by transferring the Ark there. David danced ecstatically as the Ark was carried to Jerusalem. At that moment he was not only king for Israel, but priest-king. His wife Michal, however, despised him for his undignified conduct. Therefore David said to her:

Before the Lord who chose me above your father . . . I will make merry . . . And I will behave even more humbly . . .

(Samuel II VI:21–22)

As a result of this, according to *II Samuel* VI:23, Michal never bore a child.

David would have built a Temple for the Ark, had not the prophet, Nathan, prevented him. Instead of David's building for God, the prophet said, God would build for David. He would build him an enduring dynasty.

Later David did purchase a threshing

floor of a Jebusite, and erected an altar on it. This became the site of the great altar of the future Temple. Whatever gold and silver he had captured, he set aside for the construction and adornment of the Temple. David also designed musical instruments used by the Levite orchestra. There is little doubt that a sizeable portion of the Psalms, our religious poetry, was composed by him.

David built a powerful border kingdom. He defeated Midian, Moab, Philistia, and Edom. Amalek he subdued forever. In Syria he established garrisons to control the native population. His chief alliances of friendship were with Phoenecia and Geshur. Maacah, the daughter of the king of Geshur, became his wife. She was to bear him Absalom, his rebellious son.

Thus Israel occupied all of the Mediterranean coast, except for the small area of Philistia and Phoenicia. In addition, Transjordan as far as the Arabian Desert acknowledged David as king. In fact his authority was recognized from the border of Egypt and the Gulf of Akaba to the River Euphrates.

After more than two hundred years, Israel knew peace. It was, or could have been a golden era. Unfortunately, the standing army and the civil servants David maintained required money. Taxes must have increased. As was the custom of those days, citizens gave of their labor as well as of their wealth.

The taxes and forced labor (corvée) must have been kept within bounds. David was still a constitutional monarch. His power was limited by public opinion and of course, by the prophets.

The power of the people must never be underestimated. It manifests itself constantly. Once when Saul condemned Jonathan for breaking his royal vow, the people opposed Saul and saved Jonathan.

In David's reign there were two revolts. These tell us how quick the people were to rise up against any real or imagined injustice. In the reign of David's grandson, popular protest shall take its most extreme form: it will split the kingdom.

It is obvious that the character of the men born in the desert, was forged on the anvil of freedom. It is also obvious that this character was passed on from generation to generation. Israel would never allow herself to be enslaved. The king had to be servant to Israel, not master.

Moses had taught them this. According to the book of *Deuteronomy,* a king was not allowed to multiply gold, horses, or wives. He was to make a copy of the Torah, and bear it before him wherever he went. The Torah, symbol of God's Kingship, was to remind him that his privileges were given to him. They were not his to take.

Most of the time David remembered this. He lived in a more royal state than Saul, but he was also found with his men within their camps. Once after a narrow escape from death, his soldiers exclaimed:

You shall not go out anymore with us to battle, lest you put out the lamp of Israel.

(Samuel II XXI:17)

Despite this command, born of love, David did continue to accompany them.

Such love speaks volumes. Perhaps you will think it was the author who felt this way. Therefore he drew David as such an endearing personality.

Perhaps. But the same pen describes the following dreadful event. David fell in love with Bathsheba, wife of one of his soldiers, Uriah the Hittite. He took her when Uriah was at the battlefield. When he learnt that Bathsheba was bearing his child, he tried to induce Uriah to return home to Bathsheba.

Uriah refused. He would not accept the comforts of home while his comrades and the Ark of God were in camp. Thereupon David sent him back to the fighting with these instructions to Joab: "Put Uriah in the forefront of the battle and retreat from him that he may be smitten and die."

After Uriah was killed, David took Bathsheba for a wife. The matter it seemed, was closed. Except . . . there was Nathan, the prophet.

Nathan appeared before David and told him this story: A rich man possessed much cattle and sheep. A poor man, but one ewe lamb. The lamb was the poor man's treasure. He fed it and raised it with love and tenderness.

When the rich man had to prepare food for a guest, he would not slaughter of his own flocks. Instead he took the poor man's lamb and prepared a meal from her.

Furious, David cried out: ". . . the man that did this deserves to die. . . ." Whereupon Nathan replied: "You are the man."

David neither blustered nor protested. Humbly he confessed: "I have sinned against the Lord."

Because of this evil deed, violence did not depart out of David's house. According to *Samuel II,* David paid with the lives of three of his sons: Amnon, his firstborn; Absalom, his third son; and Adonijah, his fourth. The baby of Bathsheba also died, although David fasted and prayed for him unceasingly. In fact, so passionately did he implore God, his servants were afraid to announce the baby's death. But they needn't have feared. He accepted God's verdict with dignity and resignation. Read about this incident.

There is no question that David was a weak father. Like Jacob, our third Patriarch, like Eli, High Priest of Shiloh, and perhaps like Samuel, he was too lax with his children. As a result tragedy stalked his family. Absalom killed Amnon for humiliating Tamar, his sister. Then Absalom escaped to Geshur, his mother's birthplace.

Joab had Absalom brought back because he knew David grieved for him. This was a serious mistake. Absalom conspired against his father. His chief counselor was

Ahitophel, a former adviser of David. Why did Ahitophel turn against David? Ahitophel was the grandfather of Bathsheba.

What is more, not only the north rallied to Absalom, but David's own tribe of Judah as well. It was in Hebron, the capital of Judah, Absalom raised the flag of revolt.

Why there? Because Absalom was born there? Hardly a politically sound reason. After all David, though not born in Hebron, was yet of Judah. He had ruled in Hebron 7½ years. Or was it because there must have been a Sanctuary there? But there were many Sanctuaries.

More likely Absalom chose Hebron to identify the rebellion with Judah and thus to rob David of the very men he would expect to support him: his own tribesmen. To make the identification solid, Absalom made Amasa, another nephew of David, General of his forces. If the other tribes swooped down from the north, David would be caught between them and Judah in the south. That may be the reason David fled from Jerusalem to Transjordan.

Many remained loyal to David. Joab and his brother, Abishai; Ittai of Gath; the two High Priests, Zadok and Abiathar; a wise Elder named Hushai, and others. The two priests and the Levites brought the Ark to David. But David refused it saying:

Carry back the Ark of God . . . if I shall find favor in the eyes of the Lord, He will bring me back and show me both it and His dwelling place. But if He say, "I have no delight in you,

behold here am I, let Him do to me as He sees fit."

(Samuel II XV:25–26)

So humbly did David accept his plight, he would not retaliate against anyone, not even against a Benjamite who cursed him. Yet in those days to curse a king was punishable by death. When Abishai, Joab's brother, would have killed this Benjamite, David restrained him. Sadly, he explained:

See my son who came forth of my body seeks my life, how much more so this Benjamite. Let him alone, and let him curse, for the Lord had bidden him.

(Samuel II XVI:11)

Few episodes in the Tanach are as tragic as this revolt of Absalom. Not the least of the tragedy was the enduring love of David for his wicked and scheming son. Even before the battle, David pleaded with his Captains to deal gently with Absalom.

As you would expect, Joab would have none of this. To him Absalom was a vicious son and rebel. He had caused the death of thousands of men. He had almost destroyed the kingdom. Joab, therefore killed Absalom. When David learnt of Joab's deed, he wept:

O my son Absalom, my son, my son Absalom. Would I had died for you O Absalom, my son, my son.

(Samuel II XIX:1)

How do you think his soldiers must have felt before such grief? And how do you think Joab reacted? Here is a description of both:

And the victory that day was turned into mourning unto all the people . . . and the people sneaked . . . into the city, as people that are ashamed steal away when they flee in battle . . . And Joab came . . . to the king, and said: "You have shamed this day the faces of all your servants who this day have saved your life . . . in that you love them that hate you, and hate them that love you . . . for this day I see that if Absalom had lived and we had died . . . then it would have been alright in your eyes. Now, therefore, arise, go forth and speak to the heart of your servants; for I swear by the Lord, if you do not go forth, no one will remain with you this night. And that will be worse for you than all the evil that has befallen you from your youth until now."

(Samuel II XIX:3–8)

David, who could recognize the truth when he heard it, obeyed.

Though Absalom's rebellion was put down, the nation was not at peace. The northern tribes were still resentful and suspicious, especially of Judah. For David forgave Judah promptly. He even appointed Amasa, who had led Absalom's army, General of his own forces in place of Joab.

Remember Abner? Yes, Joab dealt with Amasa as he had with Abner. He killed him.

Many of the northerners fought on under the leadership of a Benjamite, Sheba ben Bichri. With lightening speed, Joab defeated Sheba. Unfortunately, he could not eliminate the anger between north and south.

To add to the internal strife, two factions sprang up. One that supported Solomon, the son of Bathsheba and David, was headed by Nathan the Prophet, Benaiah, Captain of the mercenaries, and Zadok, one of the High Priests. The other, led by Joab and Abiathar, the other High Priest, supported Adonijah, now the oldest of David's remaining sons.

David favored Solomon. He saw to it that Solomon was crowned immediately. Upon his deathbed he advised Solomon to punish Joab for the deaths of Abner and Amasa. But many believe it was for Absalom's death, David sought Joab's life.

What do you think? Remember that after David's death, Joab could become a serious threat to the unity of Israel since he opposed Solomon. Except for the prophet Nathan, he was the only one strong enough to disobey and rebuke a king. He had done away with two men who might have supplanted him. And of course, he was a fearless and brilliant soldier.

However we shall never know what he might have done. For Solomon did put Joab to death. He took him from the altar itself. At the same time he exiled Abiathar the priest, also of Adonijah's party.

David died at the age of seventy, an old and weary king. During the first two thirds of his reign he secured the people and the land against their enemies. Men could sit under their vine and fig tree with no one to make them afraid. He was undoubtedly an exceptional warrior, though a too indulgent father, and in the case of Bathsheba, a very sinful man. But he must have been a magnetic personality. Men and women loved him.

He loved God. He threw himself upon His mercy. He accepted His verdict uncomplainingly. He sang of his love for God in one lyrical poem after another. Fittingly he was called the "sweet singer of Israel."

He was too complex for us to describe him completely. How shall we understand a man who could dance as he did, ecstatically, uncaring of his royal dignity? Who fasted and prayed passionately to save his baby's life, yet accepted the child's death with composure and submission? Who was determined to punish an arrogant landowner, Abigail's husband, yet was stopped by a woman's gentle voice? Who, a fugitive before the wrath of Saul, continued to love Saul, and to love Jonathan?

His personality has left its mark upon Israel unto this day. He has come closest to the image of a priest-king. The house of David was supposed to live forever. In the heart of Israel it does. The King Messiah shall be a descendant of David, the son of Jesse.

That is why we sing: "David, King of Israel, lives and endures."

How do you feel about David?

Activities

THE MESSIANIC VISION

The concept of the Messiah is central to Jewish history. In her darkest hours, Israel comforted herself with the sure knowledge that the Messiah would come and redeem her.

In the concentration camps men and women sang of their faith in his eventual arrival. They used the words of the great Jewish philosopher, Maimonides (Rambam):

I believe with perfect faith in the coming of the Messiah. And though he tarry, and despite everything, I believe.

Others believed, not so much in a Messiah, but in a Messianic Age in which all mankind would be redeemed. We will speak of this vision in our next Chapter.

What we must realize now, is that unless we understand how important this waiting for the era of peace and truth was for our people, we shall never truly comprehend her history. It shaped Israel's character and deeds.

The Messiah, as you have just read, is supposed to be of the seed of David: an Israelite born in Bethlehem, Judah. How strange, therefore, that this very Messiah, according to the Tanach, shall be a descendant of two non-Hebrew nations: Moab and Ammon.

The *Scroll of Ruth,* which we shall discuss in another chapter, explains how the great-grandmother of David was Ruth, a woman from Moab. According to *Kings I,* Solomon married Naamah of the kingdom of Ammon. Her son was Rehoboam, the heir to the throne. Thus, tradition holds, that the blood of Moab and Ammon shall mingle with Hebrew blood in the person of the Messiah!

Of all the women of Israel, the *Talmud* chose Ruth and Naamah as the "two pure doves of Israel!"

Activities

Project

• There are several theories about how and when the Messianic Age shall be achieved. See if you can find out what they are?

Questions

• "Mesheach Adonai" is the origin of the concept of the "Divine right of kings." This concept will not only affect Jewish history, but world history as well. It is why nations insisted that heirs to their thrones be of the royal blood, no matter how lacking the heir might be. Indeed to kill a king was more than murder. It was "deicide," the killing of a god. This is certainly how Shakespeare saw it in his drama *Macbeth* when the king is killed the author cries:

Confusion now hath made his masterpiece
Most sacrilegious murder hath broke ope
The Lord's anointed temple, and stole thence
The life o' the building.   Act II, Scene III

• When the Jews of Yemen hailed David Ben-Gurion then prime minister, as "King David who lives forever," Ben Gurion objected violently. Not only because he was not descended from David's dynasty, but because he objected to the idea of monarchy.

1. How do you feel about the reestablishment of "the House of David" in modern Israel?
2. What would or could David have done if the other four Philistine kings had accepted David as their ally against Saul?
3. What do you think David meant by "drinking the blood" of the three Gibborim? Why did he offer the water as a libation to God?
4. What does the loyalty of a Philistine like Ittai tell us about David?
5. What political reason could David have had in punishing the murderers of Ishbaal?
6. Was David justified in trying to replace Joab with Abner or Amasa? How, do you suppose, did Nathan discover that Uriah had died because of David's order?
   Was Joab justified in condemning David's tears for Absalom? Could you have spoken as Joab did?
   Read about Joab in *Samuel II.* Write an analysis of this warrior.
7. Name three other warriors of David's family. How were they related to David?

Readings for Students

The Legends of King David, S. Skulsky, Samuel Simson Ltd., Tel Aviv.

Stories of King David, C. Freehof, J.P.S., Philadelphia.

The New World Over Story Book, ed. Schloss and Epstein, Bloch Publishing Co., New York. (p. 194, The Revolt by F. C. Hyman).

Scroll of Ruth.

Samuel I and Samuel II.

David, by Bosch, Juan, Hawthorn Books, 1965.

And it Came to Pass, Bialik, Hayyim N., Hebrew Publishing Co., 1938.

Readings for Teachers

Samuel I and Samuel II.

Kings I.

A History of the Jewish People, Margolis and Marx. J.P.S. 1944. Phila.

My People: The Story of the Jews, Abba Eban. Behrman House, 1968, N.Y.

Scroll of Ruth.

chapter 16 Solomon

SOLOMON, WHOSE NAME MEANS peace, was appropriately named. Unlike his father, David, he was not a man of war, nor was he interested in military campaigns.

He could afford to ignore the battlefield. David had already subdued his neighbors. Egypt, which might have threatened him from the south, was too weak to raise her sword. Mesopotamia, in the north, was divided into several states. Not one of them was strong enough to venture outside her territory.

Solomon maintained peace through his diplomatic skill. He made alliances with surrounding countries and often married the daughter of these allies to strengthen his treaties. One of the most unusual weddings took place between him and Pharaoh's daughter.

It was not uncommon for a Pharaoh to wed the daughter of alien rulers. But rarely, if ever, did a Pharaoh give his daughter to another. In the 14th century B.C.E. a Babylonian king wanted a princess of Egypt. The Pharaoh replied: "From of old, a daughter of the king of Egypt has not been given to anyone."

Solomon's marriage was, therefore, a very important political event. It is obvious that by this wedding this Pharaoh acknowledged that Israel was the greatest power between Mesopotamia and Egypt. More, this Pharaoh attacked the Philistines, reached the Philistine-Israelite frontier, captured the city of Gezer, and gave it as a present to Solomon, his son-in-law. This was the first time Gezer became part of Israel.

Though the king of Gezer is included among the 31 kings Joshua defeated, the city was never occupied. Neither in the days of Joshua, Judges, or David, did Gezer lose her independence.

In contrast to David, and of course, to Saul, Solomon was a very sophisticated and worldly person. Under him the arts and sciences flourished. He was interested in all cultures, and attracted to himself the wisdom and lore of other nations.

He reached out to the world through commerce as well as through diplomacy. He bought horses and chariots from Egypt and resold them to Syria. Since Phoenicians were expert sailors, he launched a fleet of ships with Hiram, king of Phoenicia. It sailed from Ezion-Geber, a port on the Gulf of Akaba, to ports along the African and Indian coasts. These ships brought back such luxurious goods as sandalwood peacocks, and ivory. Gold and silver came from the mysterious land of Ophir. Some believe Ophir was in southern Arabia, others, in India.

The queen of Sheba, who carried royal gifts to Solomon, is supposed to have come upon a trade mission. Solomon's fleet might have cut in upon the caravan trade so important to her economy. Whatever she sought, she must have acquired, for we read: "King Solomon gave to the Queen of Sheba all her desire. . . ."

Hebrew sailors sailed with other foreign expeditions. They went as far as Tarshish, supposed to be in southern Spain. Thus Israel became one of the chief bases for commerce from east to west, and from north to south.

To protect the trade that crossed his land, Solomon fortified three cities: Gezer, Megiddo, and Hazor. Hazor and Megiddo protected the trade routes from Egypt to Damascus. Gezer was a frontier town. From the hill on which she stood, can be seen the plains leading to Lydda (the modern Lud) and the historic valley of Ayalon where *Joshua* tells us, Joshua commanded sun and moon to stand still. Most important, Gezer was situated on the road to Jerusalem. Thus she was both defense post and shield for Jerusalem.

The same architect must have laid out these three cities. Their fortifications and six-chambered gates were similar. One of the most exciting finds in Gezer is a farmer's almanac, inscribed in Hebrew. It listed the seasons of the year according to their agricultural work.

Solomon also built refineries near the Timna-Eilat area. These smelted copper and iron. The construction of the refineries was so brilliantly engineered, they are in use today, 3000 years later. This industry was very profitable for Israel, both in her international trade and in her industrial development.

Solomon was also a master builder. He erected luxurious palaces for himself and for his wives. He imported artists, skilled workers, and raw materials. According to *Kings I,* one of the most magnificent of his possessions was his throne of gold and ivory:

There were six steps to the throne, and the top of the throne was round behind; and there were arms on either side by the place of the seat, and two lions standing beside the arms. And twelve lions stood there on the one side and on the other upon the six steps; there was not the like made in any kingdom.

(Kings I X:19–20)

All his drinking vessels were of gold, as were his targets and shields. He had fourteen hundred chariots and twelve thousand horsemen. It is even recorded in *Kings I* that he had a thousand wives!

His most significant building project for Israel, was the Temple. Some call it his private chapel. For the people it was their holy House, and the center of their religious life.

When Solomon dedicated the Temple on Succot about 953 B.C.E., his prayer reveals both his thinking and attitudes. Among his opening lines is the following:

But will God in very truth dwell on the earth? Behold heaven and the heaven of heavens cannot contain You; how much less this house that I have built . . .

(Kings I VIII:27)

After pleading with God to forgive Israel for whatever sins she may commit, he added this telling sentence:

. . . concerning the stranger that is not of Your people Israel . . . when he shall come and pray toward Your house, hear in heaven . . . and do according to all that the stranger asks . . .

(Kings I VIII:41–42)

These are not the words of a villager, nor of him who thinks only of his nation. Within these verses speaks the man who has beheld other civilizations, who has glimpsed the wide world beyond.

So flourishing was this Solomonic period, many look back at it as an era of prosperity and peace. Had not the population grown to eight hundred thousand, double its former size? Were there not many new cities and villages throughout Israel? As David was the father of music and Psalms, Solomon was considered the father of wisdom, justice, and literature. Tradition attributes three Books of the Tanach to him: *Song of Songs; Proverbs;* and *Ecclesiastes. Kings I* describes him thus:

. . . he excelled all the kings of the earth in riches and wisdom. And the whole earth sought the presence of Solomon to hear his wisdom which God had put in his mind.

(Kings I X:23–24)

However, a closer look reveals a different picture. True he built great structures, store cities, fortresses, palaces, the Temple. True he developed industry, sent forth ships and caravans, accumulated vast amounts of horses and chariots. And true he married many foreign princesses to secure Israel's safety. But these cost dearly. And someone had to pay.

Who but the people? Taxes increased enormously. Drafting of labor became more oppressive. Worse, to collect taxes and regulate labor, Solomon divided Israel into twelve districts, ignoring tribal lines. Over these new districts he appointed overseers. Can you imagine what this must have meant to descendents of the men born in the desert?

When these measures did not yield enough, Solomon had to give King Hiram of Phoenicia twenty towns on the Galilee for 120 talents of gold. Supposing you were a native of those towns? How would you have felt?

Furthermore his foreign wives brought their various gods with them. Foolishly, Solomon allowed them their individual shrines outside of Jerusalem. Many claim this opened the way to idolatry among the people. Others point out that these alien cults were limited to the palace. In any event, the introduction of idolatrous practises in any part of the land had to weaken the character of the nation.

Inevitably, Solomon became more tyrannical. He had broken the commandments laid down in *Deuteronomy.* He had increased gold, horses, and wives. Instead of destroying pagan shrines, he permitted them to be installed. Thus he ignored the Torah which he was supposed to have before him always.

In addition the northern tribes accused Solomon of favoring Judah. One of Solomon's own men, Jeroboam ben Nebat, rebelled against him. A prophet named Ahiyah, promised Jeroboam that he would be king over the ten northern tribes.

Solomon would have killed Jeroboam, but the young man fled to Egypt. There he found refuge with the Pharaoh Shishak (or Sheshonk), probably successor to Solomon's father-in-law. Jeroboam remained in Egypt until the death of Solomon.

Activities

THE LION OF JUDAH

One of the titles of the Emperor of Ethiopia, is the "Lion of Judah." He traces his ancestry to Menelik, son of the Queen of Sheba. Menelik's father was supposed to have been Solomon. When Ethiopians bless each other they say: "May the God of Israel watch over you." Israel and Ethiopia maintain good relationships today.

GEZER'S FARMER'S ALMANAC

These two months are (olive) harvest.
These two months are planting (grain).
These two months are late planting.
This month is hoeing up of flax.
This month is harvest of barley.
This month is harvest.
These two months are vine-tending.
This month is summer fruit.

This almanac was probably written in the second half of the 10th century B.C.E. in the reign of either Solomon or his son, Rehoboam.

Try to identify which months of the Hebrew calendar correspond to each of these periods.

Readings for Students

Legends of King Solomon, S. Skulsky, Samuel Simson, Tel Aviv.
Stories About King Solomon, L. Freehof, J.P.S., Philadelphia.
The New World Over Story Book, edited by Schloss and Epstein, Bloch Publishing Co., N.Y.
(p. 217, The Cedar's Surprise by M. Campbell)
(p. 259, *The Broken Tablets* by M. Stern)

(p. 224, King Solomon and the Shamir by M. Stern)

Kings Prophets and History, by Kamm, Josephine, McGraw-Hill, 1965.

Readings for Teachers

Kings I.

King Solomon, by Thieberger, Frederic, East and West Library, 1947.

chapter 17 Division, Defeat and Exile

REHOBOAM, SOLOMON'S SON, INherited the throne and with it, the problems his father had left him. When he went to Shechem to receive the allegiance of the northern tribes, he was sternly received by a delegation of Elders. Among them stood Jeroboam ben Nebat, back from Egypt. These northerners demanded that he reduce both taxes and the period of compulsory labor.

Instead of listening to his older counsellors, Rehoboam took the advice of his young courtiers. Arrogantly, he replied:

My father made your yoke heavy, but I will add to your yoke; my father punished you with whips, but I will punish you with scorpions.

(Kings I XII:11)

As you can imagine the call to revolt rang out across the whole land. ". . . What portion have we in David! . . . to your tents O Israel!"

Only Judah and Benjamin refused to desert the house of David. The rest rejected Rehoboam as their ruler. They formed the separate kingdom of Israel and elected Jeroboam ben Nebat as their king. Judah and Benjamin took the name of Judah or Judea. Thus began the series of catastrophes which was to end with the defeat and exile of both nations.

Jeroboam quickly realized he could never maintain a separate kingdom if the people continued to flock to the Temple at Jerusalem. Therefore he established two shrines: one at Bethel, and one at the northernmost point in Dan. In both he installed a golden calf.

Were these idols? Hosea, a prophet of Israel, thought so. But if they were, where was the god that should be standing or riding upon them?

There is no mention of such an image. Indeed, some historians see no difference between them and the figures of the Cherubs which were upon the Ark of the Lord. They might even have had wings, like the Cherubs. . . . Clearly, they represented the vehicle, not the divine rider.

While Hosea denounced these calves, Elijah and Elisha, two early and powerful prophets of Israel, did not. They did not even call upon the people of Israel to worship in Jerusalem. Nor did Amos, a Judean prophet, who spoke in Israel.

Most of the material concerning this period comes from the Tanach. Books of certain prophets, like Isaiah, Jeremiah,

Amos and Hosea, tell of conditions of those days. Their prophecies are quick to protest social and political evils. *Kings I & II* supply us with a description of the governments of each nation. And *Chronicles I & II,* the last Books of Scriptures concentrate on the kingdom of Judah.

We are all, of course, affected by what we consider desirable or undesirable. But we may not, in writing history, omit the great achievements of a king because we dislike him, nor may we omit the unhappy events of a king, because we favor him. This is what the author of *Kings* and *Chronicles* do. Nevertheless their account of the two kingdoms in their proper order, is a boon to our studies. Let us examine *Kings I and II* very carefully.

There are forty-seven chapters in the two books of *Kings.* The first eleven cover Solomon's reign, a period of forty years, (961–922 B.C.E.). Seventeen others deal with another forty year period from about 875–835 B.C.E. These years tell of the House of Omri.

Kings came and went in Israel. Of the seventeen kings there, only eight inherited the throne. The other nine were murdered. Indeed, for fifty years after the splitting of the kingdom, Israel was the scene of civil war. During this period, she lost a part of Transjordan to Aram and to Moab. She also warred against her southern sister, Judah.

In 876 B.C.E. a man named Omri seized the throne. He brought order to the country and made a mutual assistance pact with Judah. According to the Mesha Stele, a Moabite record, Omri conquered Moab, and took back his lost Transjordanian lands.

At Samaria, Omri began the construction of an elegant new capital. He maintained friendly relations with Phoenicia, the kingdom of Tyre and Sidon. He strengthened this alliance by marrying his son, Ahab, to Jezebel, a princess of Tyre.

Samaria's fortifications and the palace which Omri and his son built are the finest examples of architecture from Ancient Israel. Obviously this dynasty was both wealthy and powerful. Ahab was mainly responsible for repulsing the rising Assyrian nation. With two thousand chariots he drove her back when she tried to march into Damascus and Israel.

Neither political ability nor military strength impressed the author of *Kings I.* In a few words he summed up the twelve years of Omri:

"He bought the hill Samaria of Shemer . . . and built a city which he named Samaria after the owner, Shemer. Then Omri did that which was evil in the sight of the Lord . . . As for the other acts of Omri . . . and his power . . . are they not written in the Book of the Chronicles of Israel."

(Kings I XVI:24–27)

Kings I goes on to describe Ahab as a weakling: a man ruled by his wife, Jezebel. Clearly it is with Jezebel that the author is obsessed. As well he might be. For this

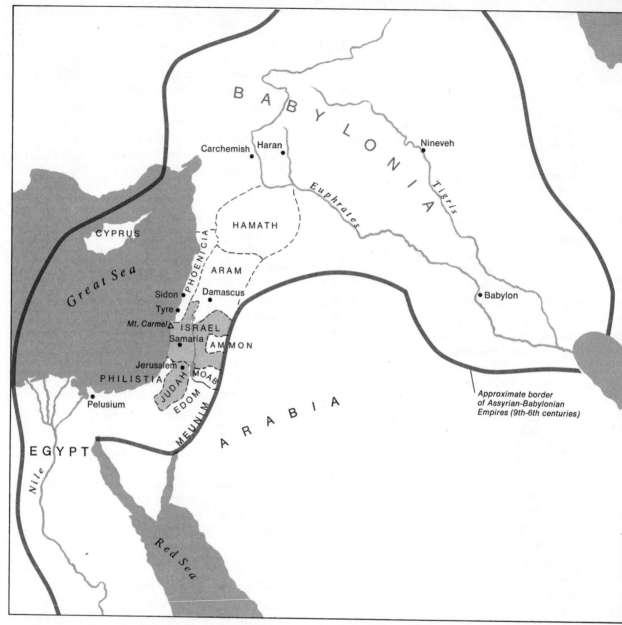

Map 3   Israel and Judah (Around 900 BCE)

Phoenician princess must have been a born missionary; perhaps the first in history. Like Solomon she must have come in contact with many cultures and religions in Tyre. Was not Phoenicia the greatest international trading power of the world? Already Phoenicia had colonized North Africa, Spain, and Sardinia.

The worldly Jezebel despised Israel for a backwoods nation. Why she worshipped a God you couldn't even see! And how she worshipped! Yahweh's priests didn't cut themselves; didn't whirl and chant about the altar. Nor did they know any magic which could control their Yahweh. Furthermore, Israel's God had no history: no wives, nor family.

To remedy this ridiculous situation, she imported 450 prophets of her god, Baal Melkart, and of his wife, the Asherah. So persuasive did she become, there were supposed to be only seven thousand people in Israel who did not bow the knee to Baal.

Who could oppose her? No ordinary man, to be sure. Only someone like Elijah, the mysterious prophet from across the Jordan. Dressed in a hairy mantle and leather belt, Elijah was the very opposite of the elegant and painted Queen. Harshly, he condemned the house of Ahab, predicting the burning drought that scorched the land. To Ahab, he was the "troubler of Israel." But to Jezebel, he was a mortal enemy.

This "troubler" brings the people to their senses. According to *Kings I,* he challenges them and the 450 pagan priests on Mt. Carmel:

How long will you dilly dally between two opinions? If the Lord be God, follow Him, but if Baal, follow him.

(Kings I XVIII:21)

To expose the folly of idolatry, he arranges a sacrifice on the mountain. The priests of Baal Melkart do the same. The pagans called on the name of their god. Elijah called upon Yahweh. The true God would accept His sacrifice by consuming it with heavenly fire. Here is a description of the proceedings: and the prophets

. . . "called on the name of Baal from morning even until noon, saying: 'O Baal answer us' . . . and they danced in a halting way about the altar . . . And . . . Elijah mocked them and said: 'Cry aloud for he is a god; either he is musing, or he is gone aside, or he is on a journey, or perhaps he sleeps, and must be awakened.' And they cried aloud and cut themselves . . . till the blood gushed . . . but there was neither voice nor any to answer . . ."

(Kings I XVIII:26–29)

When Elijah's sacrifice was consumed, the people acknowledged Yahweh, and put the pagan priests to death. Of course Jezebel was furious. She vowed she would kill Elijah. *Kings I* relates the flight of the prophet and even his despair. For he could be as afraid as any man. Nevertheless, he raised an enormous opposition to her and Ahab. His "sons of the prophet" must have helped him, moving across the country and stirring up the people. Elijah appointed Elisha to succeed him, but would not permit him to say goodbye to his parents. For Elijah, service to Yahweh meant total dedication.

After Carmel, the next great clash between Ahab and Elijah is not over cult, but over deed.

Ahab craved a vineyard next to his palace which belonged to a man named Naboth. But this was Naboth's inheritance, and he would not sell it. Ahab sulked and refused to eat. He knew very well that according to Torah, Naboth could not be forced to sell.

Jezebel, however, did not see it that way. Her god, Baal-Melkart, was not concerned with a man's possessions. Certainly not with a commoner's. . . . He took what he wanted. So too did her father, Ethbaal, for like god, like king. Confidently, she assured Ahab:

Don't you govern the kingdom of Israel? Arise and eat bread, and let your heart be merry; I will give you the vineyard of Naboth.

(Kings I XXI:7)

And she did. She had two false witnesses accuse Naboth of cursing God and the king. After this mock trial, Naboth was put to death.

However, this was not Phoenicia. This was Israel. Baal did not rule in Israel. Yahweh did. We read in *Kings I* that Elijah was sent by God to Ahab and commanded to speak these words:

Have you killed and also taken possession. Thus God says: 'In the place where dogs licked the blood of Naboth, shall dogs lick your blood . . . Behold I will bring evil upon you, and will cut off . . . every man child . . . As for Jezebel, the dogs shall eat Jezebel in the moat of Jezreel' . . . When Ahab heard those words, he rent his clothes, and put on sackcloth . . . and fasted . . . and went softly.

(Kings I XXI:19–27)

Ahab was killed fighting the Syrians (Aram), and his blood ran into the bottom of his chariot. When they brought him to Samaria for burial, they washed his chariot by the pool of Samaria, the place where Naboth had been executed. The dogs licked Ahab's blood, as they had Naboth's.

Opposition to the house of Omri continued even after Elijah's death. Elisha, Elijah's successor, chose a general named Jehu, to overthrow this dynasty. He even had Jehu anointed king; the only king of Israel ever anointed.

Jehu was a dashing, determined, and ruthless soldier. He not only killed Joram, the son of Ahab, but also King Ahaziah of Judah, who was visiting Joram. He rooted out the remaining sons of Ahab and all who served Baal Melkart. So bloody was this revolution, it was denounced by a later prophet, Hosea.

This is the first and only time a prophet (Elisha) used the army to overthrow a dynasty. As a result, never again did any king or queen in Israel or in Judah attempt to use the power of the throne to displace Yahweh as king.

As the author of *Samuel I* could not conceal his admiration for the Philistines at Aphek, so the author of *Kings II* could not hide his for Jezebel. For she died like a queen. She painted her eyes, set her hair, and taunted Jehu thus:

Is it peace . . . you murderer of your master?

(Kings II IX:31)

She was thrown out of the window into the vineyard of Naboth. Later Jehu commanded:

Look now after this cursed woman and bury her, for she is a king's daughter.

(Kings II IX:34)

But by this time, there was little left of Jezebel; the dogs had eaten her. The prophecy of Elijah was fulfilled.

Jehu's bloody deeds, however, hurt Israel. By murdering Jezebel and her priests, Jehu made enemies of Phoenicia. By killing Ahaziah, the king of Judah, he infuriated Judah. Without these allies, Israel was helpless before Aram. It was not difficult for Aram to annex the whole of Israelite Transjordan.

By the time Jehu's son reigned, Israel was paying a huge tribute to Aram. So lowly did the king of Israel sink, he was permitted only ten chariots. Contrast this with Ahab's two thousand.

With Jehu's grandson, Joash, Israel began to recover. Joash himself, recaptured the Transjordanian territory. But it was his son, Jeroboam II, who was to rule a powerful and wealthy kingdom for forty years. Under Jeroboam II, Israel expanded not only northward, cutting off slices of Aram and the kingdom of Hamath, but southward, as well, annexing parts of Judah.

How did this change in Israel's fortune come about? First, Assyria's power suddenly dwindled. Second, Aram and Hamath warred against each other, and, of course, weakened themselves. Third, Israel joined Phoenicia in trading, and both prospered enormously. And last of all, Jeroboam II collected huge tolls from caravans going to Arabia.

All of this raised the standard of living dramatically. But it also brought about a marked difference between the rich and poor. As wives of the rich lolled on ivory couches, drinking wine and feasting like fat cows, the masses hungered. As the wealthy moved between winter and summer homes to escape heat and cold, the poor froze or sweltered in miserable hovels.

With Jeroboam II's death in 746 B.C.E.

the Assyrians began to regain their strength. In 732 Tiglath-Pileser, the Assyrian king, conquered northern Israel and deported her population both east and west of the Jordan. He also put Hoshea, a puppet king on the throne of Israel.

But in 721 Israel revolted. Assyria defeated her and brought her national existence to an end. The conquering king was Shalmaneser, although his son, Sargon II claimed the victory. Sargon II boasted he took 27,290 Israelites captive. These exiles are referred to as "the lost ten tribes." We shall explore this subject at the end of this chapter.

The capture and exile of Israel was interpreted as the punishment of God upon a sinful nation. Obviously, this raised serious religious problems. For Assyria, after all, was a vicious conqueror, not unlike the Nazis of our century. A historian described her as the nest of a bird of prey from where:

. . . set forth the most terrible expeditions which have ever flooded the world with blood. Ashur was its god, plunder its morality, cruelty and terror its means. No people were ever more abject . . . no sovereigns more despotic . . . more pitiless, more proud of their crimes. Assyria sums up within herself all the vices. Aside from bravery, she offers not a single virtue.

Certainly Israel was not as evil as Assyria. Idolatry, terrible as that was to sons of the *Covenant,* was mainly of the palace.

Nor could there have been that many. For *Kings II* tells us both worshippers and pagan priests fit into one temple. Furthermore, when prophets reminded king and commoner of the *Covenant,* they listened. Even an Ahab "went softly."

Nor was there any evidence that Israel was less observant than Judah. Sabbath and new moon, tithing of the fruits, offerings to God were as frequent in Israel as in Judah. According to the prophet, Amos, Israel brought her sacrifices to Yahweh at the appointed times. Why then should the wicked Assyria have been triumphant over Israel? Keep this question in mind as we turn to the kingdom of Judah.

Judah's history was not torn by dynastic war. All her kings were direct descendants of David. Only a daughter of Jezebel ever challenged the right of David's son to the throne. Prophets rebuked individual kings, not the family line.

The strongest king of Judah since Solomon was Uzziah. According to the last book of the Tanach, *Chronicles II,* he reigned 52 years, during which he expanded agriculture, cattle-raising, and commerce. He subjected Philistia, which controlled the caravan route of the coast, and defeated Arabia, Ammon, and a country called Meunim. Naturally, his military machine had to be superior. Throughout the desert as well as in Jerusalem, Uzziah built and fortified towers. He also introduced the siege engine which threw arrows and huge stones. But the Chronicler tells us "when his heart was lifted up," God punished him with leprosy. His son, Jotham became regent, although Uzziah probably retained the reins of power.

It was Jotham's son, Ahaz, who was threatened by a coalition of Aram and Israel. Ahaz turned to Assyria for help. With this act, Judah became vassal to Assyria.

Some Judean rulers win a partial approval of the author of *Kings.* Two, however have his wholehearted endorsement. The first was the son of Ahaz, Hezekiah. Indeed Hezekiah is considered the best king since David.

At first Hezekiah continued his father's policy. He paid his tribute to Assyria and bought peace. With this peace, tradition asserts, he taught the true faith of Yahweh to Judah. He tried to unite north and south, building cities and aqueducts, and extending commerce. He was guided in this policy by the prophet, Isaiah: *Isaiah* XXX:15 "In sitting still and rest shall be your salvation," Isaiah advised. "In quietness and confidence your strength."

But to patriots this sounded cowardly. Eager to throw off Assyria's yoke, they conspired with other nations especially with Egypt. Despite Isaiah's pleas and warnings, they convinced Hezekiah. Ultimately the king joined the alliance against Assyria.

Thus, when the Philistine king of Ashdod withheld tribute in 714 B.C.E. Hezekiah and the other allies did the same. Sargon, the Assyrian, reacted promptly. He crushed

Ashdod so severely, the allies ran for cover.

But these conspiring nations did not learn. Again they plotted, Isaiah walked about Jerusalem barefoot and in sackcloth to show what would happen to Judah if she challenged Assyria.

In vain. Once again Hezekiah joined the Egyptian coalition. This time Sennacherib, Sargon's son, crushed them. First Tyre and Sidon were destroyed, then the Philistine cities, then Edom and Moab surrendered. Judah's turn was next. Hezekiah was left with only his crown and the ruined city of Jerusalem. Even his daughters were taken into Sennacherib's harem.

This however, was not enough for Sennacherib. He demanded the total surrender of Jerusalem. At Lachish, Judah's frontier fortress, he awaited Hezekiah's submission.

Hezekiah would have paid any tribute: Humbly he wrote to Sennacherib:

I have done wrong. Withdraw from me; whatever you impose on me, I will bear.

(Kings II XVIII:14)

Except Jerusalem. The holy city he would not give up.

But Sennacherib insisted. He sent his general to taunt Hezekiah before the eyes and ears of the Jerusalemites:

Let not your God in whom you trust, beguile you saying: 'Jerusalem shall not be given into the hands of the king of Assyria . . . You have heard what the kings of Assyria have done to all the lands . . . shall you be delivered? Have the gods of the (other) nations delivered them . . .'?

(Isaiah XXXVII:10–11)

Of course Sennacherib hoped to destroy the courage of people and king with this open mockery. What could Hezekiah do? Nothing but turn to God. Passionately he prayed in the Temple:

O Lord our God, save from his hand, that all the kingdoms of the earth many know that You are the Lord, You alone.

(Kings II XIX:19)

Because of this prayer, Isaiah predicted Sennacherib would never step foot in Jerusalem. Instead, he said, God would lead the pagan king back to Assyria with a hook in his nose, and a bridle in his lips. As Isaiah prophesied, so it came to pass.

It is not clear where the Assyrian army was struck down. Some say before the walls of Jerusalem. The Greek historian, Herodotus, claims it took place in Pelusium, in Egypt. However, one thing is clear: a plague swept through his army. Sennacherib himself fled back to Assyria where he was assassinated by his own sons.

Jerusalem was saved; but only for a while. Assyria regained her power and remained supreme throughout the seventh century, bringing even Egypt low. Cuneiform tablets of Gezer tell of Assyrian garrisons, which, no doubt, policed Judah. In addition, Judah was forced to supply Assyria with timber and troops. But the greatest calamity of this foreign rule, was the influence of her culture upon Hezekiah's son, Manasseh.

Manasseh was so corrupted by Assyria, he is known as the Jezebel of the south. However, he did not build new temples to his gods as Jezebel did, but converted the very Temple of Yahweh. He erected special altars in its courts and set up an image of the Asherah at the north gate, where pagan priestesses wept for their god. Manasseh is the only king who divined and consulted the dead regularly. He scattered pagan shrines throughout the country and appointed priests to maintain them.

How did the people react? They must have hated this paganism. We read in *Kings II* that Manasseh shed innocent blood till he had filled Jerusalem from one end to the other.

Finally Manasseh committed the ultimate evil: he sacrificed his own son to the god Moloch. Where, you may ask, was the Torah he was supposed to have with him all the time?

So detested is he by the author of *Kings II,* he is blamed for every catastrophe that shall strike Judah. The fact that during his reign of 55 years, Judah was prosperous and secure is of no importance. His bloodshed and revolting practises overshadowed everything.

As much as the author of *Kings II* loathed Manasseh, so much did he love Manasseh's grandson, Josiah. Indeed it is Josiah he considered the second excellent ruler of Judah. With the beginning of Josiah's government, Assyria began to weaken, and Egypt tried to regain control of Judah and Aram. But it is not this international situation that interests the author of *Kings II*.

By now you know what this author seeks: the return of the people to Yahweh. And this is what Josiah accomplished. How? By following the laws of an ancient scroll found in the Temple. Most believe this was either a portion or the whole of the book of *Deuteronomy*. On the basis of this scroll, Josiah cleansed the land of idolatry. He destroyed every pagan altar of the north and south. Sacrifices were confined to the Temple in Jerusalem. The Temple itself was purified, and the Feast of Passover reinstated. It is quite clear Josiah sought the same goal as Hezekiah: reunification of north and south. Like Joshua and David before him, he knew he could not make the country one unless he restored the *Covenant.*

In 612 B.C.E. the Babylonians and the Medes destroyed Nineveh, the capital of Assyria. In 609, they annihilated Assyria completely in the battle of Haran. Egypt, who feared the rising Babylonian might more than Assyria, rushed to Assyria's assistance. Josiah, however, stopped Pharaoh Necho at Megiddo. Unfortunately, Josiah died there.

While Pharaoh Necho did not destroy Babylonia, he did gain control of Judah and Aram. In fact, he installed Josiah's son, Jehoiakim, on the Judean throne.

Judah now found herself in a dangerous position. True, Egypt protected her. But how strong was such protection in the face of a powerful Babylonia? The prophet, Jeremiah, warned Jehoiakim that Egypt was a "weak reed." Judah must not rely on her. In fact, Judah dare not even trust in the Temple.

The only sure protection, Jeremiah said, was the *Covenant.* Unless Judah turned back to God, unless she released her slaves, and supported the weak, the Temple would be destroyed as surely as Shiloh.

His prophecy enraged certain priests and courtiers. He was accused of treason and might have been executed, had not other nobles stepped in. Indeed, another prophet, Uriah, was put to death for preaching the same doctrine.

In 605 B.C.E. one of the decisive battles of world history was fought at Carchemish between Egypt and Babylonia. Egypt was shattered and driven out of Asia for good. Although tablets, now in the British Museum tell us Egypt continued to stir up trouble in Judah and Aram, and indeed, that she even fought Babylonia again, her power was gone.

Babylonia remained the foremost Empire of her day. Her king, Nebuchadnezzar, was her greatest sovereign since Hammurabi. Wherever his armies went, he built cities, temples, canals, dikes, palaces. The famous "Hanging Gardens of Babylonia" were constructed by him.

The last battle between Babylonia and Egypt probably forced Jehoiakim to swear allegiance to Nebuchadnezzar. Had he remained loyal, Jewish history would have run a different course. But in 597 B.C.E., he rebelled. He lost his life in the battle against Babylonia.

His son, Jehoiachin, tried to continue the struggle. In vain. After only three months, Jehoiachin was forced to surrender. Together with his mother, courtiers, craftsmen and seven thousand families, he was deported to Babylonia. This was the first breach in Judah.

Zedekiah, an uncle of the exiled king, and himself a son of Josiah, was appointed the last king of Judah by Nebuchadnezzar. At the beginning he swore fealty to Babylonia. And all might have gone well if the pro-Egyptian clique had not stirred up both him and the people.

But it was not to be. As it had been in the days of Hezekiah, so it was under Zedekiah. The prophet, Isaiah, had then walked barefoot about Jerusalem. Now Jeremiah strode the streets with a wooden yoke about his neck. The yoke symbolized the rule of Babylonia. When a false prophet broke this yoke, Jeremiah prophesied that God would put an iron yoke upon Judah in its place.

Jeremiah's warnings did no good. Zedekiah, probably against his will, was forced

to join an anti-Babylonian coalition. Chief among these allies, was, of course, Egypt.

One must sympathize with Zedekiah. Patriotic fever was whipped up by false prophets in Judah. Among the exiles in Babylonia constant intrigue with Egypt and the smaller nations of the west, percolated. They encouraged revolt by spreading rumors about Nebuchadnezzar's domestic troubles. They might even have conspired with Babylonian plotters against the king.

This last possibility may explain the letter Jeremiah sent to the Jews of Babylon:

Build houses and dwell in them; plant gardens . . . take wives and bear sons and daughters . . . and seek the peace of the city . . . and pray unto the Lord for it, for in her peace shall you have peace.

(XXIX:5–7)

Jeremiah also cautioned as follows:

Let not your prophets . . . and your diviners fool you, nor listen to the dreams you choose to dream . . . for they prophesy falsely unto you . . . I have not sent them, says the Lord.

(XXIX:8–9)

It was good advice, as history proved. But then it was not easy to choose between true and false prophets. Indeed, it seemed, if anything, Jeremiah was the false prophet. For Egypt, whom he had called "a weak reed," did come to Judah's aid.

How easy at such a moment, for the

people to listen to the dreams they chose to dream. And, certainly, how easy to denounce Jeremiah again; to charge him again with treason, and this time, to throw him into prison. So strong was the feeling against Jeremiah, even Zedekiah did not dare to consult the prophet openly.

At a secret meeting, Jeremiah continued to urge the king to surrender. Even then, he assured him, he could ward off bloodshed. Even then, he could save the Temple and Jerusalem.

To no avail. Events had gone too far. The rebellion continued. Babylonia returned to Jerusalem, Egypt proved herself "a weak reed." On the 17th of Tammuz in 586 B.C.E. a breech was made in the walls of the city. On the 9th of Av, the Temple was destroyed. Zedekiah, after being forced to witness the execution of his sons, was blinded and dragged off to exile. Together with him went a large part of the population.

Nebuchadnezzar appointed a man named Gedaliah as governor of Judah. A seat of government was set up at the ancient sanctuary of Mizpeh, five miles northwest of Jerusalem. Fugitives began to return: resettlement and rebuilding might have begun. But again super-patriots intervened. They assassinated Gedaliah.

Panicked by this new defiance of Babylonia, some fled to Egypt and dragged the old prophet, Jeremiah, with them. Though a few remained, the desolation was serious enough to be fatal.

Surely at this point, the Jew should have disappeared into the haze of history. Moab would. Edom would. So too would Philistia, Ammon, Hatti, and this very powerful Babylonia. Amalek and Assyria already had. And most believed the northern kingdom of Israel had, as well.

But the Jew did not disappear. Why? Was it because the *Covenant,* not given in the land of Israel, continues everywhere? What do you think?

We know the Judeans will not be allowed to forget the terms of the *Covenant.* Prophets will see to that. Their words, harsh and severe, when necessary, could also be comforting and full of hope. They were, after all, the heirs of Abraham, Moses, Samuel, Nathan, and Elijah.

We have referred to prophets often in this chapter. Now we must get to know them.

Activities

THE LOST TEN TRIBES

Itzhak Ben-Zvi, a former president of Israel, tells us that there is a tradition among the Jews scattered in the mountainous regions of Caucasia, that they are descended from the tribes exiled by Shalmaneser. These are the Jews of Georgia, Daghestan, Azerbaijan, and Armeni. Explorers and scientists see a kernel of historical truth in this tradition. The exiled Jews of Israel probably travelled from Assyria to the Ararat region and penetrated into the most remote passes of Caucasia.

Among the Jews of Persia this same tradition exists. The Jews of Demavend trace their history to Gilead of the tribe of Manasseh in Transjordan. The Jews of Urmia, Azerbaijan, on the border between Turkey and Iran consider themselves direct descendants of the exiles of Samaria.

Benjamin of Tudela, a famous Jewish traveller, states that:

. . . in the hills of Nisbur there are four tribes of Israel, namely the tribes of Zebulun, Dan, Asher, and Naphtali . . . all descendants of the first exiles who were carried to this country by Shalmaneser, King of Assyria . . .

Well before Benjamin of Tudela, we find reference in the *Book of Tobias,* written sometime between 200 B.C.E. and 50 B.C.E., to several families belonging to the tribe of Naphtali. A different source, that of the Christian explorer, Artelly, tells us that the tribes of Dan and Naphtali invaded parts of Tatarland. Another Christian, a historian this time, reports that King Firuz of Persia went to war twice with the tribe of Naphtali, and was twice defeated.

Besides these Jewish survivors, many of the exiles are believed to have been forcibly converted to Islam. We find traces of Jewish customs among various groups in Persia, Caucasia, and Afghanistan. There are others who practice Islam openly and Judaism secretly. These are known as crypto (hidden) Jews. We shall have a great deal to say of crypto Jews in later Chapters.

Questions

1. If Rehoboam had listened to his older counsellors, how might the course of Jewish history have been changed?

    This 'iffy' question raises the ghost of Michal, David's wife. Because she scorned David when he danced ecstatically before the Ark, she never bore a child of David. How might such a child have affected the kingdom? Consider who Michal's father was?

    This Unit contains many 'iffy' questions. List three at least.
2. Jezebel swore she would kill Elijah. Why didn't Ahab turn him over to her when he had the chance?
3. Should Elisha have been allowed to say goodbye to his parents? What principle is involved? Does total dedication to God destroy human bonds?
4. Was Naboth justified in refusing to sell his vineyard to King Ahab? Read the story in Kings I and review Chapter XII before you answer.
5. Why did the division of the kingdom into Judah and Israel end in tragedy?
6. One thousand craftsmen were deported with Jehoiachin. For what famous project did Nebuchadnezzar probably use them?

Project

• Find out the origins of the Jews returning to Israel today. See if there are any who trace their history back to the exile of the northern kingdom of Israel.

Readings for Students

The New World Over Story Book, ed. Schloss and Epstein, Bloch Publishing Co., New York. (p. 57, The Stones by F. C. Hyman) (p. 253, In Naboth's Vineyard by M. Stern)
In Assyrian Tents, by Pendleton, Louis, J.P.S. 1929.

Joel of the Hanging Gardens, by Edmonds, T. G., J. B. Lippincott Co., 1966.

Readings for Teachers

The Biblical Archaeologist Reader, Wright and Freedman, A Doubleday Anchor Original, Garden City, N.Y. 1961.
The Exiled and the Redeemed, Itzhak Ben Zvi, J.P.S., Philadelphia, 1957.
The Book of the Acts of God, Wright and Fuller, Doubleday & Co., Garden City, N.Y., 1957.

Unit V

By the rivers of Babylon,
There we sat down, yea, we wept,
When we remembered Zion . . .
For there they that led us captive
asked of us words of song,
And our tormentors asked of us mirth:
"Sing us one of the songs of Zion." . . .

PSALM 137

chapter 18   The Nature of Prophets

THE WORD "PROPHET" IS FAMILIAR TO you by now. Moses was a prophet, the greatest of prophets. Samuel, Nathan, Ahiyah, Elijah, Elisha, Isaiah, Jeremiah, Ezekiel . . . all bore this title "prophet." There are many we have not as yet mentioned, like the woman, Huldah. Tradition even names Miriam, the sister of Aaron and Moses, a prophetess.

Before we try to understand the prophet and the nature of prophecy, let us see how tradition arranges them. The following Books of the Tanach are called Early Prophets: *Joshua, Judges, Samuel I* and *II, Kings I* and *II.* Actually these are historical books. But because they contain many incidents about prophets like Samuel, they are grouped together under this classification.

The Later Prophets are divided into Major and Minor Prophets. The three Major ones are *Isaiah, Jeremiah,* and *Ezekiel.* The twelve Minor are: *Hosea, Joel, Amos, Obadiah, Jonah, Micah, Nahum, Habakkuk, Zephaniah, Haggai, Zechariah,* and *Malachi.* Their order in the Tanach is not the same as in history. For example, Amos precedes Hosea, not Hosea, Amos.

The three Major and eleven of the Minor (Jonah is omitted) are also known as Classical or Literary Prophets. What distinguished them from the Early Prophets, is that they denounced the evil deeds of man against man. Prophets like Amos, Jeremiah, and Micah, burn with anger against the wealthy who oppress the poor.

This extreme difference between men was a new feature of Israelite society. For years after Joshua had divided the inheritance among the people, the land was owned by families and tribes. With the monarchy and the rise of royal officials, a change took place. As in the case of Ahab and Naboth, kings seized the property of their subjects. The favorites of the king passed laws to make it possible for them to steal a man's heritage. They not only robbed; they made it legal.

Thus arose a new class of rich and arrogant men. It was against them Isaiah cried:

Woe to them that decree unrighteous
decrees . . .
To turn aside the needy from judgment
And to take away the right of the poor of My
people
That widows may be their spoil
And that they may make the fatherless their
prey . . .   (X:1–2)

Why should we be concerned with them today? Supposing they did protest against evil? Did this truly affect history? Had Israel been completely just and merciful, would it have mattered to Assyria? Do cruel and warlike nations hesitate to attack righteous men?

For the prophets such a question would have been foolish. For them Assyria, Babylonia, or any nation, was only a tool of God. If Assyria defeated Israel and exiled her, she did it because she was in Isaiah's words: "the rod of God's anger." For the prophets, Assyria was controlled by Yahweh. History was in His hands.

Nevertheless they also said man's deeds affected history. Had Israel been completely just and merciful, it would not have mattered to Assyria, but it most certainly would to God. For what happened to Israel, according to the prophets, was the result of Israel's treachery. She had betrayed the *Covenant.*

As for Assyria, though she was "the rod of God's anger," she would be punished for her cruelty. So too would Babylonia. These nations may not have been, like Israel, partners to the *Covenant,* but they had freedom of will. It was their greed and brutality that made them conquerors. For these they would have to pay.

The prophets spared no one. Gradually we shall see how they developed the view that not only the nations were responsible for their deeds, but so was each man and woman. That is why the prophets never hesitated to denounce anyone, whether king, false prophet, priest, or the masses of men. In Chapter XXXIV:18–20, Jeremiah speaks out against Judeans who had not released their slaves as Torah commands:

And I will give the men that have transgressed My *Covenant* . . . the princes of Judah, and the princes of Jerusalem, the officers, and the priests, and all the people of the land . . . so I will even give them into the hands of their enemies . . .

All Israel understood that God doomed entire nations for cruelty and injustice. Had He not done this to Sodom and Gomorrah? For Israel, too, the moral law was also fundamental. It had been given at Sinai. But idolatry was a different matter. Idolatry was no crime for the rest of the world. For Israel, it was unforgivable.

In fact, according to the first Five Books, idolatry is the most serious crime. *Leviticus* and *Deuteronomy* tell us that idolatry will cause the collapse and exile of the nation.

In the Early Prophets we see this too. You remember how the author of these historical books cried out constantly against Baal. Of course, they were aware of David's dreadful sin against Uriah, of Ahab's murder of Naboth. But these were not continuous sins for which the whole nations must suffer. There was only one such national sin: idolatry.

The Classical Prophets added to this concept. They said yes, Israel's history was affected by idolatry. But it was affected by murder and theft as sharply. Not only idolatry would lead to captivity, sins against man would as well.

Nor was it only for the most vicious crimes. Everyday sins of deceit, false weights, slander destroy a nation. So too do oppression of orphan, widow, stranger, Levite.

Fearlessly the prophets named names. Whether they were kings like Jehoiakim or Jeroboam II; whether priests like Amaziah in Bethel, or Pashur in Jerusalem; whether false prophets like Hananiah or Shemaiah; they accused according to the deed.

For the prophets justice and mercy were absolute and constant demands. This point of view shaped the character of the Jewish people throughout its history. Funds for the poor had to be administered by the most responsible, and wisest. Festivals could not be properly observed that did not make provision for the needy. What we call charity was for Israel, not choice, but commandment. As for justice, it becomes the foundation of Jewish Law. It made no distinction between rich and poor. Few, if any nations, were as careful, as exacting as Israel, when man's life or property was at stake.

Of course, neither justice nor mercy originated with the Classical Prophets. To love your neighbor as yourself; to tithe; to leave the corners of the fields for the poor; not to carry false weights; nor to slander; are Torah commandments. But these laws could have been ignored. Surely kings like Ahab or Manasseh ignored them. It was the prophets who opposed kings and their officials.

They made these commandments more important than the cult. Most men understood that sacrifices of the wicked were unpleasing to God. What they didn't understand, and what the prophets emphasized, was that these cultic acts were of no value in themselves. They had no magical power. To worship God was good; indeed, a divine commandment. The Torah says God is gracious to man by accepting his prayer or sacrifice.

The Classical Prophets said God doesn't *need* sacrifices. Only pagan gods do. Pagan gods depend on the cult. Their priests officiate over the mysteries of the life, death, and resurrection of the gods. Pagan festivals celebrate events in the lives of gods. Sacrifices renew the strength of the gods. No pagan prophet would have used these words of Amos:

I hate, I despise your feasts,
And I will take no delight in your solemn assemblies.
Yes, though you offer me burnt-offerings and your meal-offerings
I will not accept them . . .
But let justice well up as waters
And righteousness as a mighty stream.

(V:21–24)

At approximately the same time Isaiah was saying the same thing to the worshippers at the Temple in Jerusalem:

To what purpose is the multitude of your
sacrifices unto Me? . . .
I am full of the burnt offerings of rams . . .
Your new moons and your appointed
seasons . . .
Are a burden unto Me . . .
Wash you, make you clean . . .
Seek justice, relieve the oppressed
Judge the orphan, plead for the widow
(I:11–17)

You can see very clearly how the prophets raised right living to an absolute religious value. Why? Because they regarded the good life as godlike. Justice and compassion were the essence of Yahweh. Therefore man had to strive for both.

Finally the prophets are important to us today, because they remind us that before nations can live in peace, they must cleanse themselves of their evil deeds. Judgment precedes redemption.

The influence of the Classical Prophets is not only felt in Israel, but in Christianity and Islam as well. Wherever men hold conscience higher than even national policies, there the Prophets live.

Why such men sprang up at this time in history is still a mystery to some historians. They were not magicians. Although on occasion they did predict the future in detail, as Isaiah did about Sennacherib, they were not diviners. Divination was a pagan practice.

Prophets spoke mainly of what must happen when nations or individuals misbehave. That is why their words did not always come to pass. For people could repent. According to *Jonah,* the whole city of Nineveh repented and was saved.

Since men could change, God, the prophets taught, might change. His decisions did not have to be final. We see, therefore, that the essence of prophecy is not prediction, but the declaration of religious truth.

Were all prophets alike? Hardly. A prophet is also a man. He carries upon himself the burdens every man must carry. He is as easily hurt, as fearful as all human beings.

Moses, driven to despair by the people, cries out:

"What shall I do unto this people? They are almost ready to stone me!"   (Exodus XVII:4)

Elijah, fleeing from Jezebel, prays:

"It is enough, O Lord, take away my life . . ."
(Kings I XIX:4)

Jeremiah laments that he had to prophesy evil:

"Woe is me my mother, that you bore me, a man of strife . . . to the whole earth."
(XV:10)

Some tried to refuse their burden. Moses, you remember, pleaded that no one would believe him and that he could not speak well. Jeremiah also tried to avoid his charge:

"Ah, Lord God, behold I cannot speak for
I am a child." (I:6)

Jonah disobeyed outright by running away.

Others like Isaiah, welcomed the prophetic role. According to the *Book of Isaiah,* when God asked "Whom shall I send, and who will go for us?" Isaiah replied, "Here am I, send me."

What then bound these men together? First and foremost, it was the burden they bore. God, they said, forced them to speak His word. Or to put it another way, they spoke because they could not be silent. Jeremiah described it thus:

And if I say "I will not make mention of Him,
Nor speak anymore in His name,"
Then there is in my heart as it were a burning fire
Shut up in my bones,
And I weary myself to hold it in,
But cannot. (XX:9)

Secondly, they saw all evil through a kind of magnifying glass. What might seem to us a small injustice, was to them, mountainous. Why? Because whenever the prophet looked at any man, he saw him in relation to God. How much more so, when he looked at his fellow Jew? Was not Israel a partner with God? Did she not have to keep her part of the *Covenant?*

Third, the language of the prophets was either shriller or more explosive. They could not speak calmly in the face of evil. Crimes against the poor and the weak were, to be sure, crimes against men. For the prophets, they were mainly crimes against God.

You see, the prophets demanded not an easy comfortable acknowledgment of God, but a constant attitude of obedience. They expected Israel to turn to Him with all her heart, her soul, her might, and at all times.

This expectation is not really new. We saw it in the lifetime of Abraham. You should recall these words:

Shall I hide from Abraham that which I am doing . . . seeing that Abraham shall surely become a great and mighty nation and all the nations of the earth shall be blessed in him? For I have known him to the end that he may command his children and his household after him . . . to do righteousness and justice . . .
(Genesis XVIII:17–19)

This paragraph analyzes the nature of prophecy. For one, the prophet is informed of the intent and deeds of God. For another the function of the prophet is explained: he must teach righteousness and justice. And finally, the aim of prophecy is made clear: it is to create so splendid a nation that all nations of the earth shall be blessed in Israel. This aim shall be summed up by an unknown prophet of the Exile:

I will also give you for a light to the nations
That My salvation may be unto the end of the
earth. (Isaiah XLIX:6)

It might therefore, be accurate to conclude that prophecy began with our Patriarch, Abraham.

It is clear from all you have read, that the prophets took man very seriously. How else when man can affect God and His decrees. Did not the plea of the man Abraham for Sodom and Gomorrah affect God, according to *Genesis?* Could not ten righteous men have saved the cities? Furthermore, man could make God suffer. Indeed, the prophet suffered for the pain man caused His Creator. Perhaps this seems bold of him. As though God needed man's sympathy. But it is basic to the prophetic view of history. For a God who could not be hurt by man was an indifferent Being. The Greek god, unlike the God of the *Covenant,* could not be affected by man.

The prophet had no theory about God. He did not try to explain His nature. What he tried to do was to explain how God felt about man.

Because the prophet took man that seriously, he made sure that man understood what was expected of him. The righteous man outside of Israel, on the other hand, suffered because he did not know what the gods demanded of him. A famous Babylonian prayer contains these words:

. . . O that I only knew that these things were well and pleasing to a god! What appears beautiful to man, is abominable to the god, and what is odious to man's heart is most pleasing to the god. Who has learnt to understand the will of the gods in heaven . . .? When have stupid mortals even understood the ways of the gods?

In contrast to this confusion, listen to Jeremiah:

Woe to him who builds his house by un-
righteousness
Who makes his neighbor serve him for nothing
(XXII:13)

Probably the prophet who summed up most precisely what man must do to be most fully a man, was Micah. He said:

It has been told you, O man, what is good,
And what the Lord requires of you:
Only to do justly, and to love mercy, and to
walk humbly with your God." (VI:8)

The words of Micah and the other prophets echo down the corridors of history. They have brought comfort to Jew and non-Jew. For Israel in exile, they became a shield against the pressures of each day.

We cannot discuss each of the Classical

Prophets. Therefore we shall limit ourselves to three of the Minor prophets: Amos, Hosea, and Micah; to two of the Major: Isaiah and Jeremiah; to two of the Exile: Ezekiel and the unknown prophet we call Second Isaiah or Deutero-Isaiah; and to two of the Return: Haggai and Zechariah.

Activities

Questions

• Tradition declares the period of prophecy closed. Do you agree? Can you think of anyone of your century who meets the qualification of a prophet? Be sure to look up *Deuteronomy XVIII 15–22.*

Readings for Teachers

Great Ages and Ideas of the Jewish People, Edited by Leo Schwartz, Random House, N.Y., 1956.
The Biblical Age, Chapter III, by Kaufman.
The Relevance of the Prophets, R. B. Y. Scott, The Macmillan Co., N.Y., 1944.
The Goodly Fellowship of the Prophets, John Patterson, Charles Scribner's Sons, N.Y., 1948.
Spokesmen for God, by Hamilton, Edith, W. W. Norton & Co., 1949.
Priests and Prophets, by Hoschander, Jacob, Jewish Theological Seminary of America, 1938.

chapter 19 Amos and Hosea

CLASSICAL PROPHECY AROSE IN THE middle of the eighth century B.C.E. It lasted for 300 years: 750–430 B.C.E. It manifested itself about the same time in the Northern and Southern kingdoms. Its first prophet was Amos; its last, Malachi.

These prophets regarded themselves as carrying on the traditions of Moses and Joshua. They spoke as did Moses and Joshua, to a people who had not sent for them. They believed they were agents of God, sent by Him because He loved Israel.

Aram (Syria), was Israel's northern neighbor. She warred against Israel, thus causing most of Israel's political problems. These wars started during the reign of Ahab, and did not end until the time of Jeroboam II. When Assyria began to threaten all nations, Aram united with Israel against Assyria.

Worse than the political disorders, was the social decay: robbing of the poor by the rich. Decent men were horrified. Was this the people of the *Covenant*? Could they allow a few to become fat, while the masses starved? The unique group of men who challenged this society were these prophets of Judah and Israel.

Amos and Hosea spoke to the northern kingdom of Israel at the time she was hurtling to her end. They cried out precisely because they saw her danger. Not because of Assyria's power. Rather because the evil within Israel's society was so great. It was Israel's evil that would make Assyria the instrument by which God would punish her: "the rod of God's wrath."

Amos was born in Tekoa, a small village on the edge of the desert of Judah, about twelve miles from Jerusalem. Contact with the outside world was maintained by the caravans that passed close by. He described himself as a herdsman, and we can see his origins reflected in the images of his language. They were drawn directly from nature:

Will a lion roar . . .
When he has no prey . . .?
Will a bird fall in a snare . . .
Where there is no lure for it? (III:4–5)

he asks, predicting the disaster that is about to overtake Israel.

He left Tekoa in Judah to speak against the corruption of Israel in the days of Jereboam II. Three themes stand out in his prophecy. The first is that God is a God of all nations: as He punished the other nations for their evils so would He punish Judah and Israel. No, more, because Israel's was the *Covenant,* her fate would be worse:

You only have I known of all the families of the earth
Therefore will I visit upon you all your iniquities   (III:2)
Because they sell the righteous for silver
And the needy for a pair of shoes
That pant after the dust of the earth on the head of the poor
And turn aside the way of the humble . . .
                                                        (II:6–7)

Amos, like all the prophets, was a fierce nationalist. He loved his people. He spoke as violently as he did, because he wanted desperately to bring Israel back to Torah. He wanted to save her.

He believed in the *Covenant.* He accepted Israel's special relationship to Yahweh. Yet this did not make the Creator of the universe only Israel's God. Yahweh did not demand the same standards from the other nations that He did from Israel, but He was still the God of all nations: the God of history.

Amos' second theme was that God is the God of justice. Not justice as a general idea, but as a specific command. If a man does not obey this command, he not only corrupts himself, but he hurts his Creator.

Without justice, Amos knew Israel could not endure. The rich might lie upon couches of ivory, their wives might drink wine and get as fat as the cows of Bashan, but the day of reckoning must come. The only way to prevent it was to:

Hate the evil and love the good
And establish justice in the gate;
It may be the Lord, the God of Hosts
Will be gracious unto the remnant of Joseph   (V:15)

Notice the words "it may be." This is the hope Amos held out for Israel. We can call it the prophetic "it may be." No matter how dark the prediction, repentance accompanied by deed, can stave off the evil decree. If however, they continue to:

. . . trample upon the poor
And take from him exactions of wheat . . .
. . . afflict the just . . . take a ransom
. . . turn aside the needy in the gate
                                                        (V:11–12)

the Day of Judgment will overtake them.

The vision of this Day is the third of Amos' themes. This message came as a shock to Israel. For this Day, known also as the Day of the Lord, was supposed to be one of joy, not of sorrow. On that Day, Israel was to triumph; her enemies to be brought low.

Amos foretold the very opposite. Israel would have to pay dearly for all her sins. His prophecy reached into the two strongholds of the nation: her palace and her temples. The herdsman dared to attack throne and altar:

The high places of Isaac shall be desolate
And the sanctuaries of Israel shall be laid
waste;
And I will rise against the house of Jeroboam (II)
with the sword.   (VII:9)

Outraged, Amaziah, the high priest of
Bethel, ordered Amos back to Judah:

. . . flee away into the land of Judah . . . eat
bread and prophesy there, but prophesy not
again any more at Bethel, for it is the king's
sanctuary, and it is a royal house.

(VII:12–13)

Clearly, Amaziah considered Amos a
professional prophet: one who earns his
bread by prophesying. This was distasteful
to Amos:

. . . I am no prophet, neither am I a prophet's
son; but I am a herdsman and a dresser of
sycamore trees: and the Lord took me from
following the flock, and the Lord said unto me:
'Go prophesy unto My people, Israel.

(VII:14–15)

No matter how dark his words, Amos'
final message is full of comfort. It is not
only that his love for Israel triumphs over
his anger, but that he knows once Israel
has paid for her crimes, she would be redeemed. The exiles would return. Judah
and Israel would be united once more:

They shall build the waste cities and inhabit
them

And they shall plant vineyards and drink the
wine thereof
They shall also make gardens and eat the
fruit thereof . . .
And they shall no more be plucked up . . .

(IX:14–15)

Hosea also dealt with the northern kingdom. His favorite names for her were
"Ephraim" or "Samaria," the capital. Unlike
Amos, he was born in Israel. He was a
father of three children, familiar with farming. Because of some of his images, it has
been suggested he was a baker. Like Amos,
he tried to prevent the fall of Israel by
warning her to turn back to God.

Hosea's own experiences were the stuff
of his prophecies. He saw the same cruel-
ties and oppressions Amos saw during the
reign of Jeroboam II. But unlike Amos, he
lived on after Jeroboam's death, witnessed
the crowning of four kings, and their as-
sassinations.

"A vulture is over the house of the Lord,"
he cried out in horror. In his eyes none of
these men were legitimate kings, since
only God could elect a monarch. Before
Israel's foreign policy, he was dismayed.
He pleaded for Israel not to ally herself
with either Egypt or Assyria, the rival empires of his day.

However, the most important insight Hosea revealed, was that God loved His people. How can a man measure the heights of
such divine love, or plumb its depths? He
can, if he himself knows love. And if he

continues to love even after the beloved betrays him.

This is exactly what happened to Hosea. He married Gomer, a woman he loved dearly. Yet she abandoned him for other men. She forgot how good he, her true husband, had been to her. Despite her infidelity, he discovered that he continued to love her. And when she in turn, was abandoned by her false lovers, he took her back.

If he, a mortal, could know such love, how much more so the Creator of man, the Source of life itself? And this knowledge which he learnt from his own life, he taught, or tried to teach to Israel. He reminded her that it was God who had chosen her, redeemed her from slavery, brought her to this land of plenty. Like Gomer, Israel must remember who took care of her:

. . . that it was I that gave her
The corn and the wine and the oil
And multiplied unto her silver and gold
Which they used for Baal . . .   (II:10)

You can see from this verse who was the false lover after whom Israel went. Of course, Baal: the god of the land rather than the Creator of heaven and earth. It might be more accurate to say that the people tried to combine the worship of Yahweh with that of Baal.

Yahweh, for them, was God of the people of Israel, the sole God of the political society. Baal, they considered the god of the land, a god who granted many children and plentiful crops in return for ugly forms of worship, incense, and the sacrifices of human beings.

One historian believes there were two Hoseas. According to him, Chapters I-III are the prophecy of this first Hosea. It is he who takes Gomer for a wife. The second is the author of Chapters IV-XIV. According to this scholar, the second Hosea emphasizes that Yahweh is the Lord of nature as well as the Master of history. The reason the people forgot this fact was their lack of knowledge. Over and over again this "second" Hosea dwells upon this lack:

My people are destroyed for lack of knowledge . . .
Because you have rejected knowledge
I will also reject you . . .   (IV:6)
For I desire mercy, and not sacrifice
And the knowledge of God rather than burnt offerings.   (VI:6)

What was this knowledge? It was not only to be obedient, but to have sympathy and commitment. Nor was it knowledge about God, but awareness of Him.

In the beautiful prophecy of Chapter II, in which the "first" Hosea saw God as the husband of Israel, the knowledge of God can be described by the relationship between husband and wife:

On that day you shall call me Ishi (my husband)
And I will betroth you unto Me forever

Yes, I will betroth you unto Me in righteousness
and justice
And in lovingkindness and in compassion.
And I will betroth you unto Me in faithfulness.
And you shall know the Lord . . .

(II:18, 21–22)

To "know the Lord," then, meant duties, responsibilities, and the lasting relationship which marriage is supposed to be. Anything that betrays that bond is a form of infidelity. Between husband and wife this is called adultery. Israel's knowledge of God would keep her faithful to Him.

How could the prophet have been so bold? How could he have created such an image? Did it emerge only out of his own experience with an unfaithful wife? Or did the *Covenant* contain this imagery? What do you think?

Both Amos and Hosea spoke to a people with historical memories. Both reminded them of the Exodus, of the wilderness. Amos referred to Israel's selection by Yahweh, to the Conquest of Canaan, and to her settlement. Hosea mentioned the prophet (Moses), Israel's creation as a nation, the *Covenant,* Sinai, and even one specific incident at Baal-Peor, found in the *Book of Numbers* XXV:1–3. From the period of the Conquest Hosea recalled the establishment of the monarchy. It is Hosea who denounced the bloody revolution of Jehu.

Yet the emphasis is different. For Amos history is determined mainly by man's deeds. Hosea adds that God participates in history because of His love for man. This divine love pursues man even though man hurts God by disobedience.

For Amos, the principal sin was injustice; for Hosea, idolatry. Indeed, Hosea is the only prophet who considered the golden calves set by the first Jeroboam, to be idols. Very plainly he said:

They that sacrifice men, kiss calves   (XIII:2)
Your calf, O Samaria is cast off . . .
The craftsmen made it and it is no god:
Yes, the calf of Samaria shall be broken into
chips.   (VIII: 5–6)

Amos cried out against evil deeds. Hosea protested there was no knowledge of God, no inner attachment to Him. Amos spoke of what God does; Hosea of what God feels for Israel.

Hosea too, concluded his prophecy with words of comfort. Repentance, he taught, shall return Israel to God:

Take with you words
And return unto the Lord
Say unto Him "Forgive all iniquity
And accept that which is good:
So the words of our lips will we offer instead
of bulls." (XIV:3)

In turn God will respond:

I will love them freely . . .
I will be as the dew unto Israel
He will blossom as the lily . . .

His beauty will be as the olive tree
And his fragrance as Lebanon . . .

(XIV:5–7)

Activities

Questions

1. What prayer on Friday night contains the marriage image of God and Israel?
2. What Book of the Tanach do we read on the Sabbath of Passover that speaks of the courtship of Israel by God?
3. Which of the Early Prophets was paid for his prophecy?
4. What was the relationship between him and the king of his day?
5. What difference was there between professional prophets and prophets like Amos?

6. Another name for husband is Baal. Indeed, this is the more common form.
   Why should Hosea have used 'Ish' instead of 'Baal'?

Readings for Students

Hosea.
Amos.

Readings for Teachers

The Prophets, by Heschel, A. J., J.P.S., 1962.
The Jews, ed., Finkelstein, Louis, J.P.S., 1949. Vol. I.
The Biblical Period, by Albright, William F. (pp. 35–41).
Hosea.
Amos.
The Book of Amos, by Hammershaimb, Erling, Schocken Books, 1970.
Amos of Tekoa, by Routtenberg, Hyman, Vantage, 1971.

chapter 20 Isaiah and Micah

ISAIAH, IN CONTRAST TO AMOS, SPOKE mainly to Judah. Tradition maintains that he was related to the royal house. His father, Amoz, was supposed to be the brother of Amaziah, not the High Priest of Beth-el, but one of the kings of Judah. Everything and everyone connected with Isaiah refers to prophecy. His wife was called a prophetess, his father was thought to be a prophet, the names of his two sons contained a prophecy of comfort and warning. His own name which means help or deliverance of God, reflects one of his most important messages.

Isaiah began to speak in 742 B.C.E., the year in which King Uzziah died; not long after the death of Jeroboam II of Israel. Uzziah was succeeded by Jotham, and Jotham by Ahaz, who ruled from 735–715 B.C.E.

At that time Assyria dominated most of the western states of the Fertile Crescent. In 737 B.C.E. a usurper named Pekah sat on the throne of Israel. He, together with Rezin, king of Aram (Syria) became the leaders of an anti-Assyrian coalition. They were joined by Ashkelon and Gaza.

Ahaz, however, refused to participate. Pekah and Rezin, therefore, went to war against Ahaz. They hoped to depose him,

and install a puppet of their own who would fight with them against Assyria. Had they been successful, the house of David would have come to an end.

Pekah and Rezin devastated Judah and laid siege to Jerusalem. Edom from the south, and Philistia from the west, annexed portions of Judean territory. Ahaz was terrified. What could he do. Isaiah tried to reassure him:

. . . be quiet, do not fear, and do not let your heart be faint, because of these two smoldering stumps of firebrands. (Pekah and Rezin) For thus says the Lord God: '. . . it shall not come to pass.'

(VII:4, 7)

Ahaz, however, was not reassured. He sent treasures from the Temple and the palace to Tiglath-Pileser, the Assyrian king, and pleaded:

I am your servant and your son. Come up and rescue me from the hand of the king of Aram, and from the hand of the king of Israel . . .

(Kings II XVI:7)

Tiglath-Pileser needed no encouragement from Ahaz to crush the "two smoldering stumps of firebrands." As you already know, he defeated both. Then he deported the Israelites of the Galilee and of Gilead. After that, he executed Rezin and his advisers. Rezin's royal gardens were destroyed and the Syrians (men of Aram) were deported as well. Tiglath-Pileser also captured Ashkelon and Gaza and subdued Edom.

When Ahaz went to Damascus, the capital of Aram, to pay his respects to Tiglath-Pileser he copied the altar he saw there and ordered it installed in the Temple at Jerusalem.

What Ahaz did in appealing to the Assyrian king was blasphemy in the eyes of Isaiah. How could Ahaz be servant and son to Tiglath-Pileser when God was his Master and Father? It was God who ruled and decided: not Pekah nor Rezin nor Tiglath-Pileser. Isaiah saw every political situation from the peak of faith. God was the Holy One of Israel. The emphasis is on both "Holy" and "Israel." Only God is The Holy One. And only Israel did He hallow. Consequently Israel, and no other nation, is a holy people. It is important to bear this in mind when looking at history through Isaiah's eyes.

Hosea, remember, had been revolted by both Egypt and Assyria. But Hosea, you might say, was not skilled in international affairs. He was, after all, a farmer, or perhaps, a baker. Isaiah, however, was skilled. He was a statesman. He had access to the throne. Yet he too advised neutrality. Ahaz, he urged, should join neither the anti-Assyrian coalition nor Assyria herself. You should recall he advised Hezekiah, the son of this very Ahaz, to do the same.

Why was Isaiah so set against alliances? For three reasons. First, and foremost, because to depend on man was to deny God. And for Israel hallowed by God, this was especially evil. Secondly, to become vassal to a foreign power, could mean accepting their gods. Did not Ahaz show this tendency by copying the pagan altar? And last, it could mean having to participate in the wars of the ally.

Isaiah's messages are contained in Chapters I-XXXIX of the *Book of Isaiah.* There are many themes that run through these verses.

Like Amos and Hosea, he loved his people. Jerusalem, for him was God's city. Judah was His elect. The house of David was the Anointed of God. Like Amos especially, Isaiah saw God as the God of history.

What makes Isaiah different, is that he combined with this love of Judah, the vision of the Messianic age, or as he called it "The End of Days." This meant two things. First, that the whole world would come back to the knowledge of God. For according to tradition, when the world was created it was monotheistic. Idolatry was supposed to have spread because men were ungrateful and disloyal. Therefore, the End of Days would bring the end of the kingdom of the pagan. All men would acknowledge Yahweh. All would learn

Torah. And secondly, since men would know they have but one Father, they would understand they are brothers. They would live together as brothers should: in peace.

Thus Isaiah is the first to conceive of Judaism as a universal religion. For Isaiah idolatry meant that man trusted in his own capacities, in the work of his own hands. Had he lived today he would have meant nuclear bombs, missiles, space ships. In his day he probably thought of the ships that sailed to Tarshish at the end of the Mediterranean, of high towers that Uzziah built, of the engines of war.

But these brought no blessing, Isaiah said. Man can live the good life only when he accepts the commandments of God, the Holy One of Israel. This vision of what the ideal age must be is Isaiah's legacy to mankind. That his vision glows upon the Temple mount of Jerusalem we should expect. For Isaiah, Jerusalem had to be the center unto which all nations would come to be judged by the Lord of history.

And it shall come to pass in the end of days,
That the mountain of the Lord's house shall be
    established as the top of the moun-
    tains . . .
And many peoples shall go and say:
'Come and let us go up to the mountain of
    the Lord, . . .
And He will teach us of His ways
And we will walk in His paths.'
For out of Zion shall go forth the law,
And the word of the Lord from Jerusalem.
And He shall judge between the nations, . . .

And they shall beat their swords into
    plowshares,
And their spears into pruning-hooks;
Nation shall not lift up sword against nation,
Neither shall they learn war any more.

                              (II:2–4)

Indeed, so blessed was peace, it would extend over the animal world as well:

And the wolf shall dwell with the lamb,
And the leopard shall lie down with the kid;
And the calf and the young lion and the fatling
    together;
And a little child shall lead them.
And the cow and the bear shall feed;
Their young ones shall lie down together;
And the lion shall eat straw like the ox;
And the infant shall play on the hole of the
    snake . . .   (XI:6–8)

Isaiah loved the dynasty of David. Therefore, he concluded, it was from this house the Messiah would come. This Davidic king, was, as you know, a political agent of God. At the End of Days he would become His spiritual agent:

And there shall come forth a shoot out of the
    stock of Jesse . . .
And the spirit of the Lord shall rest upon him.
The spirit of wisdom and understanding . . .

                              (XI:1–2)

Like Amos, Isaiah could not bear social corruption. But he does not denounce this evil as much as Amos. We know why today. From the excavations at Debir, we see that the population of Judah between 750–589 B.C.E. lived much on the same level. Aside from the king, no one class possessed the kind of wealth that caused men to resent or hate each other.

What hurt Isaiah most of all, was that men could think worship or sacrifice might be substitutes for righteousness:

"To what purpose is the multitude of your
    sacrifices to Me . . .
I am full of the burnt offerings of rams,
And the fat of fed beasts;
And I do not delight in the blood
Of bullocks, or of lambs, or of he-goats
                                (I:11)
I cannot endure iniquity along with the
    solemn assembly . . .   (I:13)
Seek justice, relieve the oppressed,
Judge the fatherless, plead for the widow.
                                (I:17)

It has become the fashion to ascribe to Isaiah contempt for ritual or for the observance of the Shabbat, or for the Temple procedures. This is a very grave error. Bear in mind that his prophecy of "The End of Days" will not only take place in Jerusalem, but on "the mountain of the Lord."

More than that, his vision of God, and his acceptance of his prophetic mission, takes place within the Temple:

. . . I saw the Lord sitting upon a throne high and lifted up, and His train filled the temple. Above Him stood the seraphim; each had six wings: with two he covered his face, and with two he covered his feet, and with two he did fly. And one called unto another, and said:
Holy, holy, holy, is the Lord of hosts;
The whole earth is full of His glory.
And the posts of the door were moved at the voice of them that called, and the house was filled with smoke.   (VI:1–4)

Who can doubt Isaiah's devotion to the temple. It was because he loved this house, he could not bear to see its courts trampled upon by feet of evil. It was not ritual he condemned, it was the use of ritual to conceal evil.

Isaiah's final theme was concerned with the survival of Judah. No matter what, Isaiah promised, a remnant would live. In fact he called his firstborn, Shear-jashub (a remnant shall return). His son was a living message for all Judeans, a walking parable. This theme has remained a powerful consolation throughout our history.

Another Judean prophet who spoke at the same time as Isaiah, was Micah. He lived in Moresheth-Gath, a village near the Philistine border. Like Isaiah and Amos, he condemned not only the robbing of the poor by the rich, but the use of the law to legalize their theft:

Woe to schemers of evil
Working evil while still upon their beds
In the light of the morning they accomplish it
Because the power is in their hands
They covet fields and seize them
And houses, and take them away.   (II:1)

Who rob their skin from off them (the poor)
And their flesh from off their bones.   (III:2)

Unlike Isaiah, Micah despised city life. Isaiah, as you know, was an aristocrat in love with Jerusalem. Micah was a farmer who saw only corruption and injustice in all cities, and especially in Jerusalem: For him the rulers:

. . . build up Zion with blood
And Jerusalem with iniquity
Her heads judge for reward
Her priests teach for hire
Her prophets divine for money . . .   (III:10)

With the same contempt that Amos had for professional prophets, Micah declared that they:

Cry 'peace' when their teeth have anything to
     bite
But against those who do not feed them
They sanctify war.   (III:5)

Therefore, Micah prophesied that Jerusalem and her Temple would be destroyed. In fact he is the first prophet to speak thus. This prophecy will be recalled almost a century later in the days of Jeremiah.

Yet this same Micah predicted a Messianic period using the identical words of Isaiah. The "End of Days" would see all nations gathered unto the Temple mount. God Himself will teach them of His ways. And, as you recall from Isaiah, peace shall be the final blessing.

Whether Micah used Isaiah's images, or Isaiah used Micah's, we shall probably never know. It may be both drew their inspiration from the same source. For Micah also spoke of a Messianic king of the house of David:

Out of you (Bethlehem) shall one come forth
     unto Me that is to be ruler of Israel. . . .
And he shall stand and shall feed his flock in
     the strength of the Lord.   (V:1–3)

But the concept of a saving remnant is expressed differently by Micah:

". . . a remnant of Jacob shall be in the midst
     of many people,
As dew from the Lord, as showers upon the
     grass . . .   (V:6)

Micah also appealed to the history of Judah. There is a dreadful sadness in his words:

O My people what have I done unto you? . . .
Testify against Me.
For I brought you out of . . . Egypt,
And I redeemed you out of . . . bondage
And I sent before you Moses, Aaron, and
     Miriam.   (VI:3)

Micah's passion reaches its highest peak with the verses you read in Chapter 18 of this Unit:

It has been told you, O man, what is good,
And what the Lord requires of you:

Only to do justly, and to love mercy, and to
walk humbly with your God.   (VI:8)

Questions

Recall Hosea's advice: "Take with you words
And return unto the Lord."

Isaiah had words. Assyria had the army.

- Was Ahaz wrong in appealing to Tiglath-Pileser? What was at stake?
- What evidence of faith's power has the Bible
shown us so far?
- What political meaning did the pagan altar
have for Ahaz? What religious meaning?
- Where is Isaiah's vision of the End of Days
inscribed?

The famous Spanish-Portuguese Synagogue in
New York is called 'Shearit Yisroel' the Remnant of Israel.

- Why did the founders of this Synagogue
choose this name?
- In what way was Micah's vision of the remnant different from Isaiah's?

- Whom did Micah address when he listed
God's demands?
- To whom did you expect him to speak?
- What does this tell us of Micah?

Readings for Students

The Mighty Voice, M. Gilbert, J.P.S., Philadelphia.

The New World Over Story Book, Edited by
Schloss and Epstein, Bloch Publishing Co.,
New York, 1968.

(p. 28, of Donkeys, Detectives and the Bible
by Hyman).

Isaiah.

(Chapters I, II, VI, and XI).

Micah.

The Mighty Voice Isaiah, by Gilbert, Miriam,
J.P.S., 1963.

Readings for Teachers

Isaiah.

Micah.

The Religion of Israel, Kaufmann, Yehezkel,
The University of Chicago Press, 1960.

chapter 21 Jeremiah

THE PROPHET WE KNOW MOST INtimately is Jeremiah. He was of a priestly family of the village of Anathoth of Benjamin, just three miles northeast of Jerusalem. He preached about forty years, from the thirteenth year of Josiah's reign in 626 B.C.E. until after the destruction of the Temple in 586 B.C.E.

No other prophet tells us how he feels as clearly as Jeremiah. As a prophet he had to speak the word of God: he had to declare the doom that awaited Judah if she did not mend her ways. As a man, he suffered. First, for these very calamities he had to predict; and second, for the hatred he aroused with these prophecies. False prophets condemned him; priests persecuted him; even his family turned against him. No wonder he cried:

Cursed be the day
Wherein I was born . . .
Why did I come forth . . .
To see labor and sorrows
That my days should be consumed in shame?
(XX:14 & 18)

He described himself as a "gentle lamb led to slaughter." Under the shadow of the coming destruction he moaned for Judah even as he had to cry out against her:

For the hurt of the daughter of my people am
I seized with anguish . . .
Is there no balm in Gilead
Is there no physician there . . .
O that my head were waters
And my eyes a fountain of tears
That I might weep day and night
For the slain of the daughter of my people.
(VIII:21–23)

Lament though he did, he could not reverse the course of Judah. The pro-Egyptian faction, you remember, forced Zedekiah, the last king of Judah, to rebel against Babylonia.

As Isaiah saw Assyria as "the rod of God's anger," so Jeremiah saw Babylonia as "the servant of God." He knew when he counselled submission to Babylonia that he would be accused of treason. Nevertheless, he would not be silent. He said the Temple would suffer the same fate as the Sanctuary of Shiloh did.

It is not difficult to understand the confusion of the Judeans. After all, Isaiah had prophesied a century ago that Assyria would never step foot into Jerusalem, that the Temple would stand. And here was this man who called himself a prophet, saying the very opposite. Indeed, Jeremiah warned them in the very gate of the Temple:

Amend your ways and your doings and I will cause you to dwell in this place. Trust not in lying words saying: 'The Temple of the Lord, the Temple of the Lord, the Temple of the Lord'.   (VII:3–4)

Such words were blasphemous in Judean ears. They seemed to scorn their Temple, God's House! Little wonder they hit him and put him into the stocks of the upper gate of the Temple.

Of course, it was clear to Jeremiah, as it had been to the other prophets, that man could rely only on God, that no cultic act could atone for corruption. Since the people had turned the Temple into a den of robbers, God must destroy it. Thus, his prophecy:

This House shall be like Shiloh, and this city desolate without an inhabitant.   (XXVI:9)

Had powerful men not protected Jeremiah, he would have been killed. Uriah, another prophet who spoke as Jeremiah did, *was* put to death. Frightened or not, Jeremiah continued to speak. Judah had to submit to Nebuchadnezzar, "the servant of God." By so doing, she would be submitting to the will of Yahweh. Indeed, it was an act of penitence, a means of atoning for the wrongs she had committed. To resist, on the other hand, would bring destruction and exile.

Like the other prophets, Jeremiah softened his prophecy. He set a limit to the rule of Babylonia. After fifty years, he said, Judah and Israel would return to their land. Jerusalem would again become the Holy City; a son of David would be her king. Then God would make a new covenant with His people:

I will put My law in their inward parts,
And in their hearts will I write it . . .
. . . all shall know Me
From the least of them
Unto the greatest of them.   (XXXI:33–34)
And I will make an everlasting covenant with
      them that I will not turn away from doing
      them good.   (XXXII:40)

So sure was he of Judah's return, he buys fields which are either already in the hands of Babylonia, or about to fall into their hands. And he buys them with all the protection of the law. He has his secretary, Baruch, record the deed of sale, has witnesses sign it, and then stores it away for the future. It is plain from this that Exile, according to Jeremiah, had no other purpose but to cleanse Judah of her sins.

As God plucks up and breaks down, so will He build and plant. The sins of those who sinned and went into exile, will not be visited upon the sons:

In those days they shall say no more
'The fathers have eaten sour grapes
And the children's teeth are set on edge'
But everyone shall die for his own sin . . .
(XXXI:29–30)

This statement of individual responsibility is found in *Deuteronomy* as well. In fact, much of Jeremiah's thoughts and very language are drawn from this Book. Remember it was in his day *Deuteronomy* was found. It may very well be Jeremiah assisted the youthful King Josiah to rid the land of idolatry. We can imagine with what hope and delight the prophet looked forward to this era of reform.

The death of Josiah at Megiddo at the hands of Pharaoh Necho, must have been a terrible blow for Judah. Certainly some must have seen it as an act of vengeance by the pagan gods whose altars Josiah had destroyed. It could not have been anything but a calamity to Jeremiah and his followers.

Like Isaiah, Jeremiah spoke of the end of idolatry at the End of Days. Nations would realize that manufactured gods are no-gods. More, he even wrote in Aramaic to the exiles in Babylonia:

. . . the gods that have not made the heavens
and the earth, these shall perish from the earth
and from under the heavens.   (X:11)

Thus, he was the first to denounce idolatry in a land of idolatry. It is no surprise,
therefore, that he shall continue this battle in Egypt as well. There he will predict evil upon the Jews whose wives made offerings to the "queen of heaven."

Jeremiah recognized how many forces tugged at man. Out of his own fears, he knew how complex man can be. What man says, he declared, was not necessarily what he meant:

The heart is deceitful above all things
And it is exceedingly weak, who can know it?
(XVII:9)

Like Hosea, he recognized that it was the knowledge of God that would save man:

Let not the wise man glory in his wisdom
Neither let the mighty man glory in his might
Let not the rich man glory in his riches
But let him that glories, glory in this
That he understands and knows Me
That I am the Lord who exercises mercy,
Justice and righteousness in the earth
(IX:22–23)

Jeremiah was undoubtedly the most unpopular man in Jerusalem. He was, as you know, struck, imprisoned, and put into stocks. He was also thrown into a pit of mud to die. At times he cried out bitterly against his enemies. He became despondent. He longed for death, as men in pain often do. But at no time does Yahweh cease to be His personal God. Yahweh's bond was with each individual, not only with the nation. As Jeremiah said, all would know Him, from the least unto the greatest.

After the assassination of Gedaliah, Jeremiah tried to guide the refugees from Judah in Egypt. He was not afraid to cry out against their idolatrous acts in this land of idolatry. Nor against the Pharaoh himself. No one knows what happened to Jeremiah in Egypt. He probably died there.

Jeremiah's sufferings and the patience with which he bore them, made him a symbol of Israel. "The *Book of Jeremiah* does not so much teach religious truth," a historian wrote, "as present a religious personality."

Activities

UNWRITTEN LAW

In addition to Written Law, every people has an Unwritten Law. For Israel, the Written Law was, and remains, Torah. The Unwritten Law is contained, mainly, in the Talmud. Yet there are examples of Unwritten Law in the Torah itself. For example, we read in *Deuteronomy* XII:21, the following:

If the place which the Lord your God shall choose to put His name there be too far from you, then you shall kill of your herd and of your flock, which the Lord has given you, *as I have commanded you* . . .

Nowhere in the Torah are these commandments spelled out. Therefore, we see, Unwritten Law goes back as far as Moses. Some say, even before Moses and Sinai.

An example of this Unwritten Law is found in the *Book of Jeremiah.* You read how Jeremiah's secretary wrote a deed for the transfer of property, and how witnesses signed it. But the Torah does not require either deed or witnesses for such a transaction.

Questions

1. Jeremiah pleaded for mercy for man, because man was so complex, so confused. Do you agree with him? Should man be judged by deed alone?
2. Why did Josiah's death shake the faith of some Judeans and not of others?

Readings for Students

Jubal and the Prophet, Hyman, J.P.S.
The Book of Legends, Goldin, Hyman E. The Jordan Publishing Co., 1937. Chap. XVIII–XIX–XX.

Readings for Teachers

Jeremiah.
A History of the Jews, Sachar, Alfred A. Knopf, New York, 1937.
Jeremiah, by Blank, Sheldon, Hebrew Union College Press, 1961.
Branch of Almond, Blumenthal, Warren B., Bookman Associates, 1961.

chapter 22 — Exile and Its Prophets

BY THE LATTER PART OF 586 B.C.E. 30,000 Jews were in Babylonia. At this time the word "Jew" became a shortened form of Judean. Besides the Babylonian community three smaller groups also survived. One was a colony of refugees who had fled to Egypt after Gedaliah's murder. These had probably dragged the old prophet, Jeremiah, with them. A second unit was a remnant scattered throughout Judah. And a third, had been enslaved and driven into other lands beside Babylonia.

There can be little doubt that the Jews in Babylonia found many Israelites Sargon had driven into Assyria back in 722 B.C.E. Therefore, it is impossible to estimate just how many of our people lived in this whole region of Mesopotamia.

The word "Exile" was now a reality. Over and over again the books of *Leviticus* and *Deuteronomy* had evoked this dreadful fate. Exile meant the ultimate punishment.

Prophets too, had threatened Israel with this word. But at the same time, Jeremiah had warned, he had comforted. If Judah repented, he had added, she would avoid this dark sentence.

While Jeremiah spoke in Judah, another prophet cried out in Babylonia. He was one of those exiled in 597 with Jehoiachin. Unlike Jeremiah, he did not comfort. He said exile could not be avoided. Indeed, Judah had to endure exile in order to pay for her unfaithfulness to Yahweh. Only through this dire punishment, he maintained, could Judah be saved. His name was Ezekiel.

Like Jeremiah, Ezekiel was the son of a priest. Until the fall of Jerusalem he uttered the most violent denunciations of Judah, and especially of Jerusalem. About seven hundred years later a Sage of Israel, Rabbi Eliezer ben Hyrcanus, prohibited the recitation of Ezekiel's prophetic chapters in the Synagogue because it condemned Jerusalem fiercely. In fact Rabbi Eliezer was so enraged at the man who chose Ezekiel's prophecy that he shouted at him: "Go out and announce the disgrace of your mother!"

However, when in 586 B.C.E. the second group of exiles arrived, Ezekiel's prophecies changed. He became the comforter and guide of his people.

Ezekiel was by nature a visionary. His most famous vision, the very first chapter of *Ezekiel,* describes the chariot and throne of God. It is known as the Merkabah. Some believe it was the description of God leaving His Temple before its destruction. The Merkabah became one of the bases of future mystical speculation.

It was his vision of the Valley of the Dried Bones that promised a complete restoration, not only of Judah, but of Israel as well:

. . . the Lord carried me out in a spirit, and set me down in the midst of the valley, and it was full of bones . . . and lo, they were very dry. And He said unto me: "Son of man, can these bones live?" And I answered, "O Lord God, You know." Then He said . . . "Prophesy over these bones, and say unto them: 'Behold I will cause breath to enter into you, and you shall live. And I will lay sinews upon you, and will bring up flesh upon you, and cover you with skin, and put breath in you, and you shall live; and you shall know that I am the Lord.'" So I prophesied . . . and as I prophesied there was a noise, and behold the bones came together, bone to its bone . . . and lo, there were sinews upon them, and flesh came up, and skin covered them above; but there was no breath in them. Then He said . . .: "Prophesy unto the breath . . . and say: . . . 'Thus the Lord God says: Come from the four winds, O breath, and breathe upon these slain, that they may live.'" So I prophesied . . . and the breath came into them, and they lived and stood up upon their feet . . . Then He said unto me; "Son of man, these bones are the whole house of Israel; behold, they say: 'our bones are dried up, and our hope is lost; we are clean cut off.' Therefore . . . say unto them: 'Behold I will open your graves, and cause you to come up out of your graves, O

My people; and I will bring you into the land of Israel . . . And I will put My spirit in you, and you shall live, and I will place you in your own land; and you shall know that I the Lord have spoken, and performed it, says the Lord.'"

And the word of the Lord came unto me, saying: . . . "Take one stick, and write upon it: 'For Judah, and for the children of Israel, his companions;' then take another stick, and write upon it: 'For Joseph, the stick of Ephraim, and of all the house of Israel his companions;' and join them . . . into one stick . . . And when the children of your people shall speak unto you, saying: 'Will you not tell us what you mean by these,' say unto them: "Thus says the Lord God: 'Behold I will take the stick of Joseph which is in the hand of Ephraim, and the tribes of Israel his companions; and I will put them unto him together with the stick of Judah, and make them one stick, and they shall be one in My hand . . .' And say unto them: 'Behold, I will take the children of Israel from among the nations, where they are gone . . . and bring them into their own land; and I will make them one nation in the land . . . and one king shall be king to them all . . . neither shall they be divided into two kingdoms anymore at all . . .'"   (XXXVII:1–22)

Notice how he binds Ephraim and Judah together. This tells us he must have found many of the children of the exiles of the kingdom of Israel in Babylonia. His description of the life of both these groups is a sad one. They are barely alive; their homes are as cold and desolate as graves. Let us see how accurate this picture was.

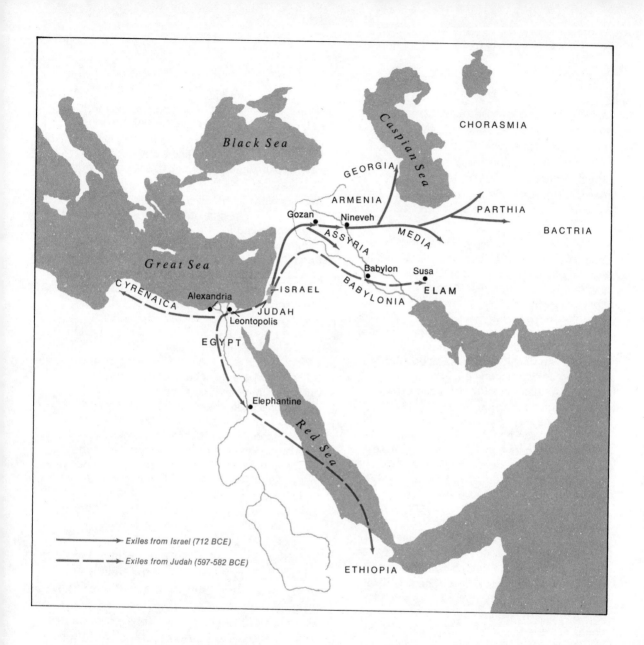

Map 4 Dispersion (712–582 BCE)

Nebuchadnezzar was a cruel general, but a reasonably merciful king. As you know, he wreaked a terrible vengeance. But once he brought his captives into his own land, he treated them kindly.

He allowed them to settle wherever they liked, to worship as they chose, to select their own work, and to arrange their own community affairs. They were not slow to do precisely this.

They settled close to each other and maintained the same customs and family relationships as in Judah. They built houses, became farmers, craftsmen, and merchants. They found, to their surprise, that they could live quite comfortably. In fact, Nebuchadnezzar himself gave allowances to many of them, from King Jehoiachin and his sons, down to the workers themselves. Clearly this exile was not the horror they had anticipated.

But all the king's kindnesses could not erase their hopes of return. Some of them probably plotted with other groups to throw off their yoke of captivity. When the second group came in 586 B.C.E. they too dreamed of going back to their native land.

The word exile is easily defined. Anyone banished from his land, and prevented from returning, is in exile, and is himself an exile. This practice of driving people from their homeland probably originated with the Hittites.

The Assyrians, as you know, exiled the northern kingdom of Israel. To populate Samaria they replaced the Israelites with their own people. In *II Kings* XVII:24, we read how these new settlers were attacked by lions. They were so terrified, they concluded that the God of this new land was punishing them for not serving Him as He had been served before.

Therefore, they wrote back to Assyria asking for a Hebrew priest who would show them how to sacrifice to the God of Samaria. Such a priest was sent to them. The settlers worshipped Him even as they continued to worship their own gods.

From this incident it is clear that exiled peoples quickly adopted the ways and gods of their new surroundings. To the pagan mind this made sense. For each god controlled his own territory. Consequently he had to be respected there. If one wanted, he could keep his native gods, but only after paying homage to the local god.

As a matter of fact, according to the unknown prophet of Babylonia whom we call Deutero-Isaiah, some Jews did renounce Yahweh. And according to Ezekiel, other Jews despaired for their future. Nevertheless, as a people, Judah remained faithful.

It was certainly a severe test for them. Yahweh's own Temple had been destroyed. His land had been conquered; His people driven out. Yet most did not accept the gods of their victors. Why they did not, is what we must understand.

Yahweh, they knew, and their Prophets in Exile reminded them, was not the God of Judah or Israel alone. He was the Creator of heaven and earth. He was in Babylonia as well as in Judah. Furthermore, exile was the fate He had promised them by word of His prophets. What they had sown, they now reaped.

They also knew that Assyria, "the rod of God's wrath," was no longer an independent nation, let alone the mighty Empire she had been. Therefore, as Assyria had been crushed by Babylonia, so Babylonia would in turn, be crushed. Indeed, they cast about for their deliverer even then. They found him in the new star that was rising: Cyrus, King of Persia and Elam. His power was spreading beyond Media and Persia, as far as the Aegean Sea and Greece. He was known as a humane ruler. No wonder their prophets predicted that he would liberate them.

There is nothing surprising about such developments for monotheists. What is surprising is that the Exile not only kept the Judeans intact as a separate and unique group, but that it deepened their faith and their insights into the meaning of God and man.

At the beginning of their Exile they had wept by the waters of Babylon. They cried, saying:

when we remembered Zion.
Upon the willows in the midst thereof
We hung up our harps.
For there they who led us captive asked of us
     words of song . . .
'Sing us one of the songs of Zion'.

How shall we sing the Lord's song
In a foreign land?   (Psalms CXXXVII:1–4)

Yet at the end of forty-nine years, they learnt they could not only sing God's song in a strange land, but they could sing it with greater fervor and understanding. Exile gave them insights they would never have had within their own land. The "knowledge" of the Lord of which Hosea and Jeremiah spoke, became a real and living experience.

Let us see how this came about. Consider first what would happen if you were expelled from your native surroundings. Home, soil, shape of trees, curves of hills, all would be different. The very quality of the air would be strange. Not to mention language, school, or sports.

You would not only be a foreigner, you would feel yourself a foreigner. You would no longer move about freely and naturally. You would realize very keenly, even bitterly, how you had directed, or misdirected your life before. You would discover that your previous way of life contained meanings and directions you had not truly understood. Your past would become more meaningful in an alien environment.

Thus Exile would make you more aware of yourself. Out of this new knowledge, you might resolve to preserve as much of your identity as possible. You would become in Exile what you were born to be. If so, you would become yourself.

Now let us look at what happened to the

Jews in Babylonia. They had been deprived of their Temple. But they still needed their bond with God. Also they craved comfort, fellowship, and guidance. What would they do? Only what they could. Fortunately they had already learnt how to worship without the sacrificial service of the Temple. This had already been done in Elisha's day. And though we know that not all the altars were removed with the discovery of *Deuteronomy* in Josiah's day, many were. In their place independent forms of prayer sprung up. Priests substituted the *laws* of sacrifice for sacrifice. In addition they recited Psalms, or portions from their Sagas, or from their codes. Most telling, was the creation of individual prayers.

The model, therefore, was already known to the exiles. And they had priests with them. But more important, they had the prophet Ezekiel. It was to him they flocked on Shabbat, holidays, and New Moon.

At the very beginning, the Babylonian leaders decided they too would not offer sacrifices. Only in Jerusalem could that worship be conducted. In the meantime, they would concentrate on prayers, psalms, historical records, and codes of law. Once again the priests substituted laws governing sacrifice for sacrifice. Thus, as they gathered in small groups, they developed a type of worship which answered the needs of exile. Hosea's words became a reality:

Take with you words
And return unto the Lord . . .
Say unto Him, 'Forgive all iniquity
And accept that which is good:
So the words of our lips will we offer instead
    of bulls.

(XIV:3)

What a lesson they learned! The Temple, their pride and joy, was not, after all, indispensable. Their bond with God did not depend on stones or gold or bronze or marble. Their hearts became the Temple of the Lord. Or better still, God Himself became their "little sanctuary."

Furthermore, if they could worship in this "impure land," they could worship in any land any time. And if prayer was as powerful as sacrifice, then the cultic acts of the priests were not that all important. Each man could be his own priest.

What has happened? Yes, the individual Jew becomes priest, Temple, and even at times, author of prayer. Since this was so, then the responsibility for irreligious conduct falls once and for all upon each person. No one could be blamed for anyone else's misdeeds, neither for his father's nor his son's.

Deuteronomy and Jeremiah had said this. Ezekiel emphasized it in sharp accents:

The soul that sins, it shall die. The son shall not bear the iniquity of the father, neither shall the father bear the iniquity of the son.

(XVIII:20)

This led to the further conclusion that the individual who sinned could atone, not only by sacrifice, since that was not possible in Babylonia, but by confession and by mending his ways. And not only the individual. The whole people could atone. Was that not what Judah was doing now? Ezekiel, who had said that Jerusalem and the Temple must be destroyed, that Judah must go into exile, saw his words come to pass. Judah was atoning. Therefore, Ezekiel proclaimed a new doctrine:

Have I any pleasure at all that the wicked should die? . . . and not that he should return from his ways and live? . . . Cast away from you all your transgressions . . . and make yourselves a new heart and new spirit.
(XVIII:23, 31)

If you think hard, you can begin to see what other changes had to take place. The authority of the priest without Temple and cult, had to decrease. It did. In his place the head of the family or clan now stood. Instead of the national rule of a Davidic king, separate communities governed themselves. This is known as self-autonomy.

Yet they felt as one. Why? Because they took upon themselves, willingly and happily, the fulfillment of rituals. As though they realized that observing the same religious practices would keep them together in an alien land. Even their festivals changed. In Israel and Judah they had been of an almost purely agricultural and local nature. Now they took on religious and national significance.

Take for example, Shavuot. It celebrated the wheat harvest, the offerings of the first fruits, and Sinai. In Babylonia one could not bring first fruits to a Temple that did not exist. But one could rejoice over the gift of the Ten Commandments and Torah. One could concentrate on Sinai. Indeed, Torah, though not as yet declared officially sacred, became more meaningful: a prop and a guarantee. . . . If the prophets assured them the *Covenant* existed, Torah was the source of their assurance. And so the exiles turned to their scrolls with an eagerness they had not displayed in Judah.

How fortunate they were to have Scriptures. In their gatherings for worship they were able to read aloud from them. The Psalms expressed their hopes and dreams; their faith in their ultimate redemption. In Jerusalem they used to go to the Temple for sacrifice and confession. Here, in addition to prayers and readings, they studied. In fact, study of Torah became a form of prayer. God's will had become more vital to their daily lives in Babylonia than it had been in Judah.

Out of these groups devoted to prayer and study, we believe the shape of what would become the future Synagogue developed. For all that the priests taught there, it became the institution of the layman. A Christian theologian calls it "the greatest and most durable system of lay leadership and lay education in religious history."

Nor was the history of their last years in Judah lost upon the exiles. The four days which had marked the beginning of the siege of Jerusalem, the fate of the city, the destruction of the Temple, and the murder of Gedaliah, became days of mourning and fasting.

With all this remembering, or perhaps because of it, no Jew relinquished his hold on the land of Israel. They turned to Jerusalem when they prayed. They kept careful records of families for their awaited return. Ezekiel was only one of many prophets who kept alive this hope. He did it in a very practical way. He drew up blueprints for a new Temple. He described in detail how they could worship in it. He divided the whole land assigning territory in Jerusalem to priests, Levites, and to a ruler he called Nasi. He measured out equal boundaries of the tribes and drew a plan of the frontiers of the country.

His words of comfort glowed. The land would give forth enormous harvests of grain and fruit. Her waters would teem with fish. The Jews and the strangers who will join Israel would enjoy blessings of material and spiritual bounties.

Those Jews who remained in Judah tried to dismiss the exiles. "They are far from the Lord," they said, "unto us (alone) is the land given for a possession."

But Ezekiel answered them firmly:

Thus says the Lord God: Although I have removed them far off among the nations, although I have scattered them among the countries, yet have I been to them as a little sanctuary in the countries where they are come.   (XI:16)

Never again could monotheism be restricted to one land. From then on God would be worshipped everywhere. This older Ezekiel was far different from the younger.

But the man who sustained the exiles most, was Ezekiel's successor, the Babylonian Isaiah, known also as Deutero-Isaiah or Second-Isaiah. His prophecies begin with Chapter XL of the *Book of Isaiah* and continue until the end of the Book.

His voice is one of the most eloquent in the whole Tanach. We do not know who he was, or where he lived. We only know that he is one of the most important religious personalities of the world.

Yet this second Isaiah only saw himself as a "limmud," a disciple or a kind of apprentice to the First Isaiah. He expanded on the visions of his Master. He joined what he called "former things" to "new things" and to "coming things." For example in XLII:9, he says:

Behold the former things are come to pass
And new things do I declare
Before they spring forth, I tell you of them.

The "former things" are the defeat of Babylonia which First Isaiah predicted, when he said:

And it shall come to pass in the day that the
Lord shall give you rest from your travail, and
from your trouble, and from the hard service
. . . that you shall take up this parable
against the king of Babylon, and say
How has the oppressor ceased! . . .
The Lord has broken the staff of the wicked.
The sceptre of the rulers,
That smote the peoples in wrath
With an incessant stroke,
That ruled the nations in anger,
With a persecution that none restrained.

(XIV:3–6)

The "new things" refer to the change in fortune for Israel. From captivity she will be led forth. God would remove all obstacles to freedom:

I will make waste mountains and hills,
And dry up all their herbs;
And I will make the rivers islands,
And will dry up the pools,
And I will bring the blind by a way that they
    knew not . . .
I will make darkness light before them,
And rugged places plain   (XLII:15–16)

The future things "before they spring forth," refer to the complete redemption of Israel. Indeed in that day, all Israel shall be "limmudim" disciples. But not of the prophet. Of their only Master: God.

And all your children shall be (limmudim)
    taught of the Lord
And great shall be the peace of your children.

(LIV:13)

With such singing words did this Isaiah comfort Israel. But what was new about his message? Other prophets comforted. True. But only Isaiah never used the prophetic "if." In his eyes Israel has atoned. Therefore her delivery is a sure thing. God Himself has decided it. Israel does not participate in this decision.

God is not only the Holy One of Israel, He is also the Redeemer of Israel. As you know it was First Isaiah who addressed God as the Holy One of Israel. He had hallowed Israel, alone. Thus, Israel was the only holy nation. Now, as Redeemer, He is duty-bound to rescue His people. For in ancient days, the redeemer was the male relative who had to make good any family loss. If a member of a family was killed, it was his duty to slay the murderer. If a relative was enslaved, he had to buy his freedom.

Neither of these images of God is new. In *Leviticus* XIX:2, we read: "You shall be holy, for I, the lord your God, am holy." In *Exodus* XIX:6, we read that Israel was to be a "kingdom of priests and a holy nation." Also in *Exodus,* we saw how God redeemed His people from bondage. Indeed, He had already redeemed Jacob as *Genesis* XLVIII testifies. What is different, is the coupling of these two images: The Holy One of Israel, and Redeemer.

Fear not, you worm Jacob
And you men of Israel
I help you says the Lord,
And your Redeemer, the Holy One of Israel.
(XLI:14)

Thus says the Lord, thy Redeemer
The Holy One of Israel
I am the Lord your God
Who teaches you for your profit
Who leads you by the way you should go.
(XLVIII:17)

Notice that where First Isaiah had stormed against Israel calling her a "sinful nation" because she had spurned her God, Second Isaiah announces only good tidings.

What further distinguishes this later prophet, is his all out war against idolatry. True, for Hosea idolatry was the cardinal sin. But it is the Second Isaiah who goes into fine detail concerning the absurdity of this worship. Idols were nothing but wood and stone. He allowed them no myths. They were empty and ridiculous. Thus in XLIV:14–19, we read:

He plants a bay tree, and the rain does nourish
    it.
Then a man uses it for fuel;
And he takes of it, and warms himself;
Yes, he kindles it, and bakes bread;
Yes, he makes a god, and worships it;

He makes it a graven image, and falls down
    unto it.
He burns half of it in the fire;

With half of it he eats flesh:

He roasts roast, and is satisfied;
Yes, he warms himself, and says: 'Aha
I am warm, I have seen the fire';
And of what remains he makes a god, even his
    graven image;
He falls down unto it and worships and prays
    unto it,
And says 'Deliver me, for you are my god.
They know not, neither do they under-
    stand; . . .
And none considers in his heart . . .
Shall I fall down to the stock of a tree?
(XLIV:14–19)

Even Israel needs reminding of the absurdity of idols. Unto her he says:

Remember these things, O Jacob,
And Israel, for you are My servant . . .
I have blotted out, as a thick cloud, your
    sins . . .
Return unto Me, for I have redeemed you.
(XLIV:21–22)

Even Cyrus, the conqueror of Babylon must know God is the only Master of the universe. But together with this message, Deutero-Isaiah adds the historical reason for Cyrus' office:

For the sake of Jacob, My servant,
And Israel Mine elect,

I have called you by your name,
I have surnamed you (with such titles as 'My
    anointed' and 'My shepherd') though you
    have not known Me.
I am the Lord, and there is none else,
Beside Me there is no God:
. . . from the rising of the sun, and from the
    west,
. . . there is none beside Me;
I am the Lord, and there is none else;
I form the light, and create darkness;
I make peace and create evil;
I am the Lord that does all these things.
                                        (XLV:4–7)

With the same accents Second Isaiah reminds Israel:

Thus says the Lord, the King of Israel
And his Redeemer the Lord of hosts:
I am the first, and I am the last,
And beside Me there is no God.   (XLIV:6)

Everything the prophet says about creation and history is directed at the eventual redemption of Israel. Sometimes he blends creation and history together, as we have just seen him blend history and theology when addressing Cyrus. An example of the former is found in Chapter XL. First he announces the good tidings of redemption. Then for those who doubt His power, the prophet adds:

Who has measured the waters in the hollow of
    his hand,
And meted out heaven with the span,

And comprehended the dust of the earth in
    a measure,
And weighed the mountains in scales,
And the hills in a balance?   (XL:12)

Scornfully, he continues:

Who has meted out the spirit of the Lord?
Or who was His counsellor that he might
    instruct Him?   (XL:13)

And just as strongly, he replies. Obviously no one:

Behold the nations are as a drop of a bucket,
And are counted as the small dust of the
    balance;
Behold, the isles are as a mote in weight. . . .
All the nations are as nothing before Him;
They are accounted by Him as things of
    nought, and vanity.   (XL:15–17)

Since the object of all this is to reassure Israel, he adds:

Why do you say, O Jacob,
And speak, O Israel:
'My way is hid from the Lord,
And my right is passed over from my God?
Have you not known? have you not heard
That the everlasting God, the Lord,
The Creator of the ends of the earth,
Faints not, neither is weary. . . .
He gives power to the faint . . .
Even the youths shall faint and be weary,
And the young men shall utterly fall;
But they that wait for the Lord shall renew
    their strength;

They shall mount up with wings as eagles;
They shall run, and not be weary;
They shall walk, and not faint.   (XL:27-31)

However, it was not enough to assure Israel. Second Isaiah is concerned with all mankind:

Yes, He says: 'It is too light a thing that you
      should be My servant
To raise up the tribes of Jacob,
And to restore the offspring of Israel;
I will also give you for a light of the nations,
That My salvation may be unto the end of the
      earth.'   (XLIX:6)

We see here what has been called "a theology of world history." God's servant, Israel, or the prophet himself, is to spread the message of God's saving power. Is this the same as the "End of Days," when the mountain of the Lord's house shall be established as the top of the mountains, and all nations shall flow unto it?

No, not quite. At the End of Days, God will teach all the nations. In the days of Second Isaiah, both the prophet and the people, Israel, shall serve as teachers.

There are many theologians who see most of Second Isaiah's lessons centering about the figure of the Servant of God. Through him, the prophet explains why Israel suffered. Especially the young exiles had to be answered. After all, they were certainly not responsible for the capture of Jerusalem or for the destruction of the Temple or for this Exile.

To them the prophet said, according to these theologians, that not only did one become wiser and better through suffering, but that Israel's special function was to bear the sorrows of mankind. Thus, suffering became a summons.

Those who refuse this summons, who recognize no obligation to mankind or to God, whether individuals or nations, are eventually discarded by history. Which is why nations like Amalek, Assyria, and Hatti, were left behind. But he who heeds the summons acquires this new and radiant knowledge.

Thus in Babylonia, Jews had the opportunity of teaching this knowledge to the world. By submitting to their captivity, they would not only be redeemed, but would become an example for all men. If we accept this interpretation of Second Isaiah, we must admit that he could never have agreed with Amos' conclusion:

You only have I known
Of all the families of the earth
Therefore will I punish you
For all your iniquities . . .   (III:2)

He would have changed the last line. Instead of "for all *your* iniquities," he would have said "for all *their* iniquities." Israel had not been punished in measure. Her pain far exceeded her guilt:

She has received from the Lord's hand
Double for all her sins . . .   (XL:2)

Clearly, this was not justice. But it was what God had ordained for Israel. It did not seem fair. But then man cannot understand God.

For My thoughts are not your thoughts,
Neither are your ways My ways . . .
For as the heaven is higher than the earth,
So are My ways higher than Your ways
And My thoughts than your thoughts.

(LV:8–9)

This, therefore, is what Israel had to understand: she is the Suffering Servant of the Lord. Here is the prophet's description of him:

He was despised and rejected of men
A man of sorrow and acquainted with grief;
Surely he has borne our griefs
And carried our sorrows . . .
But he was wounded for our transgressions
He was bruised for our iniquities . . .
With his stripes are we healed.   (LIII:3–5)

Nevertheless, Israel's suffering is not a penalty. It is a privilege, a sacrifice. When Israel shall finally be redeemed, all nations will understand her role and their dependence upon her. She will become a shining example to all ages and to all peoples:

Kings shall shut their mouths because of him
    (Suffering Servant)
For that which has not been told them they
    shall see.
And that which they have not heard they shall
    understand   (LII:15)

In line with this train of thought, it is possible to ascribe to Second Isaiah two significant contributions to religious concepts. One, that Israel was a sacrificial lamb of God for all the world. And two, that through suffering one acquires true knowledge, both for oneself and for others.

Consistent with this is the praise and glory Second Isaiah heaps upon Israel. She is God's love, His heritage, His holy people, His servant, a Light to the nations, and His witness. Verse after verse sings with these images. But he does not stop with Israel. With his "theology of world history," he cannot help but see all men. He cries

Turn to Me and be saved
All the ends of the earth   (XLV:22)

For all men could be God's servants:

The glory of the Lord shall be revealed
And all flesh shall see it together. . . .

(XL:5)

The foreigners who join themselves to the
    Lord,
And to be His servants . . .
These will I bring to My holy mountain . . .
For My House shall be a House of prayer
For all peoples.   (LVI:6–7)

And yet, as though contradicting himself, or as we might say, with the paradox that all great minds use, the Second Isaiah adds:

The heaven is My throne
And the earth is My footstool

Where is the House that you may build unto
    Me? . . .
But on this man will I look
Even on him that is poor and of a humble
    spirit . . .   (LXVI:1–2)

Notice he speaks of "this man," not "this Jew."

Because he spoke so poetically, don't think he was not a realist. He knew the people must not only hear comforting words, they must experience them. Therefore, God had to send a messenger who would make Israel's redemption come to pass.

And God did. He sent them Cyrus, King of Elam and Persia. Before his might, the city of Babylon fell without a battle. Babylonian Jewry was overjoyed. The Second Isaiah called this king, "Mesheach Adonai," The Lord's Anointed.

Cyrus, in turn, welcomed their tribute. He knew he could achieve two goals through the Jews. First, he could repopulate the ruined province of Judah by sending them home. And secondly, with a grateful people resettled there, he would secure the southern frontier of his empire against Egypt.

Thus he returned the 5400 vessels of the Temple looted by Nebuchadnezzar. And with this proclamation, he sent those who were ready, back to their native Judah:

Thus Cyrus, king of Persia says: 'All the kingdoms of the earth has the Lord, the God of heaven, given me; and He has charged me to build Him a house in Jerusalem, which is in Judah. Whoever there is among you of all His people, his God be with him, let him go up to Jerusalem, which is in Judah, and build the house of the Lord, the God of Israel, He is the God who is in Jerusalem. And whoever is left, in any place where he lives, let the men of his place help him with silver, and with gold, and with goods, and with beasts, beside the freewill offering for the house of God which is in Jerusalem.'   (Ezra I:2–4)

Activities

ARCHEOLOGY AND EZEKIEL

A critic named Torrey, accused the prophet, Ezekiel, of painting too bright a picture of the life of the exiles in Babylonia. Nor, he asserted, could there have been farmers or craftsmen among them, as Ezekiel said. To cap it all, Torrey doubted that Ezekiel could have known about the Persians since they had not "made an appearance on the stage of history."

From the discovery of the archeologist, Weidner, we know all of these accusations are unfounded. Weidner cleared the ruins of a remarkable vaulted building near the famous Ishtar Gate of Babylonia. In the structure below this vaulted building 300 cuneiform tablets were discovered. These list the rations distributed to hundreds of captives and craftsmen from all parts of the Near East. One of the Jews listed is described as a gardener. Among these records King Jehoiachin and five of his seven sons are named as recipients of very generous supplies from Evil-Merodach, then king of Babylonia.

Now we see that craftsmen were well paid. Jews were gardeners or farmers and lived reasonably well. As for Persia, Torrey did not know that this nation was mentioned on inscriptions of a king of Assyria back in 640 B.C.E. On these same cuneiform tablets below the vaulted building, the names of three Persians appear.

It is apparent that Ezekiel had opportunity enough to speak of Persia.

Torrey makes other charges. His article containing them is titled: *Pseudo-Ezekiel and the Original Prophecy.* Pseudo means false.

What title would you suggest if you were writing an essay on Torrey?

Projects

Act out the Valley of the Dried Bones. Pantomime or dancing can be very appropriate.

Write a playlet showing how the people gathered for worship and study. Who might be present. From what Book would they be reading?

Questions

1. Since the Exile was by no means so dreadful, why did Ezekiel use such strong language?

   To what period in Jewish history could the word "grave" be applicable? Do you think this vision had come to pass? Explain.

2. In what way is the synagogue a lay institution to this very day? Who also said God could not be housed in a Temple? When and where?

3. Most agree the Suffering Servant is the nation, Israel. This is the way W. F. Albright, a leading Christian historian puts it:

   ". . . the people of Israel which suffers poignantly in exile and affliction; he is also the pious individual who atones for the sins of the many by his uncomplaining agony; he is finally the coming Saviour of Israel . . ."

4. Others interpret the Suffering Servant to be Moses, Jeremiah, Jehoiachin, Cyrus, or even Zerubbabel, of whom we shall speak in the next chapter. In what way do Moses, Jeremiah, or Jehoiachin qualify? Whom would you choose? Why?

5. How has Christianity interpreted this prophecy of Second Isaiah?

6. What is the significance of "this man" in the verse of Second Isaiah?

Readings for Students

Isaiah. Chap. XL to end of book. Excerpts from Ezekiel.

Readings for Teachers

History and Destiny of the Jews, Kastein, Josef, Garden City Publishing Co., Inc., New York, 1936.

The Biblical Archeologist Reader, Wright and Freedman, A Doubleday Anchor Original, Garden City, N.Y., 1961.

Isaiah (Chapters XL to end of Book.)

Ezekiel

The Jewish Community, Salo W. Baron, J.P.S., 1948.

The Prophetic Faith, Martin Buber, Harper Torchbook, 1960.

From the Stone Age to Christianity, Albright, William F., A Doubleday Anchor Book, Garden City, N.Y., 1957.

Ezekiel, Davidson, A. R., University Press, Cambridge, 1906.

The Suffering Servant of Isaiah, by Driver and Neubauer, Hermon Press, 1877.

Unit VI

Behold, I will open up your graves, and cause you to come up out of your graves, O My people. And I will bring you into the land of Israel . . . And I will put My spirit in you, and you shall live . . .

EZEKIEL XXXVII:12, 14

chapter 23   Return to Zion

ACCORDING TO THE BOOK OF EZRA, 42,360 Jews left for Judah from the city of Babylon, now part of the Persian Empire. Sheshbazzar of the royal family of David, was appointed by Cyrus to manage this migration. At its head was Zerubbabel, grandson of King Jehoiachin, and Joshua, grandson of Seriah, the last High Priest. After four months they arrived in Jerusalem, on the first day of Tishri, 538 B.C.E.

Although more Jews remained in Persia, these who returned were hardly poor. They were not seeking economic betterment. They had over 7000 slaves, herds of cattle, gold and silver. They could have continued to prosper in Persia. Why then did they leave?

Simply because they longed for Zion. Above all they yearned for their Temple. They wanted to reestablish the daily sacrifice. That is why the first thing they did was to build an altar. And for the first time since the Exile, they celebrated Sukkot.

Some months later, they laid the foundation for the Temple. This took place 50 years after the first Temple's destruction. Those who had seen that one, wept. This building could hardly compare with the House they remembered. But the younger men rejoiced. Tears and laughter mingled at that celebration. However, no further building followed for nearly twenty years. Why? Who or what prevented it?

Before we answer this, let us take a bird's-eye view of the Persian Empire and then of Judah. Persia was the greatest Empire yet known to history. To govern her far-flung lands, Persia replaced each of the countries she conquered by making it into a Persian province, called a satrapy. Each satrapy was ruled by a governor, or Satrap, whose literal meaning was "protector of the kingdom." Satraps kept in touch with the central power through frequent exchange of orders and reports. They were actually like the monarchs of the lands they had dispossessed. Persia's king was known as the Great King, or the King of Kings.

Cyrus, founder of the Persian Empire, established twenty satrapies. Under later kings many changes were made. Some satrapies disappeared, usually because of rebellion. Others were created. Twenty, however, seems to have been the number maintained.

Satraps not only administered civil law, but were the commanders of the local satrapal army. When the Satrap's office became hereditary, the threat to the Great

Map 5 The Persian Empire (538–332 BCE)

King could not be ignored. To counteract this danger, certain officials of each Satrap were commanded to take orders directly from the Great King. More effective control was obtained by an official known as the "king's eye" (or king's ear, or king's messenger). This king's eye made a careful inspection of each satrapy regularly.

The most important satrapy for our history was the fifth, known as Across the River, or Beyond the River. This satrapy was the region between the Middle Euphrates and the Mediterranean. It included Phoenicia, Syria, Judah, Cilicia, and Cyprus. Its chief cities were Sidon, Tyre, and Arvad.

By far the most vital country was Phoenicia. Phoenician ships formed the core of the Persian fleet: 300 triremes out of a total of 1200. A trireme was a ship of war with three rows of oars on each side.

Egypt, together with Libya and the towns of Cyrene and Barca, comprised the sixth satrapy. During Xerxes' reign, Egypt's 200 triremes constituted the second largest portion of the Persian fleet. While Egyptians were trusted as sailors, they did not make reliable soldiers. Persia, therefore, retained whatever mercenary units already existed in Egypt. One such mercenary colony that transferred its allegiance to Persia was made up of Jews. It had been commissioned by a Pharaoh in 600 B.C.E., and was stationed at the Ethiopian border. Some call it the colony of Elephantine (or Yeb) as well as Sin (or Syene). We will discuss these colonists later.

There is no certain record of troops from Judah in Persian service. In an epic poem about Xerxes' expedition against Greece, mention is made of a regiment from the "Solymian hills." But this probably referred to the "eastern Ethiopians." Nevertheless, Jews had arms, and when ordered by the Satrap, had to appear with swords, spears, and bows. The district governor of Judah had his own personal guard. He lived in a house overlooking the Temple Hill and was known by the Persian title of all district governors: Tirshatha. The first Tirshatha of Judah was Zerubbabel. The Satrap over him was Tattenai.

The district of Judah was approximately a quadrilateral. It was 35 miles long from Bethel in the north to Beth-Zur in the south. Its width of 25 miles stretched between the Valley of the Salt Sea in the east and the lowland (Shephelah) in the west. Its area, therefore, was about 900 square miles, of which a good part was desert. Why was it so small?

With Judah's defeat, many of her neighbors had annexed parts of her land. Ammon and Moab helped themselves to her eastern territory, while Philistia did the same on the west. The southern hill-country south of Beth-Zur was gradually occupied by Edom. As for the central hill-country and the rich Shephelah, these had been completely ruined by the Babylonians.

The northern hill-country was attached to the district of Samaria, whose people were called Samaritans. These were the descendants of the Assyrians whom Sargon had settled in Samaria after he had destroyed the northern kingdom of Israel.

You remember that *II Kings* told us that when these same settlers had been attacked by lions, they had begged for a Jewish priest to show them how to worship Yahweh. But they did not stop offering to their own gods, even, according to *II Kings,* sacrificing their children to them. Thus, they blended the worship of Yahweh with that of their own idols. This blending we know as syncretism.

They must also have intermarried with whatever Israelites remained in Israel. Because of their worship of Yahweh, syncretistic though it was, and because of their marriages, they claimed kinship with Israel. This was a logical claim for them. For in ancient days to worship the same god, meant to belong to one family, tribe, city or nation. All relationships grew out of the religious structure of the family. Gods were related to certain families, and tribes, and only to those families and tribes.

Therefore since they too served Yahweh, and their wives or husbands were originally of the Yahweh cult, they thought it only proper that they be allowed to join the Judeans in building God's House. But the Jews refused. The Samaritans could worship in the completed Temple; they could not participate in constructing it. One historian maintains that the Jews rejected this aid, not because the Samaritans were considered pagans, but because the Samaritans wanted to build the Temple in Shechem, the holy city of their territory.

Whatever the reason, the Samaritans were insulted. They determined upon revenge. Sanballat, Tirshatha of Samaria, together with leaders of other hostile nations denounced the Jews to the Persian king. They accused them of plotting rebellion against Persia. Tobiah the Ammonite, was one ally of Sanballat. He was called Ammonite because he lived in Transjordan near Rabbat-Ammon. There is reason to believe he was a Jew. We shall deal with him and his family in Unit VII.

Cambyses, son of Cyrus, became king in 529 B.C.E. Most of his reign was taken up with the conquest of Egypt. He was not the tyrant many historians describe. He did not kill Apis, the sacred bull of Egypt, as charged. Whether he was petitioned by the Jews for permission to rebuild the Temple, we cannot say. According to Josephus, an ancient historian, Cambyses forbade the building of either the Temple or Jerusalem because of Samaritan pressure. The king is said to have committed suicide on his way home from Egypt, near Mt. Carmel.

His throne was usurped by a man pretending to be Smerdis, his brother. After just eight months, this false Smerdis was assassinated by Darius, a devoted warrior of Cambyses. It is this Darius who will become the next king.

In addition to the external threat of the Samaritans, there were, at this time, Jews who opposed building a House of Yahweh. From the *Book of Haggai,* the first of three prophets who preached in Judah after the Exile we learn of them. According to Haggai, they said:

"The time is not come, the time that the Lord's House should be built"   (I:2)

These may have been men who were so discouraged either by attacks of their enemies, or by their own poverty, or by the desolate conditions of the country, that they could not find the energy or enthusiasm to build. For indeed, what faced them in Judah each day was hardly the dream they had dreamed in Babylonia.

During the 49 years of Exile, Jerusalem had remained a mass of ruins. The Jews who had remained in Judah had done nothing to clean up the city. The returnees found pitted roads and untended soil. Even the razed stones of the Temple still gathered dust. There was no order anywhere: no structure either of trade or industry, or agriculture, into which they could fit. Whatever they had brought back with them had been quickly consumed. Just to eat each day, to erect a home, to pay taxes to Persia, proved too much for them. What was even more discouraging was the greed of some of their fellow Jews. These were men who lent them money, then demanded such high interest, they were compelled to surrender their homes in payment. When this was not enough, these creditors took them and their children as slaves. It was as though Isaiah, Amos, and Jeremiah had never prophesied. As a result, many abandoned Jerusalem. These settled in rural areas and tried to eke out a living from the neglected land.

Besides these impoverished Jews, there were those who did not think a Temple urgent. These were the men who had accepted the teachings of Second Isaiah wholeheartedly. After all, if the heaven is God's throne, and the earth His footstool, then what sense was there in trying to build Him a House? At the very least it could wait.

Haggai the prophet, was neither a follower of Second Isaiah, nor for that matter, of Jeremiah. Jeremiah had warned the Judeans not to trust in the Temple of the Lord. Haggai, on the other hand, said that they would never prosper without a Temple. In fact, he said, they now suffered because they had not provided God with His dwelling place:

You looked for much, and lo, it came to little . . . Why? Because of My House that lies waste, while you run every man for his own house. Therefore, over you the heaven has kept back, so that there is no dew, and the earth has kept back her produce . . ."   (I:9–10)

There is, as you can see, no mention of justice or mercy. We hear no echo of Amos, Isaiah or Ezekiel.

Haggai spoke in 520 B.C.E., the second year of the reign of Darius Hystaspes, king of Persia. Many parts of Darius' empire were rebelling then. Haggai probably believed this was the beginning of the Messianic era. He so stirred up Zerubbabel, the Tirshatha, as well as Joshua the High Priest and all the people, that they began to construct the Temple. He predicted the overthrow of the kingdoms of the earth, and more directly, promised Zerubbabel he would be exalted by God:

And the word of the Lord came . . . unto Haggai . . . 'Speak to Zerubbabel . . . saying "I will shake the heavens and the earth; and I will overthrow the throne of kingdoms, and I will destroy the strength of the kingdoms of the nations; and I will overthrow the chariots, and those that ride in them; and the horse and their riders shall come down, every one by the sword of his brother. In that day . . . will I take you, O Zerubbabel, My servant . . . and I will make you as a signet; for I have chosen you, says the Lord of Hosts.

(II:20–23)

He did not mention Persia or Darius by name. But then he dared not. We think his nationalistic fervor encouraged Zerubbabel to try to cast off the Persian yoke.

At about the same time, Zechariah, the second of the Post-Exilic prophets, spoke. But his message was no fiery call to arms.

God, Zechariah declared, wanted justice and mercy. Fasting and cultic acts, he emphasized, were no substitute for righteousness:

Return unto Me, says the Lord of Hosts, and I will return to you. . . .   (I:3)

Neither Haggai nor Zechariah mention each other. But Zechariah gives us a hint of his reaction to the message of Haggai. For on the 24th day of the eleventh month, exactly two months after Haggai had predicted world disaster, Zechariah announced:

We have walked to and fro through the earth, and behold all the earth sits still and is at rest.
(I:11)

No catastrophe had overtaken Persia. Jerusalem, Zechariah added, would be comforted with good words:

I return to Jerusalem with compassion: My House shall be built in it says the Lord of Hosts.   (I:16)

Like Ezekiel, Zechariah saw many visions. Like Jeremiah and Amos, he stressed truth and peace:

Speak every man the truth with his neighbor; execute the judgment of truth and peace in your gates; and let none of you devise evil in your hearts . . . and love no false oath, for all these are things I hate, says the Lord.
(VIII:16–17)

Like First and especially Second Isaiah, he stressed the day when Judaism would be a universal faith:

Yes, many peoples and mighty nations shall come to seek the Lord of Hosts in Jerusalem, and to entreat the favor of the Lord. . . . In those days . . . ten men . . . shall take hold of the skirt of him that is a Jew, saying: "We will go with you for we have heard that God is with you."   (VIII:22–23)

Would Haggai have agreed with Zechariah? Let us examine two questions Haggai asked of the priests, and see if we can answer this ourselves. Here they are:

If one bear hallowed flesh in the skirt of his garment and with the skirt do touch bread or pottage or wine or oil, or any food, shall it become holy?" And the priests answered and said: "No." Then said Haggai: "If one that is unclean by a dead body touch any of these shall it be unclean." And the priests answered and said, "It shall be unclean."   (II:11–13)

What do these questions mean? There are differences of opinion. But it would seem that what was ritually holy could not impart its holiness. But what was ritually unclean, could make anything it touched unclean. If we apply this to Israel and the nations, the message is plain. Israel was hallowed by God. But that holiness was limited to Israel. She could not impart her holiness to others.

On the other hand, the nations about her, ritually unclean as they were according to Haggai, could destroy Israel's holiness. There is no difference between this separatism and that of Athens for example. Did not Athens conceive of its gods as hallowing only Athenians.

Should our analysis of these questions be correct, then Haggai would have been aghast at Zechariah's prophecy.

If Zerubbabel did rebel against Persia, because of Haggai's superpatriotism, it was a foolhardy act. Darius had had enough of rebellious uprising. He was hardly likely to put up with one in Judah, that gateway to his most dangerous enemy: Egypt. We don't know for sure. But we do know that Haggai and Zerubbabel the Tirshatha, disappear from history. Whether they were banished or executed or simply died a natural death, has remained a secret.

Zechariah probably tried to prevent any hot-headed deed on Zerubbabel's part. His warning is plain in this advice:

Not by might, nor by power, but by My spirit, says the Lord of Hosts.   (IV:6)

As we see, alas, his words were in vain.

Nevertheless, the Temple was completed. In 516 B.C.E., exactly 70 years after the beginning of the Exile. Tradition counts this as the fulfillment of Jeremiah's prophecy.

The Samaritans, despite their persistent

hostility, had failed to interfere with the construction of the Temple. For one thing, Jews in Persia were able to influence the king. For another, the Jews had remained undaunted. When Tattenai, the Satrap of Across the River, challenged them, saying: "Who gave you a decree to build this house and to finish this wall?", they said: "Cyrus." They also suggested that a search be made for the original document containing this royal decree.

This was done. The document was found in Ecbatana (modern Hamadan). Thereupon King Darius ordered Tattenai not to obstruct the building of the Temple. Anyone who did so, he warned, would be hung, and his house destroyed. To underscore this command, Darius himself contributed to the Temple: animals for sacrifice, as well as wheat, salt, wine, and oil.

It is the High Priest who now became the leader of Judah. He and a Council of Elders administered whatever power Persia allowed her Jewish subjects.

It has been suggested that the struggle for control was not so much between Judah and her foreign enemies, as much as between the Tirshatha, Zerubbabel, and the High Priest. It is, of course, a possibility. What is a fact is that not only the High Priest emerged as the dominant figure in Judah, but that his fellow priests benefitted as well. They became the richest landowners, the heads of the Temple, and the agents of Persia.

You may remember that Levi was not granted any tribal land by Joshua. How then did these sons of Levi manage to own property? At first, from necessity. When they returned to Judah, the people found they could not support a priestly class. Therefore, the priests had to earn their own bread: they had to till the soil. Once having acquired their land, they refused to surrender it even after they began to receive tithes and other gifts. These two sources of income enriched them steadily.

Why should Persia have allowed the priests to take over the leadership? First, because all rulers prefer to deal with one section of their subjects most loyal to them. Priests were usually such a conservative influence. Moreover, ancient kings were in awe of all men who dealt with gods. Because of this awe, they usually did not tax anyone connected with the Temple. They even, as we have seen, made generous donations to the Temple. Darius did both.

As a result, Joshua and his fellow priests became the most powerful group in Judah. The High Priest and his family were descended from Zadok, a son of Aaron. It was this Zadok who became the only High Priest of Israel in Solomon's reign.

These men of Zadok shall be known as Zadukim, Sadducees. Being responsible for the Sacrificial Service, they emphasized Temple and cult. It may not be fair to claim that they did not agree with King Solomon's prayer that ". . . the heaven and the heaven of heavens cannot contain You, how much less this house . . ." or with

Second Isaiah's pronouncements. For they knew too that Yahweh ruled the universe. However, they did maintain that He dwelt first and foremost in His House in Jerusalem. And though He ruled all men, He was Judah's God primarily.

For those who followed Second Isaiah, however, the emphasis was on all men everywhere. Unlike Haggai, they welcomed all nations into the *Covenant.* The Temple, though dear to them once it was built, was not as vital as it was to the Sadducees. Furthermore, they must have opposed the concentration of wealth in the hands of priests. After all, had not God Himself proclaimed that He was the inheritance of Levi, not property? These men probably looked toward the royal House of David for leadership.

The books of *Ezra and Nehemiah* are our main sources for the period of the post-Exilic days. Like the sons of Zadok, the author of these books believed in a more exclusive God. For him too the Temple was the chief dwelling place of Yahweh. The priesthood represented for him the best and truest leadership of Judah.

Let us now meet Ezra and Nehemiah, the main personalities of these two books.

Activities

Questions

1. Considering the role of the Temple in the life of the people, who do you think was correct: Second Isaiah or Haggai?

2. How did the following people provide Israel with the means of group worship: Moses, Joshua, Samuel, David, Solomon, Jeroboam II, Hezekiah and Josiah?
3. What happened to Abiathar, the other High Priest appointed by David? Some claim he was the author of *II Samuel.* What proof could be offered for such a theory?
4. Compare Second Isaiah and Haggai, using their own words to illustrate their views.
5. Do you think we need a Temple today? Would you approve of a Sacrificial Service? Before you answer, remember most of the sacrifices were eaten. What did the sacrifices bring home to man?

Readings for Students

Selected portions of Haggai and Zechariah as well as Second Isaiah.

Readings for Teachers

The Rise and Fall of the Judean State, Zeitlin, Solomon, J.P.S., 1962. (Vol. I, pp. 332–337)
The Pharisees, Finkelstein, Louis, J.P.S., 1940. (Vol. II)
From the Stone Age to Christianity, Albright, William F., A Doubleday Anchor Book, Garden City, New York, 1957.
History of the Persian Empire, Olmstead, Arthur T., Phoenix Books, The University of Chicago Press, 1960.
Haggai.
Zechariah.

chapter 24 Ezra and Nehemiah

EZRA IS KNOWN AS EZRA HASOFER, Ezra the Scribe. In the book of *Ezra,* he is described as "a ready scribe in the law of Moses." (VII:6). A Scribe was not someone who merely copied Scripture. He was one who taught the law. Some think he was the official Scribe of the Jews to the Persian court. Today we might call him Secretary of State for Jewish Affairs. As such he would have been directly responsible to the king for the Jewish community.

Ezra, whom we date at the beginning of the fifth century, is considered by tradition, the first Scribe. According to one historian, the High Priest, Simon the Just, who lived around 200 B.C.E., was the last. The Scribal period, therefore, lasted roughly 300 years.

In a royal charter of the Greek king, Antiochus III, (200 B.C.E.) we find a special group known as "Scribes of the Sanctuary." They were non-priests who advised on the laws and customs of his Jewish subjects. Since these Scribes influenced the king, they had a special standing among their fellow Jews. And since Jewish law and customs were derived from Torah, the Scribes became the authority for Torah. Simon the Just, though a priest of the house of Zadok, was more a Scribe than a Zadokite.

Ben Sira (190 B.C.E.) was a teacher who wrote *Ecclesiasticus.* This book was widely read, though it was never admitted into the Canon (Tanach). According to Ben Sira, a Scribe was not only an interpreter of law, but one who explained riddles and dreams, advised kings and assemblies; and taught wisdom. Ben Sira wrote glowingly of the High Priest, Simon the Just. But his ideal Scribe was not Simon. It was Daniel.

Nevertheless for the 300 years between Ezra and Simon the Just, teachers and Scribes had been mainly priests. Malachi, the third of the post-Exilic prophets, described the priests thus:

The law of truth was in his mouth
And unrighteousness was not found in his lips;
He walked with Me in peace and uprightness,
And turned many away from iniquity.
For the priest's lips should keep knowledge,
And they should seek the law at his mouth;
For he is the messenger of the Lord of Hosts.
(II:6–7)

Ezra was such a priest. He was of the high priestly family of Seraiah. Some years after Sheshbazzar had led Jews back to

Judah, Ezra decided "to teach in Israel statutes and ordinances." (*Ezra* VII:10)

Why? Were there no priest, no teachers in Jerusalem. And why should he desert his people in Babylon? Two possibilities present themselves. First, that like any Jew, he yearned to live in Zion. And second, that he was worried about conditions in Jerusalem.

Both are correct. But more than either, was his desire to introduce Torah to Jerusalem as the law of the land.

Artaxerxes I of Persia (465–423) must have approved of his plan. He sent him with gold and silver vessels, ordered the treasurers of Across the River to give Ezra enormous allowances of wheat, oil, wine, and salt. In addition, he made him, not a Tirshatha, but an Administrator of the Law for the Jews of Judea. It suited the king, as we have seen, to appoint priests from among his subjects as his agents. But most significant for the Jews of that day and ours, Artaxerxes I proclaimed Jewish law to be the law of Israel. Any violations would be as serious as a violation of a Persian decree.

With 1754 men and their families, Ezra began his preparations for departure at the beginning of the first month of Nissan. There are 500 straight miles between Babylon and Judea. However, there were no direct flights then. The roads twisted and turned, stretching into 900 miles. It took almost four months to cover that distance.

Thus, at the beginning of Av, the fifth month, they arrived at Jerusalem. They sacrificed 12 bullocks for the tribes of Israel, as well as rams, lambs, and goats for sin offerings. The gold and silver vessels were deposited in the Temple, and the orders of Artaxerxes for Temple supplies were relayed to the Persian Satrap.

If Ezra had been driven to Jerusalem by his concern for his people there, his worst fears were realized. The Temple, though completed, was not maintained properly. Jerusalem, an open city was unprotected from her enemies of Samaria, Ammon, Edom and Dedan, an Arabian country. But worst of all, the people, with priests and Levites showing them the way, had intermarried with the other nations. They had abandoned the *Covenant.* The children of their foreign wives were learning pagan ways, worshipping pagan gods.

Ezra was appalled. He tore his garments, plucked the hair from his beard and head, and fasted all day. In the evening he fell upon his knees and wept and prayed. Can you compose his prayer? You could if you think back upon the whole of Jewish history preceding Ezra. Now listen and see if these words match your composition:

. . . for our sins we . . . have been delivered . . . to the sword, to captivity . . . and now . . . grace has been shown . . . to leave us a remnant to escape . . . God has not forsaken us in our bondage but has granted mercy to us . . . to set up the house of our God, and to repair her ruins . . . And now, O God, what shall we say . . . Shall we again break Your commandments and make marriages with the peoples that do . . . abominations.

(IX:6–14)

His prayer reached the hearts of the people. They put away their foreign wives and children. *Ezra* counts 113 men who had intermarried. To our amazement, the list was headed by Joshua, the High Priest.

While this was a painful separation, it in no way compared with the laws of other people against intermarriage. In Athens, for example, an alien who married an Athenian woman was sold into slavery and his property seized. If an Athenian married with an alien woman, she was sold into slavery, and he was fined 10,000 drachmas.

Was Ezra's decree necessary for the survival of Judaism? There is a difference of opinion. Most believe it was. The mixture of paganism and Judaism would have destroyed the pure monotheism of Israel.

Yet there were some who did not agree. Do you remember Ruth, great grandmother of King David of the *Scroll of Ruth?* (Chapter 15). This Scroll told of Ruth, the Moabite woman who left her home and country to follow after Naomi, her mother-in-law.

Ruth married Boaz of Bethlehem and bore Obed. Obed fathered Jesse, who in turn, fathered David. Yet Ezra would have forbidden the marriage of Ruth and Boaz. And Ruth, according to this Scroll, became the great grandmother of David, from whose house the Messiah shall descend. Thus, Ruth became an ancestress of the Messiah. And not only this girl from Moab, but Naamah, a princess of Ammon. For Naamah was Solomon's wife, mother of Rehoboam.

It is generally accepted that *Ruth* was written at the period of Ezra. Certainly it reflects opposition to Ezra's action. Since Moab (Ruth) and Ammon (Naamah) are singled out in *Deuteronomy* as the two nations which may not marry into Israel for ten generations, it becomes a very pointed opposition. Five hundred years later a Sage will prove that this law of *Deuteronomy* could not be applied anymore. But in Ezra's time it must have taken courage to write this particular scroll of *Ruth.*

Another work, the book of *Jonah* was also supposed to have been composed at this time. *Jonah* is one of the most fascinating books of the Tanach. It protests the super-patriotism of a prophet, Jonah. Pagan sailors, on the other hand, behave nobly in *Jonah.* The pagan king of Nineveh speaks with prophetic compassion, while the Hebrew prophet begrudges mercy. Clearly *Jonah* proclaims God, the Father of anyone; indeed, as the loving Father of Israel's most vicious enemy: Assyria. It pleads for mercy for all living creatures, and for true brotherhood among all nations.

Most opposition, however, came from certain prophets, both men and women.

Malachi was undoubtedly among them. While he was one of the harshest critics of the priests, he thought Ezra went too far in demanding that they and others divorce their wives. Passionately he asked:

Have we not all one father?
Has not one God created us?   (II:10)

He admitted Judea had dealt treacherously, had married the daughter of a strange god. But he denied the need to break up families:

You cover the altar of the Lord with tears . . .
So that He does not regard the offering any
    more . . .
Yet you say, "Wherefore?"
Because the Lord has been witness
Between you and the wife of your youth;
Against whom you have dealt treacherously.
Though she is your companion
And the wife of your covenant,
For I hate putting away
Says the Lord, the God of Israel   (II:13–16)

Pagan women were not of the *Covenant.* Did Malachi believe that once they married Jews, they became converts? We know this was true of all ancient peoples: women took the faith of their husbands.

Ezra did not think so. He was determined to keep Israel untouched by heathen influences. His most important tool, of course, was Torah. At public gatherings he read Torah and explained it. This does not mean that these five Books were unknown to the Judeans until this time. How can we be sure? Because had they been, Ezra or anyone else, could have made sensible, logical changes in them. For example, he could have substituted "Jerusalem" for the Deuteronomic phrase, "the place which your God shall choose." Or he could have altered those laws which seem to contradict each other. Or certainly, he could have condensed repetitious laws.

That Jerusalem is not introduced, that contradictions remain, and that laws are repeated, tell us no man could tamper with these Books. They were already sacred.

Tradition maintains that Ezra established schools and sent other Scribes throughout the land to teach the people. He is also credited with introducing the Assyrian script, which is our present square type. It was designed to distinguish the Judean Pentateuch (Torah) from the Samaritan.

Though Ezra tried, he did not succeed in eliminating all super-patriotic dreams, like those of Haggai and Zerubbabel. His aim was to reconcile Judea to the foreign rule of Persia, while at the same time, impressing upon the Jews, their role as guardian of Torah. When Rome will rule Israel some five hundred years later, this same goal will be pursued by Pharisees of the school of Hillel.

Despite all he did, Ezra could not cope with every problem. He could not resist the constant attacks of Samaria and her allies. He could not protect Jerusalem whose walls were demolished, and whose gates were burned. Nor could he enforce Torah, despite Persia's support. According to the *Book of Nehemiah,* another Great Assembly was convened. During it the Judeans vowed never to give their children in marriage to non-Jews.

But they had promised this already, at the Great Assembly Ezra had summoned. Why then this second vow? Had the pagan wives returned? We don't know. But what *Nehemiah* tells us explicitly is that the Sabbath was not kept; that the rich became richer, the poor, poorer.

What was needed was a strong administrator: someone who knew how to use Persian power. Someone who could resist Sanballat of Samaria and all enemies.

Thirteen years after Ezra, such a man appeared in Jerusalem. His name was Nehemiah. He came from Susa, once capital of Elam, and now the winter capital of Persia. Nehemiah was cupbearer to Artaxerxes.

When word reached Nehemiah of the desolate condition of Jerusalem he asked Artaxerxes for permission to go to Jerusalem and build up the city. This was a dangerous request for a man so close to the king. Artaxerxes' own father had been assassinated. He, Artaxerxes himself, had killed his older brother. Who better than Artaxerxes knew about conspirators? Besides, would a man as wealthy and privileged as Nehemiah leave his home and position to go to a backwoods city of ruins?

Surely he might have other motives than the ones he revealed.

That Artaxerxes permitted Nehemiah to leave, tells us of the unusual confidence he had in his cupbearer. All he demanded was that Nehemiah tell him when he would return. This Nehemiah did.

Artaxerxes sent him forth with grants for lumber. Significantly, he also appointed him Tirshatha of Judah, the first Jewish provincial governor since Zerubbabel. Thirteen years before, Ezra and his group had made the almost four months journey unprotected by soldiers. Indeed, Ezra would have been ashamed to ask the king for such an escort, seeing that God was his Shield. Nehemiah, however, arrived with a full military retinue. Why? Did he have less faith than Ezra?

It did not take long for Nehemiah to bring political and social order to Judah. Neither Sanballat, Tirshatha of Samaria, nor Tobiah, called by Nehemiah, Tobiah the Slave, nor any of Sanballat's allies, was a match for Nehemiah. One of his first accomplishments, was the rebuilding of the walls of Jerusalem. According to the *Book of Nehemiah,* he accomplished this in fifty-two days. Josephus, however, says it took two years and four months. The builders worked with one hand, while the other held the sword. At night the men remained in the city to ward off any attack.

As Tirshatha, Nehemiah was chief of the Elders. Together with Ezra, he convened that Knesset Gedolah, that Great Assembly, we have mentioned. On the twenty-fourth day of Tishri, before the Water Gate, he gathered all the people together with their Elders. Laws were drawn up and signed. These laws prohibited intermarriage; commanded the observance of the Sabbath, and of the Sabbatical Year. They also resolved to support the Temple by paying one third of a shekel, by donating wood for the altar, by offering their first of herd and harvest, and by tithing.

What was the purpose of this Great Assembly? What, but to renew the *Covenant.* When men and women forget the basic laws of Torah, it is obvious they must be reminded of their duties. Or when people stand at the beginning of a new period of their development, it is good sense to review their role in life.

This had been done before: by Moses at Sinai; by Joshua at Shechem; by Elijah on Mt. Carmel; and by Josiah in the Temple. Now that the walls of Jerusalem were up, the people reasonably safe, it seemed a proper moment for Judea to pause and take stock of herself.

At this Great Assembly prayers and confessions were uttered. Most important was the reading of the Torah. According to one historian, this reading meant that it was officially canonized: pronounced sacred. If this is correct, the 24th day of Tishri, 444 B.C.E. was a turning point of Jewish history. On that day the Pentateuch became the Constitution of Israel. This was the law

that Persian power upheld. This is why Ezra is considered the second founder of Judaism, second only to Moses.

Like all nations, Israel had an Unwritten Law as well as a Written. Some think Ezra is the founder of this Oral or Unwritten Law. But we know there were Unwritten Laws as far back as Sinai.

Nehemiah's name appears first upon the renewed Covenant. We know, therefore, that this Great Assembly took place at least thirteen years after Ezra's arrival. There can be little question that Nehemiah's authority brought people and Elders together. His strong and stern personality bristles upon the pages of the *Book of Nehemiah.* It was he who ordered all Judeans, princes as well as commoners, to cast lots. One out of every ten was to live in Jerusalem in order to defend her properly and promptly.

One of his most important achievements was the abolition of debts. In the last chapter you read of those men who lent the poor money for bread and taxes. By the time Nehemiah arrived, many of the poor were homeless, landless, and with their children, were enslaved to their debtors. You remember how Amos and Jeremiah had protested against such injustice; how Isaiah and Micah had condemned it.

Nehemiah too, was indignant. But Nehemiah, unlike the prophets, had political power. Behind him the might of Persia loomed. Nevertheless, he did not call upon this kind of power. For him there is only one strength: that of the *Covenant.* In

Chapter V of *Nehemiah,* we read how he summoned the princes and nobles:

And I held a Great Assembly against them. And I said unto them: "We after our ability have redeemed our brothers, the Jews, that sold themselves unto the heathen; and would you now sell your brothers and should they sell themselves unto us? . . . The thing that you do is not good; should you not walk in the fear of our God? . . . Restore, I pray, you, to them . . . their fields, their vineyards, their oliveyards, and their houses, also the hundred pieces of silver, and the corn, the wine, and the oil, that you demand of them.   (7:11)

They obeyed him. They would not have dared oppose him. This man, Nehemiah, did not only preach. He practised what he preached. Unlike Tirshathas who had preceded him, he took no tribute for himself. Out of his own pocket he fed the officials who helped him administer Judah. Nor did he deem it below himself or his officers to help in the building of the wall. Before the walls went up, Nehemiah with just a few of his attendants made a preliminary inspection of Jerusalem. His description of the city has been of great help to future historians.

In 433 B.C.E., twelve years later, Nehemiah returned to Susa as he had promised Artaxerxes. But either his heart was in Jerusalem, or he received disturbing news from there. Whatever the reason, he again asked permission from the king to go to Jerusalem. Like Ezra before him, he was distressed at what he found.

The High Priest had permitted Tobiah, the Slave, to live in a room of the Temple. Levites had not received their due, and had fled back to their fields to support themselves. The Sabbath was violated. Intermarriage was rife. The children of women of Ashdod, Ammon, and Moab spoke the language of their mothers. And Manasseh, grandson of the High Priest, had married Nicosa the daughter of Sanballat the Samaritan!

Nehemiah took prompt action. He threw out Tobiah; appointed honest treasurers to pay Levites and other Temple officials; ordered the gates of Jerusalem shut for the whole of Shabbat to prevent Tyrians and other traders from bringing in their wares; scolded men who had wed alien women, even unto beating them; and chased Manasseh out of Jerusalem. Manasseh fled to his father-in-law, Sanballat. According to *Nehemiah,* Sanballat built his son-in-law a new temple on Mt. Gerizim in the ancient holy city of Shechem. But according to Josephus and others, the Samaritan temple was built in the days of Alexander the Great, 332 B.C.E. With Artaxerxes' death imminent, Nehemiah returned to Susa.

This post-Exilic period highlights two important facts. One is the unique relationship of Diaspora and Zion. (Diaspora is any land outside the land of Israel) We know from Unit V, how much clearer the meaning of Judaism became to the Jews of the Babylonian Diaspora. Was not Second Isaiah's concept of the Suffering Servant, a result of Exile? Did not Diaspora enforce the knowledge that God was over all, was the Creator of the whole universe? Did not Ezra see more sharply what Jerusalem needed because he brought fresh eyes to Zion. And was not the same true of Nehemiah? His political as well as his moral genius saved Zion from disintegration.

This bond between Zion and Susa we shall see endure. It does not matter whether Susa shall become Rome, or Cordoba (Spain) or Vilna (Eastern Europe) or New York or Los Angeles. No other people in history has ever remained so loyal to its origins as Israel. At the most, Phoenicians refused to follow a Persian king when he went to war against the Phoenician city of Carthage in Africa. But most exiles, like the colonists brought to cities of Mesopotamia by Assyria, soon lost their identity with their homeland. One scholar of this period states:

The Diaspora saved Judaism from physical extirpation (destruction) and spiritual inbreeding.

At the same time many Jews of the Diaspora never return to Zion to live. Is this a paradox? What do you think?

The second fact is that were it not for the protection of the Persian Empire, our history might have taken a different course. You have seen how Samaria, Moab, Ammon, Dedan, threatened the tiny province of Judah. You know they and Philistia and Edom annexed parts of her former territory. That they could have swallowed her entirely if Persia's power did not stop them, there is no doubt. It is only fair, then, to credit Darius and Artaxerxes together with Ezra and Nehemiah for the firm foundation that was established for Israel's future unity. We shall see how this unity shall endure even after the Persian Empire disappears.

Activities

Questions

With whom do you agree, with Ezra or with the unknown author of *Ruth?* of *Jonah?* Organize a debate on this subject. Consider the following facts:
1. Political relationship of Judah to Persia; to surrounding countries.
2. Mood of people, need for guidance.
3. Influence of mother upon child.
4. The character of Rehoboam, son of Naamah.
5. The possible fate of a leaderless Judah.

Readings for Students

Builders of Jerusalem, Hyman, Frieda C., J.P.S.
The Story of Ruth, by Asimov, Isaac, Doubleday & Co., 1972.

Readings for Teachers

Ezra.
Nehemiah.
History of the Jews, Graetz, Heinrich, J.P.S.

chapter 25 The Theocracy

UNTIL THE RISE OF THE MONARCHY ancient Israel was a combination of a primitive democracy and theocracy. Elders guided their individual tribes. But the people spoke up in defense of their rights. Even women asserted themselves, as we see in the case of the five daughters of Zelophehad (*Numbers* XXVII:1–7 & XXXVI: 2–12). Nevertheless, it was more of a theocracy than anything else.

Theo refers to God; cracy, to rule. Therefore, a theocracy is a form of government in which God is recognized as the supreme civil ruler, and His laws are accepted as the Constitution of the state. Priests who said they were commissioned by God stood above all the tribes.

With the monarchy, kings were supreme. Of course, they had, as in the case of Saul, the priest-prophet, Samuel as a brake upon their deeds. David had to answer to Nathan. Later kings of both Judah and Israel were called to task by prophets like Amos and Jeremiah.

With Ezra a theocracy is firmly reestablished. True, Nehemiah controlled Judah during his two visits. After him, however, the High Priest was the acknowledged head of the country. Torah was her constitution.

What impression does a theocracy leave? Usually a grim one. Laws are rigid. Originating with God, they cannot be changed. Decisions are severe. People are limited by a very mountain of restrictions. Since God, according to the priests, dwelt in His Temple, He was an exclusive God. And so were His people.

If this is the nature of a theocracy, why then was Israel's existence neither grim nor isolated. Perhaps because people do not follow rules or adhere to definitions. It is true we do not know much about the next hundred years after Nehemiah (432–332 B.C.E.). But what we do know certainly does not agree with the image of a theocracy. Why?

For one thing, the Temple did not possess any real estate as the temples of Egypt did. Nor did Jewish priests receive any salary. Their livelihood depended on free will offerings. Even the one third shekel fell into disuse after Nehemiah. As powerful as the priests were, they still had to depend on the donations of the populace.

For another "digs" of the fifth and fourth centuries tell us that Israel belonged to the belt of a threefold culture: Greek, Egyptian, and Asiatic. This belt extended from the Nile Delta to Cilicia. Greek pottery, Phoenician amulets, Egyptian idols, weapons, household goods, were the same throughout this area. Six miles north of Jerusalem, for example, an unearthed Greek cup with a sphinx is proof that Jews used Greek pottery: even one with an image upon it.

As a matter of fact, the commercial influence of Greece was so great, that Jews used Athenian coins (owls) in the fifth century. In the fourth these "owls" were coined locally. Since they were for smaller amounts, we know they were used for domestic trade and not for international traffic. We have even discovered coins which bear the stamp of Hezekiah, a Jewish agent of the Persian government. These coins show the owl of the Athenian coins, a human figure, and to our amazement, the image of a god seated on a winged wheel. What kind of god was it? Was it the Baal of Tarsus, or can it be, it was supposed to represent Israel's God? Whatever the meaning, such coins were a clear disregard of the Second Commandment of the Decalogue.

Now if Torah was truly the Constitution of Judah, why did the Jews maintain Synagogues? Nowhere in the Torah is such an institution commanded or even described. Only the Temple of Jerusalem is God's House. What makes this situation stranger, is that the Jews truly believed they were following Torah by praying in their local Synagogues. While the hundreds of Synagogues that will spring up, never take the place of the Temple, they do give the people a feeling of some independence from the priesthood. It was in their Synagogues they gathered to pray when their village's sacrifice was being offered in the Temple.

In time they went to the Synagogues to pray morning and evening whether or not their own sacrifice was on the altar in Jerusalem. The Temple certainly regulated the time if not the content of their prayers. But the Synagogue was, as you recall, an essentially democratic institution. It became a meeting place as well as a house of study.

The spread of learning also weakened the position of the priesthood. As you read, the prophet, Malachi, reminded us that it was the priest who taught the people because he was the "messenger of the Lord." But Ezra, the Scribe, a priest himself, insisted on the people hearing and understanding the law directly.

By the fourth century, education in Torah is available to all men. Thus, the priests no longer remained the sole authorities. Laymen gradually became as knowledgeable as they. Little by little, the Scribes took over the task of education. The first Psalm praises as the ideal man not the priest, but rather the scholar:

Happy is the man that has not walked in the
    counsel of the wicked . . .
But his delight is in the law of the Lord;

And in His law does he meditate day and night.
(1-2)

As for the charge that exclusiveness is part of a theocratic form of government, the very opposite was true of the Jews. Israel of all the nations of her day, Haggai notwithstanding, welcomed the stranger. True, intermarriage was prohibited. But that was not because the man or woman was of another nation. It was because he or she was not a Jew. Once conversion took place, the marriage was sacred.

This attitude is found in Torah. It was emphasized by Second Isaiah and Zechariah. As you have read before, ancient nations tolerated all gods. Indeed, each man was considered religious who worshipped his own ancestral gods. But woe betide the alien who participated in the cult of another pagan group. If discovered he would be put to death. For the gods of the individual cities or nations did not wish to receive prayers and offerings except from their own citizens. They repulsed the stranger. His presence during a sacrifice was sacrilege.

Evidence of this ancient feeling remained in one of the principal rites of Roman worship. The priest (pontiff) had to have his head veiled when he sacrificed in the open air:

For before the sacred fires in the religious act which is offered to the national gods, the face of a stranger must not appear to the pontiff;

the auspices (divination, omens) would be disturbed.

The very reverse held for Judaism. The idolater was ignorant, foolish, even wicked for he denied the existence of one God, Creator of heaven and earth. But because Yahweh was Creator of all, He did not reject any man or woman. On the contrary He welcomed all. His House, as Second Isaiah said, was to become a house of prayer for all people.

It is important to remind ourselves that this welcome which is extended to the stranger, is rooted in Torah. Abraham became the father of a multitude of nations. *Leviticus* XIX:34 commands:

The stranger who lives with you shall be to you as the homeborn among you, and you shall love him as yourself.

And finally three Books of the Tanach: *Ezra, Nehemiah,* and *Chronicles I and II,* reveal a very interesting fact about the world of scholarship. It is generally accepted that one man, known as the Chronicler, and according to Jewish tradition, Ezra himself, wrote all three books. Indeed, these were originally one story, from Adam to Nehemiah.

Chronicles I and II concentrate on the history of the Temple and of its priesthood and on the House of David and his tribe of Judah. The author, is, on the whole, apologetic. This means he is interested in showing his people, Israel, in as complimentary a light as possible. He omits much of what discredits the good kings, as for example, the incident of Bathsheba and David. He also ignores most of the material relating to Saul and the northern kingdoms. In addition, like historians of his day, he exaggerated numbers.

In fact, the treatment of history by the Chronicler startles us so, because it is very similar to other ancient histories. Facts, figures, sources, are used in the same way by the Chronicler, as for example, by Herodotus, the Greek historian who wrote about a century before. Thus, we see that Jewish scholars were not cut off from other scholars in this Greek-Egyptian-Asiatic region.

There is a curious story by Clearchus, a pupil of Aristotle. He relates how his Master conversed with a Greek-speaking Jew in Asia Minor. It may be, as most contend, mere fiction. But it could have happened.

It is clear, that theocratic as Judah's government was, her life was neither grim, grey, nor repressed. On the contrary, she grew and developed as healthy organisms do.

In 333 B.C.E. the Persian Empire fell. A new Empire ranging from Macedonia to the Indus Valley (Punjab), broke upon the world. Its ruler was Alexander the Great, son of Philip of Macedon.

Alexander swept across the eastern lands, bringing with him the gifts of Hellenism, the only culture that was ever a serious threat to Israel.

The next chapter will take up the confrontation of these two most vital civilizations of the world: Hebrew and Greek.

Activities

MEGILAT ESTHER (SCROLL OF ESTHER)

Megilat Esther tells a story about a Persian king, Ahasueras, about his queens Vashti and Esther, and about a wicked adviser, Haman who was supplanted by Mordecai the Jew. The name, "Haman" is applied to all vicious enemies of Israel. According to Josephus, Haman is descended from Amalek the arch enemy of Israel. Hitler of our day was such a Haman.

This Megillah is an excellent example of how our people, or for that matter, how any people, forces its will upon its leaders. For *Esther* was the last book to be canonized, (declared sacred) by the Rabbis.

Had the Sages had their way, they would not have admitted *Esther* to Scripture. But you know what a delightful book it is. And what a happy holiday its story celebrates.

The people loved it so much, they refused to stop either reading it or rejoicing on the holiday of Purim. So much so, the Rabbis could not refuse to pronounce the Megillah holy. Nevertheless, as late as the third century C.E., it was recorded in the name of a Rabbi, Samuel, that *Esther* does not belong in the Canon. It could be read on Purim, but could not be written down. Needless to say, this ruling was not accepted.

The fact is, however, that we cannot verify the story of *Esther*. We cannot even agree who Ahasueras was. Some say Xerxes. But then there were two Xerxes. And neither has been known to have had a wife called Vashti or Esther. Nor can we find the name of Haman, adviser to any king, or his replacement, Mordecai.

What is authentic is the description of the Persian court: both in its physical appearance and moral climate. Towards the end of the reign of the first Xerxes, for example, this king seduced his own daughter-in-law, the wife of his eldest son. Who can say what such a man might have done in a fit of drunkenness? With a Haman encouraging him, could he not have ordered the murder of a whole people? Furthermore, some of his deeds in his war with the Greeks portray him as a foolish and inept leader. Indeed, according to Greek history, he was a weak monarch. But according to Persian records, it must be added, he was a very capable ruler who deteriorated during his latter days.

The language of the Scroll reflects Persian forms. For example the Hebrew "dath," decree, is the Persian "dat," law. The names are, for the most part, Persian or Babylonian.

Whether *Esther* is accepted by modernists as history, does not alter the essential point of the Scroll. Israel has been menaced many times by unspeakable Hamans. In many instances Israel suffered severely. At other times, as in *Esther,* Israel defeated her enemies. But above all Israel lives. And Purim still comforts the Jew.

DEVELOPMENT OF LANGUAGE

The following three words: hostis, gaest, and ger, afford us an interesting insight into the development of semantics (language). Hostis is the Greek which meant stranger and enemy. Gaest is the Anglo-Saxon word which also meant stranger and enemy. Ger, from the Hebrew root, gur, meant stranger. The root, gur, means also to dwell, to attack, to quarrel and even to be afraid.

From hostis we have our word "host"; one who receives guests. From gaest, we have our "guest": he who is welcomed in our homes. From gur the form hitgayer, is derived. Hitgayer means to convert to Judaism. Ger, therefore, means a convert.

We see, from above how alike semantic development is. What distinguishes the Hebrew ger from the Greek hostis or the Anglo-Saxon gaest, is that ger became a friend, indeed, a fellow Jew so much sooner in history.

Questions

- How does the Tanach emphasize the acceptance of the ger?
- What nation of our century still held to the ancient meaning of hostis and gaest?

Readings for Students

Scroll of Esther.
Queen Esther, Long, Laura, Association Press, 1954.

Readings for Teachers

Scroll of Esther.

The Persian Wars, Herodotus, translated by
G. Rawlinson, A Modern Library Book, N.Y.,
1942.

The Ancient City, Fustel de Coulanges, Doubleday Anchor Books, Garden City, N.Y., 1956.

The Temple of Elephantine

According to *Deuteronomy,* the Temple
which was to be established in the
"place which God would choose" (Jerusalem), would be the only place where sacrifice would be permitted. Even after the
Temple was destroyed, we read in the
Book of Jeremiah XLI:5, that the people
continued to bring meal offerings and
frankincense to her ruins.

Yet there were two other temples in Jewish history, both in Egypt. One, in the village of Leontopolis, built about 162 B.C.E.;
the other 600 B.C.E. on the island of Elephantine, also known as Yeb, at the first
cataract of the Nile. This island was about
one hundred yards from the city of Sin or
Syene.

Syene was known to Biblical writers.
Ezekiel XXIX:10 tells us:

I will make the land of Egypt an utter waste
and desolation from Migdol to Syene, even
unto the border of Ethiopia.

Syene was an important frontier post,
the end point of the Nile's boat traffic, and
the source of red granite much in demand
for sculpture, monuments and building.
The mineral "syenite" comes from ancient
Syene.

The settlers of Elephantine, as you have
read, were Jewish mercenaries. They may
have been refugees from Israel or Judah,
or soldiers sent to Egypt in return for
horses. Since these men fought for Pharaoh, he gave them permission to build their
temple. After Cambyses captured Egypt in
525 B.C.E., they became Persian mercenaries. Finally, they served Pharaoh again
when Egypt threw off Persia's yoke in 404
B.C.E.

We have many documents in Aramaic,
which describe this military colony at Elephantine. The Jewish "degel" or troop, was
divided into companies. A Persian was at
its head. Its captains had Babylonian or
Persian names. The men received salary
and rations from Persia's treasury. Nevertheless, the regiment did not live as soldiers. The Jews were merchants, brought
suits in civil courts, and dealt with military
colonists of other nations who lived nearby.
Some married Egyptian women.

Under the influence of Egypt, Jewish
women had many more rights than women
in Judea. They could conduct business,
hold property in their own names, sue in
court if cheated. They could even divorce
their husbands if they made a public declaration in the congregation. To this very
day Jewish law does not grant women that
right. Only a husband can divorce his wife,
if his wife consents.

The head of the religious community was called President. He was also treasurer of the local temple of their national God whom they called Yahu, God of Heaven. They made the same kind of offerings as are listed in the Torah. They also kept the Passover.

But their faith was very primitive. They never suspected they were violating the law of *Deuteronomy* with their Temple. They believed expensive gifts could influence God. They would not have accepted Hosea's words that God desires mercy and not sacrifice. More serious, they uttered blessings in the name of Yahu and Khnum: a syncretistic formula. Khnum was the sheep-headed god of Egypt whose temple and priests were neighbors of the Jewish temple. You can imagine how pleased the priests of Khnum were toward a temple that offered up sheep on its altar!

What is very interesting to us is the discovery of papyrus of 419 B.C.E. sent to the Jews of Elephantine containing rules on how to keep Passover. Who do you think sent this letter? The High Priest of Jerusalem? No. It was sent by King Darius of Persia! Here is a part of it:

. . . count 14 days of . . . Nisan and keep the Passover . . . Be clean and take heed. Do not work on the 15th day and on the 21st . . . drink no beer nor anything in which there is leaven . . . let it (leaven) not be seen among you . . .

Of course Darius did not know the laws of Passover. Clearly Jews close to him persuaded him to send these instructions. Why? In order to seal the laws with his authority. In that way the commandments of Torah could be kept in the same way throughout the Empire, from the Indus to Ethiopia.

In 410 B.C.E. the Egyptian priests of Khnum bribed the Persian Satrap to destroy the Jewish temple. Desperate, the Jews of Elephantine wrote to the Jewish authorities in Jerusalem for help.

We should not be surprised if Jerusalem was not too sympathetic. Sacrifices after all, were supposed to be offered only in Zion. In 408 the Jews of Elephantine appealed to the Persian Tirshatha of Judea, and, of all men, to the sons of Sanballat in Samaria. You can be sure they hinted at a bribe to these Samaritans.

So desperate were they, they even promised not to restore sacrifices if they could but rebuild their temple. By this they hoped to please both the Egyptians who worshipped almost every animal, as well as the priests of Jerusalem.

For a long time it was assumed the temple to Yahu was never rebuilt. Recent discoveries, known as the Brooklyn Papyri, however, tell us it was. We know it was in existence in December 402 B.C.E. The papyri speak of Yahu as "the God who dwells in Yeb (Elephantine) the fortress." Where a deity has his dwelling, a cult was in full operation. What happened to it eventually, is still unknown.

Activities

Questions

- Look up the description of the High Priest which is included in the Service of Yom Kippur. It was written about Simon the Just. Who do you think wrote it?
- In one place in the Torah we are commanded to keep the Sabbath because God created the universe in six days and rested on the seventh. In another place we are so commanded because God delivered us from slavery. Where are these two laws found? Why should two different reasons be offered?
- Explain how Ruth and Naamah are ancestresses of the Messiah? Find out what these two women are called in the Talmud? What might such a description reveal about the Rabbinical approach to converts?
- What is the Sabbatical Year? What purpose did it serve? Is it still observed? Should the Diaspora observe it? Can it?
- The first *Covenant* with Abraham was one which committed God. It was He Who would confer blessings on Abraham and his sons. Few commands were laid upon Abraham. Even circumcision was not so much an obligation as a sign. With Moses it is almost the opposite. The tribes accepted obligations. Of course, it is understood that the basis for this *Covenant* is the protection and support of God for Israel. But there are no additional commitments. Read *Joshua* XXIV. Upon whom did that *Covenant* rest heavily? Why did Joshua choose to renew the *Covenant* at Shechem?
- Read *Nehemiah* IX & X. Who assumed obligations at that Great Assembly?
- Who in Jewish history could view Israel's plight more clearly because he was somewhat of an outsider? Explain.
- What great Zionist leader who lived during the last 40 years of the last century and the very beginning of this century, was removed enough from the Jewish scene to see it with prophetic vision? Explain.

Readings for Students

Builders of Jerusalem, Hyman, J.P.S., 1960.
The New World Over Story Book, ed. Schloss and Epstein, Bloch Publishing Company.
(p. 234, Cupbearer to the King, by L. Spitz)
Worlds Lost and Found, Eisenberg and Elkins.

Readings for Teachers

The Biblical Archeologist Reader, Wright and Freedman, Anchor Books, Doubleday & Co., Garden City, N.Y., 1961.
(Vol. I, Chapter XI, New Light on the Elephantine Colony by Kraeling)
Ezra.
Nehemiah.
From Ezra to the Last of the Maccabees, Bickerman, Elias, Schocken Books, N.Y., 1962.
The Jews, ed. Finkelstein, Louis, J.P.S.
(Vol. I, *The Historical Foundations of Postbiblical Judaism,* by Bickerman, Elias)
Malachi.
The Jewish Community, Salo W. Baron, J.P.S., 1948.

Unit VII

And Nicanor set out from Jerusalem and pitched his camp in Bet-Horon, and the Syrian army met him there. And Judah encamped in Adasa with three thousand men, and Judah prayed and said:

"When the king's men uttered blasphemy, your angel went forth and struck down a hundred and eighty-five thousand of them. Crush this army before us today, in the same way . . ."

MACCABEES I VII:39–42

chapter 26 The Hellenistic Era

THE KINGDOM OF MACEDON WAS LESS than one fiftieth of the Persian Empire. Yet between 334–332 B.C.E., Alexander the Macedon defeated the Great King, Darius II and became master of his sprawling possessions. He would have extended his conquests beyond Persia into the Indus Valley (Punjab), had his soldiers not balked. They longed for home.

Alexander himself never returned to Macedon. He went back to Babylon which he considered his capital of the East. In the last year of his life 324–323, he divided his time between fortifying the frontiers of his enormous empire and planting the seeds of Greek civilization within the East. This civilization is known as Hellenism.

Alexander's victories went to his head. In 332 we find him in Egypt inquiring of the god, Ammon Ra, whether a common mortal like his father could have sired him.

Conquered people are usually dissatisfied. They long for a deliverer. Most of the former Satrapies welcomed Alexander as this deliverer. The Satrap in Memphis, for example, handed over the city without bloodshed. So too did most cities. Only Tyre and Gaza held out. Tyre which had resisted Nebuchadnezzar for 13 years, fell to Alexander in 7 months; Gaza in two.

Most of the meagre information about Alexander and the Jews is found in the Talmud and Josephus. That little is mainly legend. A few Greek and Roman sources are helpful, but not conclusive. The Talmud and Josephus tell much the same story:

While Alexander was besieging Tyre, he sent a message to the High Priest in Jerusalem demanding corn, men, and the tribute normally paid to Darius. The High Priest refused. He had taken an oath of allegiance to Darius, he said, and could not be false to it while the Great King was alive.

Determined to punish Jerusalem, Alexander and his army marched forth. The High Priest with an escort, came out to meet him. When Alexander saw the High Priest, he knelt down before him. His general was aghast. He had expected Alexander to execute the High Priest and to give Jerusalem over to the soldiers for spoils. How then, could he kneel before the enemy like a slave? Alexander explained that this High Priest was the same man who had appeared to him in a dream when he had still been in Macedon. It was his God who had promised him victory. Therefore, he was actually kneeling before the High Priest's God. With that he entered Jerusalem and offered sacrifices.

Most historians agree Alexander was never in Jerusalem. What gave rise to this legend was the fact that from Tyre, Alexander and his army moved south along the coast to Gaza and then to Egypt. As he went, so he returned. Which means that Alexander crossed over Palestinian soil twice. In view of this, how could he not have stopped in Jerusalem?

As with all legend, there is a kernel of truth. Since the former Satrapies acknowledged Alexander, it would have been strange, if not dangerous, had Judea not done the same. We have every right to conclude that the High Priest and the Elders did indeed, go out to some town on the coast to acclaim this new hero-king as he passed up or down Palestine.

Josephus tells us, that according to the Greek writer, Hecateus:

Alexander gave the Jews three cities of Samaria free of tax, in exchange for their friendship and loyalty . . .

We don't know the names of these cities. All we know is that the Samaritans revolted against Alexander, burning a Syrian governor alive. As a result, Alexander dealt Samaria a killing blow, and stationed a Macedonian colony of former soldiers there. Such a colony of veterans was called a cleruchy.

Alexander also granted Judea the right "to live according to their ancestral laws." This right did not originate with Alexander.

However, the phrase "to live according to their ancestral laws" probably did.

Jews recall Alexander with gratitude. Legend has it that all boys born in Judea for one whole year were named for him. Yet he was not showing Judea special favor with this privilege.

It was Alexander's policy to allow freedom of religion to all. He showed deep reverence for the gods of the lands he conquered. He made every effort to win over the hearts of his new subjects. Why? Perhaps to make them more willing to accept Hellenistic forms.

Ironically, Alexander himself, came under the influence of the East. He adopted its manners and dress. He began to award the best posts to Persians. In his attempt to merge West with East, he encouraged intermarriage. To ten thousand soldiers who wed native women, he gave gifts. He forced eighty foremost Macedonian officers to marry eighty noble Persian women in Susa. And that with Persian rites!

What might have developed had Alexander lived beyond his thirty-third year, no man can tell. His experiment in "brotherhood" seemed to fail. Immediately after his death, his officers divorced their Persian wives. Nevertheless East and West came together in certain ways eventually. We shall see how later.

Not even in death did Alexander return home. He was buried in Alexandria, the great Greek city he had founded in the Nile Delta.

He left no son. When asked who his heir would be, he was supposed to have said: "the best man." His Macedonian generals, known as Diadochi, tried to seize control of the whole or part of his empire. The two most important of these Diadochi, were Ptolemy and Seleucus. Though both laid claim to what is known as Coele Syria, they remained friends and allies until their deaths.

The territory of Coele Syria differed from period to period. At first it was simply the Persian Satrapy, Beyond the River. At the beginning of the Hellenistic period, it stretched from the Mountain of Lebanon to the Egyptian frontier, taking in the whole of Eretz Israel. At the end of this era, it will only be the Vale of Lebanon and places about Damascus.

Ptolemy declared himself King Ptolemy I Soter in 305 B.C.E. His kingdom included Egypt, Libya, the Aegean Islands, and the islands along the Red Sea coast. To protect Egypt against invasion from the north, he seized Coele Syria.

Seleucus became Seleucus I Nicator. He ruled over the largest part of Alexander's empire: all of Mesopotamia and Cilicia. He also needed Coele Syria: not only to protect Upper Syria from attack by Egypt, but also to expand southward. Because of his friendship with Ptolemy, he said he would not contest Coele Syria then.

He never contested it: neither then nor later. Ptolemy died in 282 B.C.E. Seleucus was assassinated a year later. After their deaths, however, the next Ptolemies and Seleucids fought for its possession. From 300–200 B.C.E. Coele Syria remained in Ptolemaic hands.

The Ptolemies, like the Pharaohs before them, controlled Egypt completely. Important posts went to their Macedonian favorites. But in Coele Syria it was different. There native sheiks of Transjordan and Syria governed colonies of Greek veterans, called cleruchies. These sheiks even resisted Egyptian agents. True, the Ptolemies could have punished them. But had they, on whom could they rely in case of war? And war over Coele Syria was a constant possibility.

Another reason for a more independent Syria and Judah was their ancient Phoenician and Philistine cities. They were strong enough to demand recognition as Greek cities or "poleis." (singular, polis)

Why should they want to be poleis? And what exactly did it mean to be a polis? First and foremost, it meant that the city had the same political structure as the poleis of Greece. Wealthy citizens known as the "demos" were their foundations. Their governing council, "the Boulé" was drawn from the demos. The Boulé controlled the financial, public, and religious affairs of the city.

Second, poleis looked alike. Building and shrines were of Greek architecture. Each contained a Gymnasium and Ephebeion, the chief educational institutions of poleis. Amphitheatres for dramatic productions and hippodromes for athletic contests were also vital centers. Remains of amphitheatres are found in Israel today.

Third, poleis acted as permanent centers of the Greek language. Fourth, they could mint their own local bronze coin, a very important privilege for merchants. And finally, many poleis either were or had become fortress cities.

Alexander encouraged the creation of these strongholds in order to support his empire. He settled veterans of his campaigns in them. Why? Because they were loyal to him. Such units, as we have learned, were called cleruchies. By their very presence, they kept the peace. The natives, however, hated and feared them. Their land was usually confiscated for these veterans. And they were completely at the mercy of these foreign soldiers.

Despite all these Greek forms and institutions, poleis had little influence over the masses. Wealthy natives may have aped Hellenic ways. But peasants clung to their ancient customs. Even the gods they worshipped remained the same, though some bore Greek names. In Apollonia, for example, Apollo was actually the Phoenician god, Reshef. In Ashdod and Ashkelon not even the names were changed. Dagon ruled in Ashdod; the goddess Ashtoret did in Ashkelon. Whatever Greek culture these poleis bred was of a feeble kind.

How could it be otherwise? The Greeks were either soldiers or farmers or adventurers: men who left their native lands to seek their fortunes. They represented if not the basest, certainly not the finest. Natives hardly met the best Greek minds or personalities.

For the hundred years that the Ptolemies controlled Coele Syria, the High Priest was the only mediator between the Jews and Egypt. He was also Prostates, the Greek title for tax collector.

About 242 B.C.E. the High Priest, Onias II, refused to hand over to Ptolemy Euergetes the taxes due him. Onias favored the Seleucids. Naturally, for it was Babylonian Jewry that supported the Temple faithfully. And Babylonia, of course, was part of the Seleucid empire. Babylonians and Judeans even spoke the same language: Aramaic. Onias hoped that Seleucus II, who had won a few victories over Ptolemy, would remain triumphant.

Ptolemy was furious. He threatened Judea with the most severe penalty: her division into cleruchies. He might have carried out this threat, had it not been for Joseph ben Tobiah.

Joseph was a nephew of Onias. The rift between the High Priest and King was a choice opportunity for him. First, he rushed from his estate in Transjordania to Jerusalem and urged Onias to remain loyal to Ptolemy. Then he sped to Egypt and made peace between the king and his uncle. Skillfully, Joseph endeared himself to Ptolemy until he was able to supplant Onias as Prostates. He did this by promising the king twice his usual income. All taxes above that sum would remain in his own pockets. You can see how profitable such an arrangement could be in greedy hands. And Joseph was among the greediest. He executed Elders of Ashkelon and Bet Shean (Scythopolis) when they refused to pay what he demanded.

Until now all power had been in the hands of the High Priest. Now the High Priest was forced to share that power with Joseph. For the Prostates, was, in fact, head of the civil government.

The rise of Joseph ben Tobiah signalled the rise of a new class of wealthy citizens who drew close to the Greeks. Joseph and his sons, known as Tobiads, influenced the course of Jewish history at this time, more than any other group of men. It is important to get to know them.

It seems rather certain that Joseph and his father, Tobiah, were descendants of the Tobiah of Nehemiah's day. Remember how Eliashib, the High Priest, gave that Tobiah a room in the Temple?

He must have been a Jew. Both he and his son, Jonathan, were sons-in-law of prominent Jewish families of Jerusalem. Perhaps you are thinking they were the aliens to whom Jews gave their daughters at that time. However, from the names, Tobiah and Jonathan, we know they worshipped Yahweh.

The Tobiah who lived now, 250 years later, was the head of a cleruchy in Transjordan. In a famous collection called the Zenon Papyri, a Greek describes himself as "one of Tobiah's people." This document was drawn up in "the citadel of the Lord of the Ammonites."

This same Tobiah sent rare animals to Ptolemy II, probably for his famous zoo at Alexandria, as well as slave girls to Ptolemy's treasurer. Since he married the High Priest's daughter, he most probably was of a priestly family. Priests, especially sons of Zadok, did not give their daughters to plain Israelites.

Joseph ben Tobiah was Prostates of Coele Syria for 22 years. He mingled with Greeks, ate at Ptolemy's table, and became involved with a Greek dancing girl. He might have continued as Prostates were it not for his son, Hyrcanus. As he had supplanted his uncle, Onias II, so Hyrcanus, the youngest of his eight sons, supplanted him.

So enraged were Joseph and his seven other sons, they tried to kill Hyrcanus in an ambush. Instead Hyrcanus slew two of his brothers.

This slaughter dismays us. What kind of men were these who could shed their own blood? History answers us. They were determined, self-confident, ruthless. Their ambition made them contemptuous of ancestral tradition.

Whatever wealth and power they acquired brought no benefit to Judeans. On the contrary, with the Tobiads the political power of Jerusalem was held more firmly in the hands of the rich. Which is one reason why only the upper circle of the Jew-

Map 6 Empire of Alexander After His Death
(300 to around 140 BCE)

ish community responded to Tobiad example. Hellenism, from the onset, was bound up with one social class: the wealthy.

These cheating and greedy tax collectors, these cruel and violent businessmen, were the spiritual fathers of the Jewish Hellenizing movement. It was not their love for the Greek theatre or for the other arts that motivated them. Neither was it their dedication to the Greek forms of education found in Gymnasium and Ephebeion. It was money, and the privileges that money bought them that lured.

It should not surprise us they wanted to make Jerusalem a polis. They craved a thriving commercial metropolis. If they could mint their own money, as the other thirty poleis of Palestine did, how much simpler it would be to carry on trade. Besides, if Jerusalem could become a Ptolemais or better still, an Antioch, it would receive special privileges from its royal namesake.

By 175 B.C.E. these Hellenizing Jews will succeed in converting Jerusalem into a Greek city. The Syrian Greek king, Antiochus IV Epiphanes, will grant the necessary permission. Eventually, he will do more: he will outlaw the ancestral laws of Judea, something no king before him had ever done.

Let us look at Antiochus' immediate family. Between 200–198, his father Antiochus III (the Great), defeated Ptolemy IV. Except for Hyrcanus, the Prostates, almost all Judea rejoiced. Simon the Just, son of Onias II, rejoiced, because as High Priest he was concerned with Babylonian Jewry. The Tobiads, because they wanted to be on the winning side. Besides, they hated Ptolemy, the patron of their brother, Hyrcanus.

Judea's joy was justified. Antiochus the Great was very generous. He supplied the Temple with its needs, rebuilt Jerusalem, aided its population and redeemed prisoners of war from slavery. He also lightened the tax burden, and most important, granted Jews the right to live according to their ancestral laws. According to *II Maccabees,* his son, Seleucus IV, was also generous to the Temple.

We can recognize many of the benefits the Persian kings had bestowed. We see the same partiality to the Temple. And then there is that vital phrase "to live according to their ancestral laws."

By now the ancestral laws included not only Torah, but a sizeable code of Oral Law. This code grew as Scribes applied Torah to the needs of the people.

How then, we must ask, could Antiochus IV have interfered in the domestic affairs of Judea? How could he demand, as he would, worship of Zeus Olympios? What made him try to force the sacrifice of swine upon the Jews? In short, why did he choose to ignore the ancestral laws held sacred, not only by father and brother before him, but by all since Cyrus.

The fact is, Antiochus IV would never

have dreamed of attacking Judaism had it not been for the Tobiads. The whirlwind that was to toss Judea about under Antiochus IV was set in motion by Jews who sought to live as Greeks. We call them Hellenists. It was they who tempted Antiochus. With what? Money, of course.

Antiochus IV went further than they had anticipated. Clearly they had misjudged this king. And more, they misjudged the people of Judea.

Let us see how all this came about.

Activities

Questions

1. What are the benefits of one civilization for mankind?
2. What are the benefits of many civilizations?
3. Do you think cultures and civilizations should be fused into one?
4. Support your point of view

Projects

1. Draw a separate map of Coele Syria.
2. Draw a map of the Ptolemaic empire under Ptolemy I.
3. Draw a map of the Seleucid empire under Seleucid I.
4. See if you can find out the meaning of the following names the king of Egypt and Syria used: Soter, Nicanor, Epiphanes, Euergetes, Philadelphus, and Philopator, Philometor; Theos, Eupator, Callinicus, Physcon, and Sidetes.

Readings for Students

The Book of Maccabees, transl. by Tedesche, Sidney, Prayer Book Press.

Readings for Teachers

Hellenistic Civilization and the Jews, Tcherikover, Victor, J.P.S., 1959.
The Rise and Fall of the Judean State, Zeitlin, Solomon, J.P.S., 1962.
The Maccabees, Bickerman, Elias, Schocken Library, 1947.
Antiquities, Josephus, Leavitt & Co., N.Y.

chapter 27 Pre-Hasmonean Period

THE SOURCES FOR THIS AND THE NEXT four chapters are as follows: *I Maccabees; II Maccabees; Daniel; Ecclesiasticus; The Antiquities of the Jews* by Josephus; and some Greek and Roman writers.

Daniel is part of the Tanach, or the Canon. *Maccabees* and *Ecclesiasticus* are not. Therefore, they are non-canonical. *Daniel* is written in the spirit of prophecy. But its language is obscure and difficult. Modernists believe it presents a history of the Seleucids and Ptolemies leading up to the persecution of the Jews by Antiochus IV. There are four visions in *Daniel.* Each represents the end of one heathen empire: Babylonian; Median; Persian; and Hellenistic. Their defeats are to bring on the kingdom of God.

The author of *I Maccabees* was probably a court chronicler. Like most court chroniclers, he wrote flatteringly of his patron: a Hasmonean prince. Therefore, his chief hero was the founder of his patron's family: Mattathias.

The author of *II Maccabees* was an admirer of Judah Maccabee. His book praises this hero.

Of the historian, Josephus, we shall speak later. Suffice it to say, he was an admirer of royalty, wealth, and power. For example, he wrote glowingly of the Tobiads.

What is tellingly absent is an author concerned with the people. Of course, all of these Books speak of the problems of Judea. But none saw the masses as the moving force it was. Only in Ben Sira's *Ecclesiasticus,* do we at least meet a representative of the people. And he was not of their economic or social class. He was the High Priest, Simon the Just, the first of three Simons of this period. In the preceding chapter, he, like his father, was concerned with Babylonian Jewry. Another Simon shall appear in this chapter.

Simon the Just inherited his position from his father, Onias II. Oniads were descended from Zadok. Simon ruled Judea with the help of a council called a Gerousia. This council, like the Greek Boulé, was made up of aristocrats.

There is no doubt the Tobiads sat on the Gerousia. Joseph was Prostates, the wealthiest man of Judea, and a cousin of Simon. Unlike the Tobiads, Simon the Just was a devout Jew. Indeed, he was as much Scribe as Priest.

Among the Scribes of the Sanctuary

there was an elite corp: men more dedicated to Torah and more scrupulous about observances. They were called Hasidim. Simon the Just was the head of these Hasidim.

Simon read the signs of his age correctly. He understood the ruthlessness of his Tobiad cousins. He foresaw the danger of Hellenization. There was only one way to combat this alien force: with Torah, the Law of the Living God.

As leaders before him had done, Simon called a Great Assembly. The decisions taken at this gathering were so important, it became known as *The* Great Assembly, *Ha*Kneset Hagedolah.

The most revolutionary reform was the emphasis placed on scholarship. Wealth and power had always been the qualifications for membership on the Gerousia. Now a new requirement was demanded: knowledge of the law. This does not mean members like Tobiads were expelled. They were too powerful for that. But wherever possible, Simon appointed scholars. Farmers, craftsmen, could sit on this council as long as they were men of wisdom. The name "Gerousia" was changed to "Bet Din Hagadol."

The second act of The Great Assembly was the decree ending prophecy. Prophets received the direct word of God. If scholars were now to guide the people, they could hardly compete with revelation: the direct word of God. Hence, while no one could deny the *possibility* of prophecy, this legal declaration had to be made if the Scribes and their heirs were to be recognized as the true leaders.

Prophetic works were collected and edited. Probably a standard text was produced. This would explain why copies of these books were so alike.

The third reform was directed at the priests. They were required to recite the Shema every morning before the Sacrificial Service. This was a very radical demand. As you know, there had always been a difference between priests and most prophets. Words of penitence, Hosea had preached, could substitute for animals. The Scribes inherited this prophetic point of view. They too, preferred prayer, the offering of the heart, over sacrifice. The priests, of course resented any change.

With this recitation of the Shema, the Scribes accomplished what the prophets could not. Perhaps because Simon who led them, was the High Priest himself. For even if he didn't introduce each reform, he certainly supported them.

But what was so revolutionary about priests reciting the Shema? Both the praying and the prayer. That the priests prayed with the identical words an ordinary Israelite uttered, made them as much petitioners as laymen. God was no nearer to them, than to any Jew. And the prayer itself challenged them. Let us examine its text:

Hear O Israel, the Lord who is our God, is one.

We see that God is not only our God, but God of all. He was not exclusive to Israel. Nor did His glory fill the Temple alone. It filled the universe.

Then the Shema called upon man to love God:

And you shall love the Lord your God with all your heart, and with all your soul, and with all your might.

The source of love was the whole man. It had nothing to do with ritual, nor even with Temple ritual.

Furthermore, the Shema plainly emphasized Torah, its study and its teaching, the principles of Scribal life:

And these words (of Torah) which I command you this day shall be upon your heart. And you shall teach them diligently to your children, and you shall talk of them, when you sit in your house, when you walk on the way, when you lie down, and when you rise up.

The last three verses:

And you shall bind them as a sign upon your hands, and they shall be for frontlets between your eyes, and you shall write them upon the doorposts of your house and upon your gates.

spoke directly to the individual. The priest was not involved.

The Shema was taken over by the Synagogue. In fact, The Great Assembly, arranged the order for the daily and Sabbath services of the Synagogue.

The last act of The Great Assembly was to call on the judges of the towns and villages to be teachers of the young. Simon the Just is remembered by the following saying:

On three things the world stands: on Torah, on Service and on deeds of loving kindness.

Does it surprise you that his High Priest put study (Torah) before ritual of the Temple (Service)?

Onias III succeeded his father, Simon the Just. Unlike his father and grandfather, this Onias was pro-Ptolemaic. By this time, Alexandria had become the most important Jewish community of the Diaspora. And Alexandria was in Egypt.

Like all temples of antiquity, the Temple of Jerusalem served as a bank. Since Temples were sacred, it was assumed everything under its roof was sacred. Thus Judeans kept their money in it for safekeeping. Hyrcanus also wanted this privilege. And Onias III accepted his deposit.

This enraged the brothers of Hyrcanus. Besides, they disapproved of Onias' Ptolemaic loyalty. They decided to take action against him.

Simon, the second Simon, who might have been a Tobiad brother, was overseer of the Temple. He demanded Onias appoint him supervisor of the city's markets. This would have given him control of the economic life of Jerusalem. Onias refused.

Simon, thereupon, convinced the governor of Coele Syria, that the Temple contained great wealth which should belong to Seleucus IV. The wealth to which he referred, undoubtedly, belonged to Hyrcanus.

Seleucus was in great need of money. His father Antiochus (III) the Great, had been defeated in 190 B.C.E. by Rome. Hence Syria had to pay a heavy tribute each year. Rome also held Seleucid hostages, and prohibited them from using elephants in any future war.

This last condition will be violated by the next two Seleucid kings. But while Rome might overlook elephants, it never ignored tribute.

Thus this very Seleucus IV who had been praised by *I Maccabees,* for his generosity to the Temple, now sent his agent, Heliodorus, to demand Temple funds. Onias protested. The Temple was sacred. Depositors trusted in it.

Exactly what took place we don't know. Only legend surrounds this incident. What is a fact, is that Heliodorus neither received nor seized Temple funds. *II Maccabees* tells us that when Heliodorus returned to Seleucus IV, he was asked what manner of man was fit to be sent once again to Jerusalem. This was the reply:

If you have any enemy or conspirator . . . send him there and you shall receive him back well whipped, that is if he even escape with his life . . .

The Tobiads, however, did not give up. They accused Onias of plotting against Seleucus. Violence between Tobiads and Oniads became so wide-spread, civil war threatened. The High Priest rushed to Antioch, capital of Syria, to plead for help against the Tobiads.

This was a serious error. In leaving Jerusalem, he gave his enemies a clear field. The Tobiads were not slow to take advantage of his absence. They sent Onias' brother, Jason (Joshua) to Antioch. Jason persuaded the new king, Antiochus IV Epiphanes, to appoint him to the High Priesthood in place of his brother. He promised Antiochus, no doubt with the approval of the Tobiads, 140 more talents of silver than the sum Onias paid. For another 150 talents, he bought two significant privileges. He could build a Gymnasium and Ephebeion. And he could draw up a list for a demos of Jerusalem. With these two favors, Jerusalem in 175 B.C.E. became the Greek polis, Antioch at Jerusalem.

You should remember that the demos (the citizens) and the Boulé (the council) were the props of a polis' political structure. Whom do you suppose Jason registered as citizens? Of course, aristocrats. Thus the demos was made up of upper class alone. As for the Boulé, all he had to do was to expel the scholars Simon the

Just had appointed to the Bet Din Hagadol.

The Gymnasium built on the Temple Mount itself, was an essential part of every polis. Wealthy young priests abandoned the Temple for the Gymnasium. Like Greeks, they wrestled and raced naked. They also attended the Ephebeion, wearing the broad-brimmed hat of the god Hermes.

The authors of both *I* and *II Maccabees* cited both these institutions as the outstanding features of Jason's achievements. Why? Because only their graduates could be citizens, eligible for demos and Boulé.

In addition Jason obtained permission to live according to the laws of the Gentiles (Greeks). Thus, while he did not deny Torah, he did diminish the ancestral law of Judea. He can be considered, therefore, the actual founder of the polis, Antioch at Jerusalem. Antiochus IV, for whom it was named, was its patron.

This was not, you must bear in mind, a new city. It was the same city of Jerusalem. Only now it was an official polis. To guard and protect it, Antiochus settled a garrison of soldiers in a fortress in Jerusalem. But they did not constitute a cleruchy. They did not confiscate native land, nor did they press their will upon Jerusalem with force.

In what way was Antioch at Jerusalem different from Jerusalem? Was it because the High Priest was not the head of a Bet Din Hagadol, but of a Boulé? Or was it that a new citizen body, a demos of aristocrats, controlled the city? No. What made An-

tioch at Jerusalem unique, was that the demos, if it wished, could abolish the laws of Torah.

Did it? Not in Jason's time. True, the customs of the Gymnasium were foreign to Judaism. But they are nowhere prohibited in the Torah. And while the hat of Hermes could be a sign of loyalty to a pagan god, there was certainly no cult of Hermes in Jerusalem.

Nor was the Temple cult touched. Even Jewish envoys to athletic games at Tyre did not donate money to Tyre's god (Melkart-Heracles) as was the custom. Instead they asked that the money be used for ship building.

It is clear that though Jason and his party wanted to be like the Greeks in every way, they were not yet ready to abandon their religious life. What, we must ask, did they gain? Exactly what they wanted. *I Maccabees* tells us their goal:

Let us make a covenant with the Gentiles about us: for since we have been different from them, we have found many evils.

Now they were no longer different. They were allies of the Seleucids. They governed themselves locally. They struck bronze coins for local trade. They were linked to other poleis, especially in commerce.

But Jason had outsmarted himself. For if Jerusalem was to be like Greek poleis, the

High Priest had to be like Greek priests. And Greek priests were just local agents of the polis, controlled by the demos. Jason, too, the Tobiads concluded, should be controlled. He was not that reliable. He was still faithful to the letter of Torah, if not to the spirit. He refused to hand over Temple funds to Antiochus, their patron. In fact, he must be dismissed.

They appointed a new High Priest: Menelaus, brother of the second Simon. How? By bribing the King and Syrian officials with Temple silver.

Jason refused to step down. Civil war broke out. Though Menelaus was triumphant, he lost many followers. Even Jews who had flirted with Hellenism under Jason, were repelled by Menelaus. The great mass of people detested him. He had dared to lay hands on Temple property.

Menelaus had to travel to Antioch to explain the disorders in Jerusalem. As soon as he left, the people rose up. They killed his brother, and defeated his army.

On his return, he routed the people. But he could not drive out their hatred. Neither for him, nor for his patron, Antiochus IV Epiphanes: Antiochus the manifest god. Some wits changed Epiphanes to Epimanes. Epimanes means insane. Certainly he was not normal.

At times he went about disguised as a commoner; at other times, in royal garments. He distributed either gold or pebbles. He once poured a jar of oil over public bathers to enjoy the sight of men slipping and falling over themselves. He would appear at parties uninvited, act in theatrical performances, dancing ridiculously.

For all of that, he was a wily ruler. He defeated Egypt twice. And he behaved shrewdly toward a threatening Rome.

Why should the Jews have hated him? Because he tried to destroy Judaism. Not at the beginning of his reign, but gradually. If we ask why, two reasons are offered. First, that he wanted to make his whole empire worship one god: Zeus Olympios. And second, that he was an ardent Hellenist. His ambition we are told, was to unite all inhabitants of his lands into a single body by imposing the same Hellenistic civilization upon them.

Neither is true. When Antioch at Jerusalem was established, it was not required to worship the Greek Zeus Olympios. Nor did he try to make everyone live as one people. He let Babylonian priests copy their ancient religious texts while he was burning Torah scrolls in Jerusalem. He didn't even persecute Samaritans who kept Shabbat.

Why then did he impose a pagan cult upon Jerusalem alone? Why did he go so far? The fact is his un-Seleucid conduct was a reaction to fierce Jewish opposition. Let us see how it came about.

Desperate for money for his Egyptian campaigns, and his tribute to Rome, he looted the Temple. He even stripped the gold from its walls. He was not then especially vicious. He had spoiled the treasuries of many temples. But this did not soften the pious towards him.

In 168 a false rumor swept Jerusalem: Antiochus was dead! Immediately Jason swooped down from Transjordan with 1000 men. Menelaus was unable to withstand him. He took refuge in the city's citadel.

We would expect *II Maccabees* to be delighted. True, they had no love for Jason. But Menelaus, they loathed. Yet to our amazement, it is Jason who is denounced:

"He burnt the gate of the Temple. . . . He shed innocent blood."

Surely this is odd. Are Menelaus and his Hellenizers the "innocent blood"? Of course not. It can only be that after Jason defeated Menelaus, he attacked Jerusalemites. Theirs was the "innocent blood."

The Jerusalemites triumphed. They expelled Jason from the holy city. They did away with Antioch at Jerusalem. They reinstated the ancestral laws. All this occurred while other parts of the Seleucid empire were threatened.

Little wonder Antiochus crushed Jerusalem and her inhabitants. His fear finally drove him to build a fortress upon the very Temple Mount: the Akra. In it, he settled a cleruchy!

Jewish property was confiscated. Jewish men and women were at the mercy of a Syrian garrison. But worse, the gods of these veterans were installed in their Holy Temple: Baal Shamen, lord of heaven; Dushara, god of wines; Anat, goddess of war. . . . And their priestesses of Tammuz practised ugly cults within the sacred walls!

Being orientals, the Syrians respected local gods, indeed, served them. They identified Yahweh with their own Baal Shamen. Menelaus, no doubt, continued to act as High Priest to Yahweh.

Judeans could not bear to behold this pollution. Led by Hasidim, they abandoned Jerusalem. A year after the arrival of the cleruchy, Antiochus issued his final decrees. He forbade the worship of Yahweh. Anyone possessing a Torah scroll or observing her mitzvot, would be crucified. Why? Antiochus tells us:

. . . in order to force the Jews to transgress the laws of their fathers and not to live according to God's commandments.

The Temple was renamed for Zeus Olympios. High places and altars were built throughout Judea and swine sacrificed upon them. On the 25th day of Kislev 167 B.C.E. sacrifices were offered upon an idol altar which was placed upon the altar of God. This idol altar was known as the "abomination of desolation."

In caves about the countryside, Hasidim and Judeans hid. They would not obey Antiochus. But neither did they rise up against him. There was no one leader to raise the banner of active revolt.

Nevertheless, we read that among Hasidim who fled the city there was:

Judah, who is also called Maccabeus, with nine others . . . (He) withdrew himself and with his company kept himself alive in the mountains after the manner of wild beasts; and they continued feeding on such poor herbs as grew there, that they might not be partakers of the threatened pollution.

(II Maccabees V:27)

Obviously Judah Maccabee was a Hasid. But we shall not hear of him again until 166 B.C.E.

Activities

Questions

1. Why should priests have resented a change in the Temple Service?
2. List at least four leaders of Israel who called together a Great Assembly. Give the details of two of these Great Assemblies, including aim, place, accomplishments.
3. The Shema is recited on six different occasions. Can you name four of them?
4. What do you think happened to Heliodorus? Now look up II Maccabees, and see if you are right.
5. This period was one of upheaval. Strong men pursued their own aim even if it meant destroying members of their own families. Cite two families whose members were enemies. What did they do that was the same.
6. Find the verse that contains Hosea's famous message about words being a substitute for sacrifice.

Readings for Students

Selected readings from I and II Maccabees.
(Legend of Heliodorus, II Maccabees III:7. Also in IV Maccabees, same incident with Apollonius in place of Heliodorus. Chap. IV:1–15).

Readings for Teachers

I and II Maccabees.
Daniel.
Ecclesiasticus.
The Jews, ed. Finkelstein, Louis, J.P.S.
(Vol. I, pp. 70–114, The Historical Foundation of Postbiblical Judaism, by Bickerman, Elias)

chapter 28 Hasmonean Period

IT WAS THE CUSTOM OF THE OFFICERS of Antiochus IV to set up altars in the market place of Judea, and to sacrifice a pig: an animal expressly forbidden to the Jew. They would then command the people to worship and eat of the offering. Many refused, and were crucified. The author of *Daniel* was very pessimistic. There was no hope from man, he wrote:

They shall stumble by the sword and by flame, by captivity and by spoil many days.   (XI:33)

In the winter of 166 B.C.E., agents of Antiochus came to Modin, a small village near Lydda on the road from Jerusalem to Jaffa. The altar was erected. The flesh of swine roasted. The Jews called upon to come forth and worship.

Among the Judeans stood the priest, Mattathias, grandson of Hasmon. He and his sons were known as Hasmoneans. They were not descended from Zadok. It is among his five sons: Simon, Eleazar, Judah, John and Jonathan, we find the third Simon of this Unit.

As a Jew did come forward to obey, Mattathias leaped from the crowd and slew the apostate. He then killed Syrian Greek officers, and shattered the altar. To his fellow Jews he cried:

"Whoever is zealous for the Law, and keeps the *Covenant,* let him come with me!"

Together with his sons and followers, Mattathias, abandoned home and village, and fled into the mountains. *Daniel* was wrong. Help from a man had come. Judea had her leader at last.

There were many already in the deserts and mountains. It was the way ancient people solved problems. If a peasant could not pay his taxes, or a merchant his debts, they ran away. Land was not cultivated. Harvests were not reaped. Obviously no government could operate under such conditions. For without harvests or trade, who could pay taxes?

Naturally, Antiochus' soldiers pursued these refugees. Quickly they learnt that if they attacked on Shabbat, Jews would offer no resistance. They would rather die, than fight on this sacred day.

Mattathias realized how serious such passivity was:

If we all do as our brothers have done, and do not fight against the Gentiles for our lives and our Laws, they will soon destroy us from off the earth   (*I Maccabees XI:27*)

Do not attack on Shabbat, he continued. But neither be slaughtered on Shabbat. Mattathias had no right to issue such a decree. He was not a High Priest. Yet Jews including Hasidim obeyed him.

While Mattathias and his guerrillas attacked Syrians, they focussed on Hellenists. They tore down their altars. They circumcised their infants. They assaulted them physically.

When Mattathias died, he named Judah military leader, and Simon, adviser on all other matters. Judah's other name "Maccabee," is supposed to be an acrostic. This means each of its letters מכבי is the first letter of each word of the sentence: "מי כמוך באלים יי"   "Who is like unto You among the gods, Yahweh"?

Actually, Maccabee comes from the Hebrew maccaba, which means "hammerhead." Obviously this was the shape of his skull. It was the custom, in those days, to name men because of physical features. A Ptolemy's brother was called "Physcon," "Fat-Paunch." To Antiochus VIII, the name, "Grypus," "Hook-nose," was added.

Although Judah Maccabee had no training in the art of war, he had an abundance of faith, courage, and natural military talent. He drove out Apollonius, the governor of Jerusalem, together with his army.

Thereupon, the governor of Syria, advanced upon Jerusalem with an army of mercenaries. Mercenaries, no matter how experienced, do not fight for home and country. Judah and his men did. And furthermore, as Judah said (*I Maccabees Chap. III*):

Victory in battle does not depend on the size of an army, but rather on strength that comes from Heaven . . . We are fighting for our lives and our Laws. He Himself will shatter them before us; but as for you, be not afraid.

As he spoke, so it was. Judah routed the Syrians at Bet-Horon. 800 were killed. The rest fled to the coast. Judah was now a serious menace to Antiochus.

What was Antiochus to do? Not only Judea, but Parthia in Babylonia, was rebelling. Against which should he move? Against the richer prize, of course: against Parthia. He left his general, Lysias in charge in Antioch, and set forth to war. Lysias, in turn, sent 40,000 infantrymen and 7000 cavalry against Judea.

Who could challenge such power? Certainly not an insignificant horde of guerrilla fighters. So certain were the Syrians of victory, they invited slave-traders to accompany them. You can almost hear the slavers rattling their chains behind this huge army.

Judah Maccabee prepared his men at Mizpeh, an ancient sanctuary. First he sent away those who had just married, or had just built a home, or just planted a vineyard, or were just plain timid. Doesn't this seem odd? Especially when he needed more men. But Judah was a Hasid. The Torah had to be heeded wherever possible. And it is the Torah which excuses these men from war.

He then displayed Torot upon which the Syrians had drawn idols. After this he spread out priestly garments which could not be worn in a polluted Temple. You can imagine what this did to these freedom fighters. After fasting and praying, they set out for Emmaus, 22 miles west of Jerusalem.

Judah encamped there, opposite the foe. Gorgias, one of the Syrian generals, crept out at night to take Judah by surprise. But Judah's spies alerted him. Instead of waiting for Gorgias, Judah swooped down upon the rest of the Syrians.

He slew 3000 and sent the rest flying to the plains of Judea as far away as the coast. He then put the enemy camp to the torch.

Gorgias returned wearily the next morning. To his horror, he found Judah waiting for him. Without so much as a blow, Gorgias and his men fled.

The victory was complete. The booty left behind was enormous. It included the money the slavers had brought with them. There was, as you can imagine, a sweet justice in seizing it. The gold, after all, was the purchase price for their bodies.

This defeat was an immediate threat to the Seleucids. If these untrained Jews could beat the sophisticated army of Antiochus, the whole empire might explode. For national deliverers like Judah had arisen in other provinces. There was Zipoetes in Bithynia, Mithridates in Pontus, Arsaces in Parthia, and Ariarathes in Cappadocia.

Lysias himself now took to the field. With 60,000 infantry, 5000 cavalry, and despite Rome's prohibition, with elephants. Elephants were like our tanks.

Instead of attacking Jerusalem from the north, he descended along the coast. He bypassed the hilly regions, and encamped at Bet-Zur, twenty miles south of Jerusalem. To no avail. Judah, without cavalry and elephants defeated him, slaying 5000.

Lysias offered peace terms. But to Menelaus and the Boulé! Surely this was strange. Neither Menelaus nor his associates had attacked Lysias. On the contrary, they were his allies. But Lysias could not bring himself to negotiate with Judah, a common rebel. Besides, he wasn't interested in Judah. It was Judah's followers he wanted to entice.

What did he offer? Permission to former "rebels" to return home; religious freedom; and amnesty. Jews would be permitted to use their own food and to observe their own laws. However, whoever would avail himself of this, had to do so within about ten days: until March 29, 164 B.C.E.

Why should Lysias have sued for peace? After all to lose 5000 out of 65,000 hardly crippled him. No, it was trouble back in Antioch that he feared.

Antiochus IV had lost many battles in the Upper Lands of his kingdom, and died there. Before his death he had appointed a general, Philip, to be guardian to his young son, Antiochus V as well as regent for the empire.

This was a direct blow at Lysias. He had been named to these posts. To stop Philip, Lysias had to rush back to Antioch. He did. Six months later, Judah captured Jerusalem. Menelaus and his men took refuge in the Akra. Some fled to Edom.

On the 25th day of Kislev, 164 B.C.E., exactly three years after the "abomination of desolation" had been set up on the altar of God, the Temple was rededicated. Thus Hanukah, which means dedication, entered the Jewish calendar. Not only Temple, but the whole city was purified. The poorer priests, those who had remained faithful to Torah, were allowed to officiate.

The next important step was to restore Torah as the constitution of Judea. On the 24th of Av, Jewish courts were reestablished. All Torot were brought out from their secret places. We may be sure the Hasidim were reinstated as interpreters of Law.

The Boulé once more became a Bet Din Hagadol. Hellenists were expelled. Probably those removed by Jason were now reappointed. The victory was a victory of the lower classes.

This government of Judah Maccabee was a shock, not only to Syria, but to the Greek cities of Palestine. They had co-operated all along with Antiochus. They had even tried to force Jews to worship the pagan gods of their poleis. Now, in anger and fear they intensified the persecutions of their Jewish neighbors.

Judah came to the aid of these Jews. He fortified Bet-Zur against Edom. He crossed the Jordan and destroyed cities in Gilead. He captured Hebron and Marissa, attacked Ashdod, Jaffa, and Yavneh. He would have assaulted Bet-Shean, had not the Jews of that polis (Scythopolis) testified in favor of their pagan neighbors. Simon too, rescued Jews, especially in the Galilee.

Judah and his brothers regarded the Syrian Greeks not only as enemies, but as "worshippers of heathen gods." They, therefore, shattered pagan shrines wherever possible.

Judah Maccabee became a symbol of heroism to Judea. Since the days of Zedekiah there had been neither army nor independent ruler in Judea. Now an army of peasants had been created that adored its leader. Their love was shared by the Jews of towns and villages. Indeed, Judah was to become a model for all freedom fighters. During the middle ages he would be a symbol of knighthood. In the square in Nuremberg, Germany, his statue is one of nine knights-errant: three Jews; three Christians; and three pagans.

The Hellenists, in the meantime, remained behind the walls of the Akra. For two years there was no help from Syria. However, in 162, Lysias bestirred himself.

This time he descended with 100,000 infantry, 20,000 cavalry, and thirty-two war elephants. To boost the morale of his men, he took the young king, Antiochus V with him. Before such might Judah had to abandon the fortress at Bet-Zur and to retreat behind the walls of Jerusalem.

To complicate Judah's situation, refugees swarmed into Jerusalem. And the Sabbatical year, when Jews are not allowed to farm, made food scarce. Starvation was proving a mightier weapon than elephants.

Help came again through Lysias' enemy, Philip. This Syrian general was marching against Antioch. Once more Lysias had to hurry home.

As before, he had to sue for peace. Only now he had to deal with Judah. We don't know the details of the armistice. We do know the results. It is in the form of a letter from the young Antiochus V to Lysias:

Antiochus the King greets his brother, Lysias. Now that our father has ascended to the gods (died), we desire that all the inhabitants of the state should devote themselves quietly and peacefully to their affairs, and as we have heard that the Jews are not in accord with our father's command compelling them to live in the spirit of the Greeks . . . Therefore our decision is: To restore to them the Temple and to permit them to live according to the customs of their fathers . . .

But what, you may ask, did this document accomplish? Judah had already conquered Jerusalem. He had abolished the rule of Menelaus and his Boulé. Torah was once more the law of the land.

It confirmed every act of Judah Maccabee. It abolished the polis Antioch at Jerusalem after 13 years of existence. More, it prohibited Syrians from setting up pagan shrines in the Temple. In short, it restored the Temple to the Jews.

We may be sure the Akra and the cleruchy ceased to exist as a political unit. From 167, the Akra had actually *been* the polis, Antioch at Jerusalem. Now in 162, the lands confiscated for the soldiers must have been restored to their former owners.

The soldiers, however, remained. For Judea remained within the Seleucid empire. No one, including Judah, dreamed of political independence from Syria.

What was more crucial was the civil war between Menelaus and Judah. The Syrian government had to decide who was the most dependable. By now, it was obvious to Lysias, that Menelaus was a weak reed. Nothing he had promised had been fulfilled. Instead, strife had torn Judea. One Syrian army after another had been humiliatingly defeated.

Furiously, Lysias turned on Menelaus. He hauled him to Antioch. From there he was sent to Beroea (Aleppo) and suffocated in a pit of ashes.

Still Lysias could not come to terms with Judah. In his eyes he was no more than a lowly bandit. How could he allow him to become High Priest?

He, therefore, appointed Alcimus (formerly Jakim) of the Oniad family. *II Maccabees* describes Alcimus as one "who had of his own will contaminated himself in the period of disturbances." In other words, he was a Hellenist.

Alcimus could hardly be acceptable to Judah. However, it seems he was to Hasidim. As far as they were concerned, there was no sense in prolonging the war. Torah was once more the law of the land. They were its interpreters. True, Alcimus had polluted himself. But at least, he was of Zadok: the legal house of Aaron.

After all Judah had done for Judea, it is a bitter fact that Hasidim and other Jews deserted him now. Just how badly these Hasidim misjudged Alcimus became apparent later. He was to execute sixty of them.

While Lysias might appoint Alcimus he could not install him. Judah refused to let him even approach the altar. Alcimus appealed to the new king: Demetrius I, a son of Seleucus IV.

Demetrius I had seized the throne, putting both Lysias and the young Antiochus V to death. He was hardly one to permit rebellious Judeans to depose a High Priest chosen by his government. He sent, Nicanor, an arrogant general to Judea.

Again civil war raged. Jews, even Hasidim, fought with Nicanor. Because of these Jews, Nicanor could not attack Judah on Shabbat. What an about-face this was! Four years ago a Jew who observed Shabbat was crucified by pagans. Now pagans came to heel because of Shabbat. But worse, brothers were not only fighting brothers, they were raising their swords against their own deliverer, Judah Maccabee.

On the 13th of Adar, 161, Judah smashed Nicanor's army. Alcimus fled to Antioch. In order to strengthen himself against Demetrius, Judah sent emissaries to Rome. A treaty of friendship was signed. Both agreed to assist each other if either were attacked. Rome promptly commanded Demetrius to live at peace with Judea.

This warning had an opposite effect. Demetrius moved swiftly. But seven weeks after the death of Nicanor, he sent Bacchides, another general, with 20,000 infantry and 2000 cavalry against Judah.

By now, Judah had only 800 men. His friends advised him not to face Bacchides. He too knew he could not win. Nevertheless he replied:

Let it not be so that I should do this thing, to flee before them. And if our time has come, let us die manfully for our brother's sake and not leave a cause or reproach against our glory.

(I Maccabees IX:7)

He died in battle. Ten miles north of Jerusalem, his army was routed. His brothers, Simon and Jonathan, must have snatched his body from the field. They buried him in the tomb of his father at Modin.

Had Bacchides not executed Judah's followers, Syria might have ruled Judea in peace. For Bacchides did not abolish the ancestral laws. Nor did he convert the Temple into a pagan shrine. But he did take revenge. Consequently, the masses rallied to Simon and Jonathan.

Bacchides returned to Judea in 158. This time his army was trapped between the two Hasmonean brothers. He was lucky Jonathan accepted his truce. According to its terms, Jonathan was recognized as leader of his own men. But he was not appointed High Priest, nor permitted to live in Jerusalem.

When war broke out in Antioch between Demetrius I and a pretender, Alexander Balas, both wooed Jonathan. Why? Because it was now clear that only Hasmoneans could command Judean loyalty.

Demetrius allowed Jonathan to draft men, equip an army, and take back Jewish hostages still held in the Akra. Not to be outdone, Alexander Balas addressed Jonathan thus: "King Alexander to his brother, Jonathan, greetings." He appointed Jonathan High Priest, bestowing upon him the title "Friend of the king."

On Sukkot, 152, Jonathan appeared in the Temple dressed in the robes of the High Priest. With this the civil war between the Hasmoneans and the Hellenizers came to an end. It was 15 years since Judah Maccabee had rallied the rebels, and 23 since Jerusalem had become the polis, Antioch at Jerusalem.

Judah was now a political power. The Tobiads had dreamed of such a role for Judea, but not under the control of men of the ordinary priesthood. Yet it was these men who were to wrest complete political independence from the Seleucids. It was these same men who were to establish a new dynasty.

Activities

Questions

1. Why did the Hasidim obey Mattathias, and fight back on Shabbat?
2. Look up *Deuteronomy* XX:5–8. Do you think we should apply such laws today?
3. The 13th day of Adar was celebrated as Nicanor Day to commemorate the defeat of the arrogant Syrian Greek general. Yet the 14th, the very next day is Purim. Is it likely they would have declared a holiday before another one?
   What might have happened in 161 B.C.E. to explain why Nicanor Day was declared a semi-holiday?
4. Do you agree with the Hasidim that Alcimus should have been permitted to officiate as High Priest?
5. Who do you think were the other two Jewish Knights? Yes, Joshua and David. Would you have chosen them?

Project

- Can you imagine how Judah Maccabee felt before the battle with Bacchides? Was he right in remaining to fight? Write a skit covering the arguments between him and his friends.

Readings for Students

The Epic of the Maccabees, by Mindlin, Valerie, MacMillan Co., 1962.

Readings for Teachers

Selections from I and II *Maccabees.*

chapter 29 Early and Later Hasmoneans

CHAPTER 28 IS A STORY OF PLOTS and counterplots. The Tobiads were determined men. They wanted the advantages of Greek life. But they never intended to go as far as Antiochus IV.

The Hasmoneans were also determined men. They fought for Torah and the *Covenant* with single-minded purpose. They offered their lives freely. Eleazar, for example, crept under an elephant he thought was bearing Antiochus V, and pierced it with his sword. As the elephant fell, it crushed him.

Nevertheless, we must not oversimplify. Not only religious freedom was their goal. The Hasmoneans also wanted economic freedom, and some political control. No man can bear to have his property confiscated, nor his beliefs attacked. While it is true, therefore, that the Maccabean war was the first to be fought for religious freedom, we may not say it was exclusively for that.

This Hellenistic age, as you have seen right along, abounded in powerful personalities. The first, Alexander the Great, even doubted his father, a mere mortal, could have sired him. In Bithynia, in Pontus, Cappadocia, and Parthia, extraordi-

nary men delivered their people. And in the Seleucid capital of Antioch, men like Lysias, Philip, Demetrius, and Alexander Balas competed unto the death. The Tobiads and the Hasmoneans, we can see, were typical of their age.

After Jonathan became High Priest, and hence, local governor of Judea, his brother, Simon, was appointed local governor for the coastal area from Ptolemais (Acco) to the Brook of Egypt. Between them, these two Hasmoneans controlled a sizeable portion of Eretz Israel. Jonathan was eventually lured to his death by Tryphon, another pretender to the Seleucid throne.

By the year 141 B.C.E. three important changes took place. Judea no longer paid taxes to Syria. The garrison in the Akra was expelled. The Hasmonean dynasty was legally established.

Simon razed the Akra. He and his men entered the fortress bearing palm branches. This day, and the one upon which taxes ceased, were declared semi-holidays. No one was permitted to mourn on them.

Simon was hailed as ruler, High Priest, and General, at a Great Assembly (Kneset

Gedolah) on the 18th of Elul, 141 B.C.E. This was a remarkable event, perhaps a revolutionary one. For one thing, Simon was not of the house of Zadok. Even Jason, Menelaus, and Alcimus, had been Zadukim. For another, Onias IV, the legitimate descendant of the High Priest, Onias III, was alive.

We do not have an entirely clear picture of Onias IV. We know he was a general of the Ptolemies. His home, in or near the village of Leontopolis, was a fortress. In this same village he built a temple to Yahweh, the second temple of the Diaspora. Elephantine, as you know, had been the first.

Why, we must ask, should Onias have erected a temple, and not a synagogue as Jews did throughout the Diaspora? First, no doubt, because Onias IV never forgot he was a son of a High Priest, and the true heir to that position. Second, a temple probably suited Egypt's international ambitions. The Ptolemies could say to the Judeans: "Behold the High Priest who officiates in our temple, is your legitimate High Priest. Some day we will see that you and he are united." Thus they hoped to win Judean loyalty. They had never renounced their claim to Coele Syria.

The temple of Onias (Bet Onias), however, was not accepted by Egyptian Jews. Their loyalty was to the temple in Jerusalem and to Zion. Moreover, if Onias really aspired to the High Priesthood, he was unrealistic. He was too far from Jerusalem. And by now, he would have been regarded as an Egyptian agent.

Judeans wanted no more alien rulers. Simon may not have been of the house of Zadok, but he was a Hasmonean. His father and brothers, as well as he, himself, had delivered Judea from Greeks and Tobiads.

A document drawn up between Simon and the people determined that Simon should be their "leader and High Priest forever," and that his title would be "Prince of the People Of God." In addition, his positions would descend to his heirs after him.

Do you remember Saul, first king of Israel? Or David, the second? Who had appointed them? Not the people or the Elders or the priests. Samuel had chosen them. And Samuel was a prophet of Yahweh.

Prophetic election, not election by the people, had been Israel's way. This arrangement between Simon and the people, therefore, was not Hebraic; it was Hellenic. Indeed, the very idea of such a document was Hellenic. So too was its writing.

With Simon, there is, then, this break with tradition. But not entirely. For Simon is forbidden to wear the purple or the gold brooch which was the symbol of Hellenistic kings. Furthermore, the Hasmonean reign was to endure, the document adds, only until "a faithful prophet shall arise." The people might elect. True. But only for the present. God would someday choose His king through a prophet.

From this we see, that the very Hasmoneans who had fought against Greek forms, now adopt them. Nor was this the first time. Remember how the pious had allowed themselves to be killed rather than fight back on Shabbat. Remember how Mattathias had ordered them to resist.

We would approve. Yet not until the second century C.E. did the Rabbis say: "Shabbat is given to man, not man to Shabbat." Therefore Mattathias took a great deal upon himself when he called for fighting on Shabbat. In fact, *II Maccabees* not only omits this resolution but emphasizes the observance of Shabbat. For nowhere in the Torah is it permitted to fight on Shabbat. Only the High Priest and his council could interpret Torah thus. Mattathias acted as a Greek, not a Jew. For one historian his deed "constituted a turning point in Jewish history."

His sons also issued decrees upon their own initiative. For example, they declared many semi-festivals. Were they then, like Tobiads, tampering with Torah? No. The Tobiads had tried to assimilate Torah to Hellenism. The First Hasmoneans took from Hellenic culture whatever they needed to enrich and preserve the Torah way of life.

None of the Hasmonean brothers died a natural death. Eleazar sacrificed his life to bring down the elephant he thought was carrying Antiochus V. Judah fell in battle. John was killed by an Arab tribe in Transjordan. Jonathan was murdered by Tryphon, pretender to the Seleucid throne. And Simon, Prince of Judea, was assassinated by his own son-in-law.

Judah is the outstanding brother. He punished traitors, defeated the sophisticated Syrian Greek army half a dozen times, rescued fellow Jews from Greek cities, cleansed and rededicated the Temple, and reinstated Torah as the law of the land. He is a symbol to all who love liberty more than life.

His brothers, Jonathan and Simon, enlarged Judea's borders. Peace and security blessed the land until the death of Simon. Under the rule of his son, John Hyrcanus, Judea was defeated by the Seleucids for the last time.

But the Seleucids did not last long. They were brought low by the rising new nation of the East: Parthia. From then on the two greatest world powers were Parthia in the east and Rome in the west.

John Hyrcanus took advantage of Syria's upheavals. He secured control of parts of Transjordan including the valuable Salt Sea. He protected Jerusalem by fortifying Bet-Zur to the south. He subdued Idumea (Edom) and forced the Edomites to convert to Judaism. And in the north he conquered Samaria, Scythopolis, and parts of the Galilee. The Samaritan temple on Mt. Gerizim he razed.

The international scene of Simon and his descendants was a Hellenistic one. These men had to adapt themselves to this Hellenistic world. But they could have remained full Jews. Simon did exactly that.

There was never any question in the minds of Mattathias or his five sons, that they were responsible to Torah.

However with John Hyrcanus, Simon's son, Judea became almost totally Hellenistic. In what way? For one, John Hyrcanus hired mercenaries. Not because Jews could not fight. Quite the contrary; we saw Jewish peasants defeat six Syrian armies. But mercenaries were loyal to the king alone. They had no bond with the people.

Like other Hellenistic rulers, John Hyrcanus saw himself as above the state. The army was his alone to manipulate. He did not want to consider the desires or needs of his people. It is this attitude, not their political ambitions, that marked him and his heirs as Hellenistic.

John Hyrcanus had at least, five sons. Aristobulus, the first born, was the first Hasmonean to use the title: "king." He had three of his brothers put to death. His youngest brother, Alexander Jannaeus, he confined to the Galilee.

During his one year of reign, Aristobulus conquered the Ituraeans who lived near the Lebanon, and forced them to become Jews. Alexander Jannaeus, who succeeded him, continued his conquest. By the time he was through, he controlled all of Palestine except for three cities. Like his father and brother, he destroyed many cities, expelled their inhabitants, or forced them to convert.

It is sad that the descendants of men who fought for religious freedom, should have deprived others of their right to worship as they desired. But don't think these Later Hasmoneans were extreme Jews who hated idolatry or Greek culture.

They conquered Greek coastal cities for economic reasons. These cities controlled all trade: by land as well as by sea. That is why these Greek poleis had aided Antiochus IV. They had tried to stamp out any sign of Israel's national rebirth even before it began. If Judea triumphed, they knew they would lose their trade monopoly. Thus, we see, that John Hyrcanus' campaigns against them were the continuation of this early struggle.

In the days of the Hasmonean Simon, when the Seleucids had demanded the return of Jaffa and Gezer, Simon had retorted:

We have not taken foreign soil, but the inheritance of our fathers, which fell into the hands of our foes unjustly, and now the land has returned to its first owners.
(I Maccabees XV:33–34)

There was nothing politically immoral about this position. Had his heirs remained faithful Jews, no one would have criticized them. But they were far from that. Alexander Jannaeus was openly contemptuous of Torah. He executed thousands of his own people. Pharisees had to flee from him. And he was a warrior. He had no right to wear the robes of priesthood. His court was no better than Alexandria's.

The Hasmonean period, begun in martyrdom and glory, ends beneath the dismal shadow of brutality and wickedness. The Early Hasmoneans had been heroes and deliverers. The Later were tyrants.

But Israel had her own goals. And she also had her own leaders. Hostility between Israel's Pharisaical leaders and the Later Hasmoneans was so intense, the *Mishna,* refers to the Hasmoneans only twice and to Hanukah just a few times. The *Mishna,* is the literature of the Pharisees.

The final downfall of the Hasmoneans shall be at the hands of Rome. Back in Judah Maccabee's day, Rome already had begun to measure Judea and her territory with her Roman yardstick. No matter how Israel was governed, whether by sinner or saint, it seems hardly likely she could have avoided coming under the sword of this mighty empire of the west.

But at least she might have been united. King, High Priest, Pharisees, people, all could have presented a solid and strong front to their Roman conquerors.

Activities

Questions

1. Had you been Judah Maccabee, would you have concluded a treaty with Rome? What might Isaiah have said?
2. In what way is Modern Israel similar to the Israel under the Later Hasmoneans?
3. What can Modern Israel learn from the reign of the Early and Later Hasmoneans?
4. Was Simon's reply to the Seleucids applicable today?

Readings for Teachers

The Rise and Fall of the Judeaean State, S. Zeitlin, Solomon, J.P.S., 1962. (Vol. I)

A History of the Jews, by Grayzel, Solomon, J.P.S., 1953.

Hellenistic Civilization and the Jews, Tcherikover, Victor, J.P.S., 1959.

chapter 30 Alexandria: Hellenism and Hebraism

EXCEPT FOR GREEK ARCHITECTURE, Judea never really came into contact with the best elements of Hellenic civilization. Only throughout the Greco-Roman Diaspora could the Jew meet the best of Hellenic minds. In Asia Minor, in Egypt, Libya, Greece, Rome, and even west of Rome, the Jew could, if he desired, read Greek poets, dramatists, and philosophers. He could see the magnificent sculpture and other art objects of the Hellenic world.

The three most important Jewish communities of this Greco-Roman world were Antioch, Alexandria, and Rome. Of these, Alexandria was the most flourishing center of Greek civilization. In Alexandria the Jewish community developed the most creative life outside of Israel.

The city was divided into five sections, two of which were Jewish. Not that Jews were forced into any one locale. They simply preferred to live near each other. However, since we have found the remains of synagogues all over Alexandria, it is obvious Jews lived throughout the city.

In the book *Aristeas to Philocrates,* we read that one hundred thousand Jewish captives were brought to Egypt by Ptolemy I. The thirty thousand of military age were stationed in fortresses. The rest: women, children and old men were given to Egyptian soldiers as slaves. Ptolemy II Philadelphus, the next king, freed them.

Under Ptolemy IV Philopator, the Jews were supposed to have been threatened with genocide. The *Third Book of Maccabees* tells the story. They were herded into the stadium of Alexandria to be killed by drunken elephants. Instead the elephants turned upon the spectators and trampled them.

Few, if any historians, believe this happened. However, this episode does reflect conditions under Ptolemy VIII Euergetes. And since Jews celebrated a semi-festival to commemorate their delivery, we can conclude grave danger had threatened them.

It was Ptolemy II, Philadelphus, who decided Alexandria must become another Athens. He built a deep harbor, gaining for Alexandria the dubious honor of being the greatest center of slave traffic.

Philadelphus, and Ptolemies after him, invited scholars, poets, writers and artists, to settle in Alexandria. Some did. Others visited. You may not recognize their names now. But you will meet them later on. Here are a few: Zeno, founder of the Stoic School of philosophy; Epicurus, founder of the Epicurean School; Euclid, great master of geometry; Archimedes, who discovered the first principles of differential calculus; and Aristarchus of Samos, the astronomer. It is clear that Alexandria provided the Jews with the challenge of Hellenism at its best.

But what happens when a Jewish civilization, or any civilization, meets another imposing civilization? Either it surrenders to it, or it determines to live as fully a Jewish life as possible.

Some Jews surrendered. Among them was Tiberius Julius Alexander. He was a nephew of Philo, the most brilliant Jewish scholar of Alexandria. Tiberius rose to the position of governor and general. He eventually fought against Judea.

The great majority, however, remained steadfast and loyal Jews. In order to strengthen themselves, they had to strengthen their communal life. They had religious needs which could not be met in an alien environment, unless they secured special privileges.

These needs were recognized by the Ptolemies, and later, by Rome. They granted Jews special rights. Thus, they were protected in many ways. They were able to observe Shabbat. They did not have to serve in the army. They could collect a special tax for the Temple in Jerusalem. And they were not punished in as degrading a way as Egyptian peasants.

Furthermore, when danger threatened, they could defend themselves better as a group. When someone named Apion slandered them, Alexandrian Jews sent a committee to the Emperor in Rome to defend themselves. Philo headed this delegation.

Most Alexandrian Jews were either farmers, laborers, or craftsmen. We read in the *Talmud* (Sukkah 51b) a description of the main synagogue in Alexandria:

> . . . it was a sort of great basilica . . . that at times it held twice as many as left Egypt (sic). . . . And they did not sit intermingled, . . . the goldsmiths by themselves, the silversmiths by themselves, the blacksmiths by themselves, the carpet-weavers by themselves, and the weavers by themselves; and when a poor man entered, he recognized the members of his own craft and applied to them, whence he derived his livelihood and that of his family."

There were some wealthy members too. Philo's brother who was the head of the community (The Ethnarch) was one of the richest.

The Greeks of Alexandria resented the special treatment Jews received. Yet on the other hand, Jews were not citizens like the Greeks. How could they have been? To be a citizen meant to participate in the religious rites of the city. Thus Jews paid a special poll tax under Rome, from which citizens were exempt.

What we must ask ourselves is how the Alexandrian Jewish community could remain so strong in the face of such a rich and stimulating pagan environment? After all, it is simple not to surrender to alien forces, when these forces are base and repulsive. But, as in the case of the Hellenism of Alexandria, or of the other vital poleis, why was the Jew not overwhelmed?

The answer is simple. Judaism was as strong, no stronger, than Hellenism. For all the splendor of Hellenic thought and art, the Jew knew he had a greater treasure. Nevertheless, he did not shut the door in the face of Hellenism. He welcomed whatever insights were offered, and wove them into Hebraic thinking. He had his own philosophers, dramatists, historians, and theologians. Let us meet them.

Philo Judaeus was the most gifted mind of the Alexandrian Jewish community. He could not help but thrive in so rich an environment. Because he wrote so much like a Greek, he was able to communicate with his Greek neighbors and to explain Judaism to them.

Though a pious and loyal Jew, for whom the Torah was the absolute revealed truth, he was also an admirer of Greek thought. Plato, especially he revered, even calling him "most holy." His friends used to say that one could not tell "whether Philo writes like Plato, or Plato like Philo."

Philo's intention was to show that Judaism is a philosophic religion similar to the ideas of Greek philosophy. To do this, he interpreted the Bible allegorically. What is allegory? It is ascribing symbolic meaning to words or events. It assumes that the author, whether Greek or another, intended to say something other than what is literally expressed. It was a favorite technique of the Greeks. When Philo described the Therapeutae: a sect of Alexandrian Jews, he said of them:

They read the Holy Scriptures and seek wisdom from their ancestral philosophy by taking it as an allegory . . . they think the words of the literal text are symbols of something whose hidden nature is revealed by studying the underlying meaning. (The Contemplative Life.)

Here is an example of how Philo explained the Burning Bush:

There was a bramblebush, a thorny sort of plant and of the most weakly kind, which, without anyone's setting it alight, suddenly took fire and though enveloped from root to twigs in a mass of fire . . . yet remained whole, and instead of serving as fuel to the fire, actually fed on it . . . the burning bramble was a symbol of those who suffered wrong, as the flaming fire of those who did it. Yet that which burned was not burned up, and this was a sign that the sufferers would not be destroyed by their aggressors, who would find that the aggression was vain and profitless, while the victims of malice escaped unharmed.
. . . The bramble, as I have said, is a very weakly plant: yet it is prickly and will wound if one do but touch it. Again, though fire is naturally destructive, the bramble was not devoured thereby, but on the contrary was guarded by it, and remained just as it was before it took fire, and lost nothing at all but gained an additional brightness. All this is a description of the nation's condition as it then

stood, and we may think of it as a voice proclaiming to the sufferers: "Do not lose heart; your weakness is your strength, which can prick, and thousands will suffer from its wounds. Those who desire to consume you will be your unwilling saviours instead of your destroyers. Your ills will work you no ill. No, just when the enemy is surest of destroying you, your fame will shine forth most gloriously." Again, fire, the element which works destruction, convicts the cruel-hearted. "Exult not in your own strength," it says. "Behold your invincible might brought low, and learn wisdom. The property of flame is to consume, yet it is consumed, like wood. The nature of wood is to be consumed, yet it is shown to be the consumer, as though it were the fire."

(*The Lawgiver and His Work*)

Philo maintained God was without limitation, either in time or in space, and therefore could not be described. None could say what He is, only *that* He is. To relate this indescribable God and His actions upon the world, Philo assumed there were agents to do His bidding. Chief among them, was the Word, the Logos. Through the Word the world and all living forms were created.

Exactly what the Word was, is not clear. Sometimes it was a concept, sometimes it was the son of God whose mother was the virgin, Wisdom.

The Rabbis feared Philo's allegorical interpretations of the Torah. Why? Because these interpretations stressed the inner spirit of the laws. In so doing they overlooked the actual fulfillment of these mitzvot. They were also afraid the idea of the Logos might weaken the pure monotheistic faith of Judaism.

Philo was too observant a Jew to have encouraged anyone not to observe mitzvot. Nor would he have challenged the concept of monotheism. Nevertheless, it is a fact, his writings influenced Christianity more than Judaism. It enabled the Church to interpret Scripture to suit her needs. He would also affect Islamic thinking later. Not until the Middle Ages did he become a vital Jewish influence. We shall speak of him again when we study the mystic philosophy of Kabbala.

Josephus, no product of Alexandria, also directed his work at the Greeks. Both he and Philo were intent on proving the nobility of the Jewish heritage, and of its Scriptures. So too did the unknown authors of *Aristeas to Philocrates* and *The Fourth Book of the Maccabees*.

The Fourth Book of the Maccabees is either a sermon or a lecture based on tales of heroism in *II Maccabees*. It fuses Jewish and Stoic thought. Let us see exactly how the author does this.

He begins with the Stoic principle that "religious reason rules the emotions." He proves this by citing the courage of heroes of *II Maccabees*: Eleazar, an old man; seven brothers; and their mother. All of these chose death rather than transgress Torah:

All these despised suffering even unto death, and so proved that reason rules emotions.

(I:9)

A few sentences later, he explains wisdom. First he gives the Greek definition:

Wisdom is knowledge of things human and divine and of their cause.

Then he adds the Hebraic one:

Such wisdom is education in the Law, through which we learn things divine reverently and things human advantageously.   (I:17)

As a final touch, he gives us Plato's version of wisdom:

The types that make up wisdom are prudence, justice, courage, and temperance.

The atmosphere of this book is thoroughly Greek. Eleazar, who is an Elder in *II Maccabees* is described here as a philosopher. He even conducts himself occasionally as Socrates, the teacher of Plato. The words and images are Greek. The very structure of the book is Greek. The seven brothers for example, speak at times like a chorus. Choruses, of course, were part of Greek plays.

Despite the Hellenic forms, the aim of the book is Jewish. Briefly that aim is to prove that wisdom means knowledge of Torah.

Some historians believe *The Fourth Book of Maccabees* was written in Antioch. Whether there or in Alexandria, it is a classic example of Hellenistic influence upon Judaic thought.

Another product of the Greek scene was the *Book of Tobit.* But this book was not composed for Greeks. It was intended for the Jews of the Diaspora during the Maccabean era. It tells of the hero's faithful observances of Torah in the face of Assyrian tyranny. Obviously it was encouraging the Jews to remain loyal to Judaism.

The Wisdom of Solomon is an example of Pseudepigraphic literature. This is writing ascribed to ancient authors: in this case, to King Solomon. Its Alexandrian Jewish author tried to build a bridge between Greek philosophy and the Biblical Books of *Proverbs* and *Job.* Both *Job* and *Proverbs* are part of Jewish Wisdom Literature. The author made the wise King speak on the superiority of Jewish religious "wisdom" over the pagan forms of wisdom. Here is an example of how wisdom supported two of our ancestors.

When a righteous man was a fugitive from a
     brother's wrath, wisdom guided him in
     straight paths;
She showed him God's kingdom and gave him
     knowledge of holy things;
She prospered him in his toils, and multi-
     plied the fruits of his labor;
When in their greed men dealt harshly with
     him,
She stood by him and made him rich,
She guarded him from enemies,

And from those that lay in wait she kept him
  safe,
And in his sore conflict she guided him to
  victory,
That he might know that godliness is more
  powerful than all.

When a righteous man was sold, wisdom for-
  sook him not,
But from sin she delivered him;
She went down with him into a dungeon,
And in bonds she left him not,
Till she brought him the scepter of a kingdom,
And authority over those that dealt tyran-
  nously with him;
She showed him also to be false that had
  accused him,
And gave him eternal glory.

In other Pseudepigraphic literature, au-
thorship was ascribed to Moses and the
prophets. But not only to Hebrew heroes.
Greeks like Homer, Sophocles, Plato, and
Aristotle, praised the Hebraic spirit. All of
these books had a distinct missionary goal.
They tried to show how much that was
original in pagan classics was taken from
Hebrew sources.

We also have a fragment of a religious
drama, *Exodus.* The author, Ezekiel, was
an Alexandrian Jew who used the methods
of the Greek drama in his play.

However, the most important project by
far, of this period, was the translation of the
Five Books into Greek: the *Septuagint.*
Tradition tells us it was under Ptolemy II
Philadelphus (250 B.C.E.) this stupendous
work was undertaken.

In *Aristeas to Philocrates,* Ptolemy's li-
brarian explains to the king that he has 995
books representing the best literature of
the nations. But the greatest, the Five
Books of Moses, were still missing. Thereupon the king asks the High Priest in Jerusalem to send him a copy of these books
together with men capable of translating
them into Greek.

The High Priest complies. 72 saintly
Scribes arrive with a Scroll. The king and
his courtiers marvel at their wisdom. Together the Scribes translate Scripture.

An element of divine inspiration is introduced by Philo. According to him, the
translators (no number is given) are placed
in separate rooms. Without communicating
with each other, they produce the exact
same translation. Obviously, the Divine
Spirit blesses this project.

It is called the *Septuagint,* which means
seventy in Greek. The name is in honor of
the more than 70 Sages who translated it.
So proud were the king and the Jews, the
day of its completion was supposed to
have been declared a holiday. Gradually
more books of Tanach were translated and
added to the Septuagint.

It is more likely the Jews themselves arranged for this translation. Raised in the
Hellenic environment, many no longer
spoke or read Hebrew. They needed a
Greek translation. It may also be they

wanted to impress their neighbors with their history and with the antiquity of their race. In those days to be a member of an ancient people was a mark of nobility.

A more unpleasant reason may be the anti-Semitic writings of a Greek Egyptian historian, Manetho. This Manetho maintained the Jews were descended from lepers expelled from Egypt. The Jews of Alexandria wanted everyone to know their ancestors had marched out of Egypt freely.

Whatever the motive, there is no question the *Septuagint* introduced Hebraic thought to the Hellenic world. It was undoubtedly responsible for the attraction of pagans to Judaism. What a pity Plato and Aristotle were not translated into Hebrew for the Jews of Israel! Instead of the crude and superstitious religious practises the Judeans saw surrounding them, they might have become acquainted with the noblest of Greek thought.

As in the case of Philo, the Rabbis were not happy with the *Septuagint*. The translators altered the original to fit in with their own thinking. They even omitted whole incidents they considered uncomplimentary.

In the midst of this intellectual life, the Jews of Alexandria thrived. It was said that the main synagogue of Alexandria was so big, the worshippers in the rear had to depend on a signal in order to respond: "Amen." Although not full citizens they participated in the cultural and economic life of the city. They attended theatre and sports events with their Greek neighbors.

As men like Second Isaiah and the later Ezekiel had added new dimensions to Judaism, so Philo and the authors of *IV Maccabees* and *The Wisdom of Solomon*, enriched Judaic insights. They also influenced the Greek world so strongly, the Stoic philosopher, Seneca protested:

. . . (Jews) have so prevailed that (their Jewish customs) are adopted in all the world, and the conquered have given their laws to the conquerors.

There was more than an element of truth in Seneca's lament. Judaism was a force in the Greco-Roman Diaspora. Jewish writings reached into Greek and Roman homes. The old paganism was in a state of decay. Sensitive minds throughout the Near East found the simple and beautiful monotheistic belief rational and refreshing. The religious commandments appealed to them, for they were repelled by pagan rites. Converts were welcomed into the synagogues. So too were partial converts, known as God-Fearers. We shall discuss this attraction to Judaism in the next chapter.

Jerusalem, we know, did not succumb to Athens. Neither did Jewish communities of the Diaspora. They took instead, what they thought they needed. Some of it was wholesome and fruitful, as in the election of Simon to Prince of the People of God, or as reflected in *IV Maccabees.* Some of it evil, as in the conduct of the Later Hasmoneans.

Rome, most historians believe, was the other city and civilization that did not surrender to Hellenism. But the fact is Greek influence dominated most of Roman life. So much so a Censor, Cato the Elder (234–149 B.C.E.), expelled all the Greek philosophers from Rome.

Judean Sages did not look kindly on pagan thought. How could they with what they saw? Yet they permitted Gamaliel II to teach Greek studies to hundreds of his students. Ben Sira, who lived over two hundred years before Gamaliel, knew all people possess wisdom. And we know that the Tanna, Rabbi Elazar ben Arach advised his disciples: ". . . know how to respond to an Epikoros" (one who denies God and His commandments) *Avot* II:19. Are we to conclude, then, that he encouraged grappling with foreign thought? How else could they respond?

There is much more we could say about this Hellenistic period. But the time has come to deal with the conquerors of the Greeks: the Romans. For the Judaic-Roman encounter is one of the most heroic and most tragic, and above all, most significant for Israel. Jews bear the imprint of those days until the present.

Questions

1. Of what Scroll of the Tanach does *III Maccabees* remind us? Why?
2. How does your Jewish community strengthen your Jewish life?
3. Apply Philo's interpretation of the Burning Bush to Israel's situation before the Exodus. Is it appropriate? How could the Logos threaten monotheism?
4. What brought the Jews to Egypt after the establishment of the monarchy of Israel? Give the historical background of each emigration.
5. Analyze the excerpts of *The Wisdom of Solomon*. In the first verse who was: the righteous man; the brother full of wrath; the greedy man? In the second verse who was: the righteous man; how was he sold; how did wisdom deliver him, and from what sin; into what dungeon or dungeons was he cast; what scepter did he obtain?
6. How would you define assimilation? Should it be avoided? In the light of your environment, what special problems does it create? Organize a debate on this issue.
7. Whose approach to Hellenism do you approve? Cato the Elder's, or Rabbi Elazar ben Arach? Explain your point of view.

Readings for Teachers

Judaism: Post Biblical and Talmudic Period, ed. Baron and Blau, The Liberal Arts Press, N.Y., 1954.

Aristeas to Philocrates, ed. Moses Hadas, Harper Bros., N.Y. 1951.

Third and Fourth Maccabees, ed. and trans. Moses Hadas.

Ancient Rome, Payne, Robert, American Heritage Press, Paperback, N.Y., 1970.

Of Jewish Law and Lore, Ginzberg, Louis, J.P.S., 1955.

Philo-Judaeus of Alexandria, Bentwich, Norman, J.P.S., 1910.

index

Temple Israel
Minneapolis, Minnesota

IN HONOR OF THE BIRTH OF
JONATHAN KENNEDY
FROM
RABBI STEPHEN H. PINSKY